ACED

JENNIFER LANE

Aced, Copyright © Jennifer Lane, 2015
All Rights Reserved. Except as permitted under the U.S. Copyright Act of 1976, no part of this publication may be reproduced, distributed, or transmitted in any form or by any means, or stored in a database or retrieval system, without prior written permission of the publisher.

Published by Psyched Publishing

First published, December 2015

The characters and events in this book are fictitious.
Any similarity to real persons, living or dead,
is coincidental and not intended by the author.

Library of Congress Cataloguing-in-Publication Data

Lane, Jennifer.
  Aced / Jennifer Lane – 1st ed.
  ISBN: 978-0-692-56841-5
  1. Volleyball — Fiction. 2. New Adult Romance — Fiction.
  3. Race — Fiction. 4. Psychology — Fiction. I. Title

10 9 8 7 6 5 4 3 2 1

Book Design by Coreen Montagna

Printed in the United States of America

*To readers of all skin colors:
may we find common ground.
We all bleed the same.*

"Go away!" I hollered. "I'm Netflixing." The knock on my apartment door had drowned out the dialogue, and I paused the TV show on my laptop.

"Maddie?"

Oh no. It was Lucia outside, fierce on the volleyball court but such a sweetie. I glanced at my phone, partially hidden under balled-up tissues next to me on my ratty brown sofa. She had texted several times this week, but I hadn't answered any messages from friends or family. I felt guilty for not responding—well, except for *one* person's messages. I never wanted to speak to him again.

"I'll call you tomorrow, okay?" I yelled, hoping she would leave. I hovered my finger over the play button, eager to see if Jasmine and Crosby would reunite.

A male voice floated through the door. "You okay, Ms. Brooks?"

Damn. I should've known Frank was with her. The first daughter—or whatever Lucia was called since her dad won the presidential election a couple months ago—couldn't travel anywhere without Secret Service.

"I'm fine," I called. *Liar.*

"Please, Maddie?" she called again. "I'm worried about you."

The soft warble of her voice got to me. I sighed and crossed the room to open the door. Despite my moping, I couldn't help but laugh when I saw her getup: a long, black Sherpa coat, furry boots, and a matching red, gold, and orange-striped hat and mittens. She looked adorable, and I bet her boyfriend Dane had thought so, too.

I stuck my head into the hallway; it was probably sixty-five degrees. "Aren't you overdoing it a little with the arctic layers?"

"It's, like, negative five outside! I don't know how you Midwesterners handle this." Her pink cheeks glowed.

I tilted my head in sympathy. Ramirez—Rez for short—was from Houston. "It'll get better come March."

"That's too far away." Her dimple creased as she pouted. "I thought December was bad up here, but January's way worse."

I shook my head as I opened the door wider and extended my arm. "You can come in too, Agent Vanderberg."

"No need." Frank clasped his hands behind his back and stood at parade rest next to my door.

As she entered, Lucia looked over her shoulder. "You sure, Frank? It's cold out there."

"I'll manage, Lucy." His soft smile surprised me.

"What was *that?*" I asked after I closed the door. "You forgave Frank for telling your dad about Dane?"

Her father had gone nuclear upon learning that his daughter was dating the son of Senator Monroe—a Democrat and his opponent in the presidential race—right before the final debate last October.

"That's old news." Her shrug was barely noticeable beneath her thick coat. "You would've known I forgave Frank if you hadn't holed yourself up in here."

"It's only been a few days."

Lucia's chin dipped. "You've missed practice for a week, and you know how Coach gets without you there to chill him out."

"Sorry." This was the real-world stuff I'd been avoiding with Netflix: expectations, exercise, and ex-boyfriends. I cast a longing look at my laptop.

"Didn't mean to guilt-trip you, *amiga*. I know you don't have to go to practice anymore." She clapped her mittens together. "I just miss you. We have lots to catch up on."

Now that I'd exhausted my four years of college-volleyball eligibility, I didn't have to attend off-season practice. But if I wanted to make the national team, I *needed* to practice. Selection camps for Team USA loomed, starting in April, and I couldn't afford to let myself get out of shape. "I miss you too, Rez. But besides dragging my butt to a few classes, I've checked out of everything since Saturday night."

Her brown eyes softened. "Have you heard from him?"

I flopped down on the cushion and reached for my phone, scrolling through the texts to find the ones from asshat. "How 'bout you take off your winterwear and have a seat, Texas?"

"I'm too cozy to take off my coat." She rubbed her mittens up and down the fur as she beamed. "Dane gave it to me for Christmas."

I smiled. No wonder she liked the coat so much. She folded her bundled self next to me on the dark brown thrift-store sofa I'd affectionately nicknamed "Shitty."

"I can't stay long, anyway," she added. "I was hoping you'd go to Dane's match with me?"

"Oh, right—the men's team has a home match tonight." I handed her my phone as I glanced at my crumpled sweatpants and flannel pajama top. I would not likely make it out of my apartment, even though I did want to see the men play in the new arena.

She slid off the tops of her mittens to reveal hobo gloves, and her uncovered fingertips scrolled down the face of my phone. After a few moments of silence, her head shot up. "He *said* that? His last name should be Heartless, not Hart."

"Totally." How could I have given so much of myself to Jaylon Hart? All six-foot-six, two-hundred-fifty-seven pounds of him. He was a heavyweight wrestler with corded muscle, a sexy grin, and chocolate skin. Remembering his warm gaze, my heart fluttered, then clenched. He wasn't mine anymore.

"*Long past time to end this. You and me goin' in different directions, you know it,*" Lucia read, then looked up at me. "But he makes no sense. You're both seniors, set to graduate in May. And you both dream about making the Olympics."

"I know." I'd been replaying these facts in my mind for six days now.

She resumed reading. "*Why you upset? You never loved me. I'm doing you a favor ending it.*" Her lips parted. "He dares to call breaking up with you a *favor?* Wow, Maddie, that sucks. You guys were together a long time, right?"

I swallowed, and the words almost got caught in my throat. "Three years."

"And you didn't see this coming?"

"He's been sort of…distant, I guess. But I chalked it up to his wrestling season starting. He's under a lot of pressure to defend his national championship."

Lucia frowned. "Sorry we couldn't give *you* a national championship for your senior year."

I nudged her shoulder. "Finishing third in the country ain't bad, Rez. And I still can't believe the number of blocks you had in our last game."

"*You're* the team MVP." Her shy blush morphed into lines of worry on her face. "How'll we compete next year without you?" She chewed on a fingernail. "Don't you miss volleyball?"

I sighed. "Yeah, I kind of do."

"Come with me to the match, then. It'll be a good distraction. Jaylon won't be there, right?"

"The wrestling team's in Iowa this weekend." I looked down. "I still know his schedule by heart." In memory of him, my heart thudded a longing beat. "I sound like a stalker, huh?"

Lucia patted my arm. "Not at all. It makes sense you're reeling after three years of being together. I only hope Dane and I can last that long."

"Have you *seen* the way he looks at you?"

The blush coloring her cheeks now matched the red stripe in her winter hat. She seemed extra embarrassed tonight — *what's that about?* If I wasn't going to get to finish my TV romance binge, at least the sizzling glances between Lucia and her boo could entertain me.

"Okay, Rez." *Time for me to leave my cocoon and face the real world.* "Give me a minute to get ready?"

"Yay!" She bounced on Shitty.

I headed to my bedroom and the shower. Though I hummed "I'm Gonna Wash That Man Right Out of My Hair," I didn't really believe it. Jaylon had embedded himself inside me, and a whole vat of shampoo wouldn't exorcise him. His lame explanation about growing apart didn't cut it, and how the hell could he believe I didn't love him? Sure, we'd had arguments, but so did every couple I knew, including Dane and Lucia. The unfinished feeling that had gnawed at me all week started in again.

I sighed as I swept my wet, curly hair up into a short ponytail. I stared at myself in the mirror, clad only in bra and panties. My abdominal muscles were my favorite body part, but I frowned when I noticed their grooves had lost some definition. *Time to return to the gym.* I also noticed my ashy skin, which I rectified with my favorite lotion. Breathing in eucalyptus and spearmint calmed me. But staring at my closet deflated me again. Most of my outfits held reminders of nights out with Jaylon.

"You're watching *Parenthood*?" Lucia asked from the other room.

I winced. That show made me cry every single episode, and I choked up just thinking about Crosby kissing Jasmine. Yeah, I wanted them back together. Breakups sucked.

When I didn't answer, Lucia snorted. "What are you, a middle-aged housewife?"

"Said by the nineteen year old whose favorite artist is Neil Diamond."

She was quiet for a moment. "Good point."

I grinned as I tugged on some black jeans. "Your dad's the one who got you into Neil Diamond, right? Will he invite him for a private concert at the White House?"

She gasped. "What an incredible idea! Why didn't I think of that?"

"Might as well get *something* good out of him winning the election, right?" I yanked a form-fitting black shirt over my head and added a furry tiger-print vest. "Now that you're hounded by the media and stuck with Secret Service for the rest of college."

She harrumphed. "And Dane doesn't have to be protected anymore."

"Except when he's with you and *your* agents." I selected a necklace with black stones and small gold feathers that my father had given me.

"Yeah, he said I'm lucky he likes me so much or he'd never tolerate Secret Service following our every move."

I smirked. *Sounds like Dane.* My long, black boots—my brother, Braxton, referred to them as my "bitch boots"—completed the ensemble.

"But at least he doesn't have to deal with China anymore," she added. "Those two are *aceite y agua.*"

As I exited my bedroom, I thought about Latin class and nodded. "Oil and water, *sí*. Where did China and Brad get reassigned?"

Lucia giggled. "To my brother Alejandro." Her giggles grew into guffaws.

"Why's that funny?"

"You think Dane's pigheaded? You haven't met Alex. He takes conflict with China to a whole new level. He's so overprotective of me—it's great to see *him* deal with being protected."

I shrugged. He couldn't be worse than *my* overprotective brother. I grabbed my phone and noticed again the unanswered voice mails, some of them from him. "Let's do this."

I just about drooled over Dane's quick-set to Josh. With the ball hovering perfectly at the top of the net just waiting to be slammed, of course he made a kill. *Point, Highbanks.* Raucous cheers echoed through the arena, and I couldn't help but smile at Lucia. "Thanks for bringing me here, Rez."

She smiled back. "Bet you wish you had a setter like that, huh?"

"You read my mind. He's amazing." My shoulder bumped hers. "I bet you're glad you *do* have a setter like that."

She sighed. "He is amazing."

I wanted to celebrate her happiness, but her look of bliss crushed me inside. I used to feel that way watching Jaylon wrestle—his impressive speed, glistening muscles, and steely determination filled me with pride every time. Now I'd never feel that way again.

Frank tapped Lucia's shoulder. "I'm grabbing some coffee for Allison." He gestured toward his blond Secret Service partner, who sat a couple of rows behind us. "Would you or Madison like anything?"

"I'm good." Lucia looked at me with questioning eyes.

"I'm good, too." He turned to leave but swiveled when I blurted, "Would you bring my boyfriend back?"

Frank's eyes widened, and he shifted from one foot to another. "Um..."

"Relax, Frank," I said. "Just making a joke."

"Right." He nodded. "Well, if he was stupid enough to leave, he doesn't deserve you." He turned toward the concession stand.

I shared a disbelieving look with Lucia. "Where did that come from?" I asked. "He's so cool now. What happened?"

"Frank and I came to an understanding. Dad's way too busy to worry about my love life, so Frank agreed to keep him in the dark about me and Dane."

I was glad nothing would interfere with their romance now. Lucia couldn't help it if her father was so Republican, and Dane was so Democrat. Things worked between her and Dane, and that's what mattered.

The men's coach, Phil, called a time out, and Dane looked up to wink at Lucia on his way to the huddle. His gaze floated to her left, and when his grin vanished, I turned to look. Was that *China* entering the arena?

Lucia must also have followed his gaze because she gasped. "Alex!"

Sure enough, Lucia's older brother walked behind the brown-haired female agent. And another agent, Brad, lumbered behind them both.

I'd only seen Alejandro on TV, but his presence seemed magnified in real life. He was Jaylon's height but probably weighed thirty pounds less. He moved like a panther, sleek and long in a black suit "dressed down" with no tie. His short black hair shone in the arena lights, and he appeared freshly shaven. *Hot damn!* He sure looked more suave than any college boy I'd encountered. Was that the typical dress for medical school at Johns Hopkins? Probably not. Something told me Alex did things his own way.

The agents veered off to say hello to Allison. As Alejandro approached, Lucia stood to hug him, shaking her head. "Hey, what're you doing here? You didn't tell me you were coming."

He smiled. "*Hola, chica.* Could we go somewhere to talk?"

She glanced at me. "I don't want to leave Maddie. I dragged her here, so it'd be rude to abandon her."

"So *this* is the famous Maddie." When Alejandro reached across to shake my hand, his dark eyes burned into me. "I've seen you play, but it's good to finally meet. I've heard great things about you." His handshake was firm, but his hand was soft and warm, zinging a surprising thrill right through me. I realized that for at least a few moments, I hadn't thought about Jaylon. He let go all too quickly.

His expression sobered as he looked back at Lucia. "I want to talk to you about something in private."

She folded her arms across her chest as they both sat. "I already said no, thank you. I can't right now."

He frowned and squared his shoulders. Then he leaned in to Lucia's ear and spoke to her in Spanish. She bristled next to me.

"How dare you?" she hissed.

I leaned back. What had just changed my sweet Rez into a pissy hellcat?

"*Told* you I wanted to discuss this in private," Alejandro said.

"You want to keep my sex life *private?*" Lucia railed.

Alejandro's eyes widened and darted around the stands.

"Then you should butt the hell out of it!" Lucia had lowered her voice, but her tone was still vehement. "You're my brother, not my dad." She squeaked as her hand flew to her mouth. "Dad doesn't know about me and Dane, does he?"

"Not yet." Alex seemed nervous when he glanced at me. "And I won't tell him, if you promise to stop immediately."

She and I gasped at the same time. "This is none of your business! You can't blackmail me." Lucia's voice shook, and I could tell she was close to tears. I scooped her hand in mine for support.

Alejandro blew out a breath, seeming to look for the right words. "I thought I knew you better than this, Lucy."

I squirmed. Alex might be hot, but I wanted no part of this sibling squabble. "How 'bout I leave?"

"Please stay," Lucia begged. "You're the only one who understands." She squeezed my hand and turned back to her brother. "Thought you knew me how, exactly?"

"I thought you'd follow the teachings of our parents and the church."

"I do, but I also think for myself. This decision was a big deal, and I didn't make it lightly." She gulped and dipped her head, seeming mired in guilt. But then she sat up. "You know what? I don't have to explain myself to *you*. I'm an adult now."

"Then act like it," he said.

"I am, but you're too busy judging me to see that. This is precisely why Matty and I don't tell you anything, Alex. You're such a *pendejo*."

Alejandro maintained his stoic expression, but I could see the comment stung.

"I love you, Lucy," he said, his voice strained. "I'm here to help."

"No, you're not. I don't need your help with his. *At all.* You're here to control me. Butt *out.*"

She turned away from him and stared at my feet. I could almost feel waves of fury pulsing from her. I watched Alejandro rub his hand over his face, seeming weighed down by sadness. I felt sad, too, with Lucia tense next to me and pain flitting across Alex's face. Braxton and I had frustrated each other like this many times. There was no easy solution.

Alejandro's mouth opened, but no words came out. He lifted his hand like he was about to touch her shoulder, but then he dropped it. After several moments, he seemed to realize Lucia wasn't going to speak to him. He got up with a sigh and hustled down the steps to stand near the railing overlooking the court. Brad hovered twenty feet behind him.

I glanced at Lucia, who ran her hands through her long hair. "So, you and Dane, huh?"

She looked down, her cheeks aflame. "I guess I'm a ho." She rolled her eyes.

"You know that's not true." I sucked in a breath. "Did Alejandro *say* that?"

"No." She sighed. "But he probably thinks it."

"I doubt that. And if he does, he's wrong. I'm sure he's just worried. He wouldn't fly all the way here if he didn't care about you."

She sniffed, and a tear slid down her cheek. *Stupid brother!*

"Actually, I'm surprised you both lasted *this* long, horndogs," I offered, hoping for a smile.

Her mouth twitched. "I know, right? We waited as long as we could. But then I went to DC for Dad's inauguration, and I missed Dane *so* much." She sighed. "I pretty much attacked him when I got back." She gestured to the court, where the muscles in Dane's arm rippled as he high-fived a teammate. "I mean, could *you* stay away from that hotness?"

I chuckled. "You didn't commit a crime, Rez. It's just taking the next step with the man you love."

"I wish my brother would see it that way."

I looked at Alejandro. Even angry he cut a stylish profile against the railing. He couldn't be totally immune to female attention, could he? Seemed to me like he should be receiving plenty of it. He gripped the railing with white knuckles as he glared at the court, no doubt aiming an outraged stare at Dane…

Oh yeah, there was still a game going on. Highbanks had a comfortable lead, so I tuned back in to the drama next to me as Frank returned holding two coffee cups.

"*You.*" Lucia pointed at him. "You told Alex. And you knew he was coming to yell at me, so you slithered away to avoid the confrontation."

Frank said nothing.

"I thought we had a deal," she fumed.

Her embarrassment had vanished, and damn, she was *mad!*

"The agreement involved me not speaking to your father," Frank said. "We didn't discuss your brother."

I watched Alejandro mutter something to himself, his mouth tight. He ran his hands through his hair like I'd just seen Lucia do—their family had the shiniest black hair—and a flash of silver on his wrist, an expensive-looking watch, caught my eye.

"I never imagined you'd speak to my brother! His life has nothing to do with mine." Lucia crossed her arms over her chest as she glared at Frank. "You're up to your old tricks, then. I can't *believe* you did that."

And I couldn't believe Alejandro had judged his sister so easily. He'd swooped in to question her morals, then left her to deal with the aftermath. Nobody messed with my Rez that way. Before I knew it, I was marching toward him.

As I neared, he stood taller, and I noticed a subtle scent of spice.

"Good job," I said. I stared him down as best I could, given I had to look up to meet his eyes. "What exactly are you trying to do here? You just made your sister cry."

"I just—it's my—" With a defeated sigh his head dropped, and he seemed contrite. "Sorry." But then his chin lifted, and his dark eyes glowed with warmth.

Was the bastard actually *smiling* at me?

2
Alejandro

M addie perched her hand on her hip. "Really? Your sister's over there crying. What the hell are you smiling about?"

I felt a blessed letup of the concern consuming me since Agent Vanderberg had called, and I slid my hands into my pants pockets. "Lucia told me you've been an incredible friend…that you've looked out for her. And you scolding me for upsetting her proves it. Thanks for being her friend."

The fire in her burnished eyes seemed to cool a bit. "Oh." She stroked the small feathers in her necklace, which drew my gaze to the curves of her breasts, visible beneath her vest. She was exquisite. I glued my eyes back to her face before she seemed to notice my stare. The juxtaposition of her defined jawline and her soft, full lips intrigued me. I'd known she was a talented athlete after watching her play in the NCAA championships, but I hadn't realized how lovely she was until now, up close. She smelled clean and calming.

"I'm glad Lucy has someone like you here." I continued. "I'm sorry I made her cry, but those things had to be said." And now that I had said them, I wondered if my responsibility to my father was fulfilled. When he'd asked me to take care of my siblings, I hadn't realized it would be so difficult.

She shook her head, not seeming entirely convinced. "Do you always make such an entrance?"

I forced out a puff of air. "That probably wasn't the best way to start the conversation." To confirm my gaffe, I looked to the stands, where my sister's eyes glistened as she argued with Frank. I couldn't hear them, but she was undoubtedly berating him for spilling the beans about Dane. "I know how upset Lucy was when Frank told my dad about Dane. And that was just about her *dating* him."

"So maybe you'd better not tell President Ramirez about Lucia's sexcapades, then." She raised an eyebrow in challenge.

A chuckle bubbled in my throat, but I suppressed it. This was supposed to be serious. "Doubt I'll use the word *sexcapades* with the president of the United States."

"Ah, c'mon." She smirked. "He's just a dad to you, right? You knew him before all this." She gestured to the Secret Service agents. "Just like I knew Rez before she became famous."

Now that she mentioned it, it *was* nice that she looked at my family as just regular. Or as regular as a family like mine could be. I hadn't had a girl approach me in forever—they seemed intimidated.

Granted, Maddie had come down here to bawl me out, not hit on me, but still, it was welcome. "Rez?" I smiled. "That was my team nickname, too."

She perked up. "What sport did you play?"

"Baseball."

"In college?"

I nodded. "Texas Christian University."

"The Horned Frogs! They have a great baseball team."

A spark of happiness fired in my chest, and I leaned in closer. "How'd you know *that?*"

"I'm a huge sports fan." She grinned. "My grandfather taught me everything about baseball."

I inched nearer to her.

"What position did you play?" she asked. "Wait." Her arm shot out to clasp my wrist. "Let me guess."

Her touch was warm, and I breathed in her soothing, minty scent.

She ran her tongue across her lower lip. "Pitcher?"

"Wow. I started as a pitcher, but then I got injured." My eyebrows arched. "You're good."

"Ah." She studied me. "Was it a shoulder injury?"

"Almost." I pointed to a different body part. "Elbow."

"Gotcha." She smiled. "So then you transitioned to…first base?"

My eyes widened. "You *do* know the game! You figured my height would help me snag wild throws from the shortstop."

"Plus, first basemen tend to be pretty cute." Her eyes grew big, and she took a step back. "Ah, um, I mean…"

I wasn't sure which was more attractive—her thinking I was cute, or her mortification at saying so out loud. I was just about to change the subject to save her when her hand found her hip again. She straightened.

"Wait a minute, mister—you avoided my question." The fire was back in her eyes. "Are you going to snitch on Lucia or treat her like an adult? Which she *is*."

So she'd seen right through my ploy. I'd learned the evasive maneuver in media training: *If you don't like the question, redirect it to a topic you want to discuss.* Maddie reminded me of Harris Faulkner on Fox News. She pressed politicians when they avoided her questions.

Dad had made it clear I was supposed to protect my younger sister and brother, and withholding the fact that Lucia was having premarital sex likely defied that directive. But she seemed more confident about her decision than I'd anticipated, which made me question whether to tell him. Plus, I didn't want to bother him—he was rather busy. "I'm not sure," I finally said.

"You shouldn't tell him."

"Don't you care about Lucia's reputation? Her future? She's not listening to me, but maybe she'd listen to him."

Her forehead creased. "You make sex sound shameful. It's not. It can be really…nice, wonderful even." Her mouth quivered before she looked away. Why did she seem sad? She cleared her throat. "Sex is a way to show your love. You know how it is."

Here it is. This conversation had come up with my med school friends, and they'd been horrified when I told them the truth. But I'd promised myself I would stick to my values, no matter how unpopular they seemed. "I understand what you're saying, but I *don't* know, actually." My chin crept up an inch. "I don't believe in sex before marriage."

"You…" The crease between her eyebrows deepened. "You're a virgin?"

My face warmed from embarrassment. I swallowed, then gave a slight nod, scrutinizing her face for any sign of judgment.

But she seemed fascinated rather than repulsed. "This is about your religion?"

"Yes." I wondered if she would condemn me for being Christian.

"Hmm." She eyed me. "I admire your commitment to your faith, but it must be tough to wait so long. How old are you?"

"Twenty-four." *That's not that old, right?* "How old are you?"

"Twenty-one. Well, I turn twenty-two next month." She squinted. "You're in your second year of med school?"

Pleased Lucia had shared that about me, I nodded.

"Wow. So you graduated from college in four years, then started right away at a prestigious med school."

I shrugged. "But you're also graduating in four years—tough to accomplish as a student-athlete."

"How'd you know I'm graduating?"

"Lucia won't stop ranting about the team sucking next year without you."

"Ah, Rez."

The slight huskiness of her laugh set off a flutter in my belly.

"The team will be fine next year. Your sister doesn't realize how talented she is." Maddie looked at Lucia, and I followed her gaze.

Lucia had stopped arguing with Frank, who now sat in the row behind her with China. My sister stared straight ahead, her shoulders tense, as Allison leaned in next to her. I wondered why Lucia wasn't watching the match when I realized the gym floor was empty. Both teams had disappeared to the locker rooms between games. I'd been so absorbed in my conversation with Maddie that I hadn't noticed the break in the action.

"Rez needs to work on her confidence," Maddie said. "She's really hard on herself."

My heart felt heavy to think of Lucy beating herself up. "She's always been that way." A flash of tears sliding down her apple cheeks filled my mind. "Once when Lucy was little, maybe eight, she blamed herself for Mateo going to the hospital. They were playing kickball, and he went down when the ball hit him. He didn't get back up." My pulse quickened remembering his little body splayed out on the driveway. "We were still figuring out his insulin dose and maybe missed one. It wasn't Lucy's fault that the paramedics had to come and get him. Still, she couldn't stop crying."

Maddie pursed her lips with apparent confusion, and I was about to explain the medical stuff when she nodded. "Yeah, she told me about Mateo's diabetes. He went into ketoacidosis, right?"

Surprised, I nodded. "Do you have a family member with diabetes?"

"No?" Her eyes held question marks.

"Then how'd you know about ketoacidosis?"

"I'm a bio-chem major."

"I see." *Dios, she's smart, too?* "Bet it's hard to fit labs into your schedule as a student-athlete."

"No kidding. I had to jam most of them into the summers."

I'd endured quite a few late nights as a pre-med major, and I probably put less time into my sport since I was nowhere near Maddie's caliber of athlete. "You'll be a physician's assistant, then?"

She scoffed as she stepped away from me.

"What?" I asked.

Both hands flew to her hips. "Sexist much? I'll be a physician, just like you."

"You..." My heart thumped. *I'm not sexist!* "I, I didn't mean to denigrate you...I just thought, with classes and practice and everything...you're going to med school? Lucia never told me about that." How could Maddie have a prayer of getting into med school with her insane schedule? No way she had the scores I did. "You're not applying this year, are you?"

"No, I—"

"You need to take a few more classes to get your grades up?" When her eyes narrowed, I winced. *Wrong assumption.*

"Seriously? My grades are awesome, jerk. I'm taking some time off to try out for the national volleyball team."

I closed my eyes. *Mierda.* "Oh. Lucia told me about that, but I forgot." I opened my eyes to find her watching me. Why did I keep sticking my foot in my mouth? My dad's words filled my head: *"A confident man admits when he's wrong."*

"Sorry, Maddie. Of course you'll go to med school. You'll be an excellent physician."

One hand fell from her hip. "I hope." She frowned. "My grades might be good, but my MCAT score's only average." She folded her arms across her chest. "No way I'll get into a school like Johns Hopkins."

"Hey, that doesn't sound like the future Team USA middle blocker talking."

Her frown disappeared. "Rez has told you a lot about me."

"She talks about you all the time. She's a huge admirer of yours." I was becoming one as well. Unfortunately, Lucia had also mentioned Maddie's boyfriend. Of course she had a boyfriend. She was beautiful, a superstar athlete, and smart to boot. Before I met Maddie, I couldn't have cared less about her relationship status. But talking to her now…I wished I'd met her before some dude had snatched her up.

"Rez is so sweet," she said. But the line between her eyes deepened.

"What's wrong?"

"I feel bad." She sighed. "I've been ignoring her this week."

"Why?"

When she didn't speak, I noticed the crowd noise increasing as both teams jogged in from the locker rooms. Dane and another player scooped up a ball and began to bump, set, and spike to each other. I think Lucia called that pepper? Dane towered over the other players, and I couldn't stop watching him. When an errant ball bounced my way, he looked up at me with a scowl before retrieving it. Game three was about to begin.

"I think I know why you avoided Lucia this week," I said as I gestured to the gym floor. "I'd ignore her too if forced to see her nasty PDA with *him*."

She grinned. "Aw, you still don't like Dane? But *your* side won the election."

Though the Democrats have a stranglehold on Congress. My stomach clenched.

She shrugged. "*I* think they're cute together."

I fought the urge to make a gagging sound. I didn't want to channel my seventeen-year-old brother, Mateo.

"I bet Lucia's been dying to talk about her and Dane. Now I feel even worse for going radio silent."

"You didn't know they had sex?"

"Apparently I found out after you did."

I scoffed. "I wish I'd never found out."

"Are you mad at Frank?"

"No." I shook my head. "I'm mad at myself for asking Frank to keep me informed. But she's my sister, and Dad's too busy to take care of her."

"Maybe Lucia can take care of herself?"

Her teasing smile made me pause but I still growled, "Definitely not."

She laughed as she rolled her eyes. "Big brothers."

"You have one too, then."

"Yes. His name's Braxton."

The crowd roared, and I realized again how blurry my surroundings had become as I focused on Maddie. She was like a flickering sparkler on a Fourth of July night. Everything around her seemed dull and out of focus.

"What a set!" She clapped her hands. "Dane was way off court, but he pushed the ball right to his offside hitter."

"Yeah, he's incredible," I gushed.

She caught my sarcastic tone and shook her head with a smile.

"Why did Lucy have to drag you here?" I asked. "You seem to enjoy the match."

Her shoulders slumped. "I've been a recluse all week, after…" She looked down. "After my boyfriend broke up with me."

My heart did the salsa dance. *I should feel some sympathy for her, right?* Here I was, training to become a doctor, supposed to feel sad for her loss, but my only feeling was a burst of joy. "That's…tough," I managed. "Is he a student at Highbanks?"

"He's a wrestler here. We dated three years."

"I'm sorry." Watching her lips tremble, I did feel sad for her. I fought the urge to rub my thumb across her mouth to quell the tremor. "So when Lucia said only *you* understand what she's going through, she meant you…?"

Her eyes darted up to meet mine. "That I've had sex?"

"Oh!" My eyes opened wide as heat rushed to my groin. "No, I was trying to say that you understood the, um, vicissitudes of, uh, romantic relationships —"

"Does that bother you?" She stepped closer, and I gulped. "Do you judge me for not being a virgin?"

Hell, no! I had to admit a woman who knew her way around the bedroom was sexy as hell. When blood started flowing to my brain again, I shook my head to clear it. "I know I just said premarital sex was wrong for Lucia and me, and Mateo too, but that's our family. I can't judge others for making different choices, especially if I want to be a good doctor. You have to find your own way."

She blinked as she took that in.

I hoped I hadn't sounded like a righteous twat. I wasn't sure I was convincing her of anything anyway. Hell, I was having more and more trouble convincing myself. *I wouldn't hate being another notch on your bedpost*, noted a voice in my head.

She tapped her chin. "I think I figured out the *real* reason you don't want Lucia to have sex."

"I already told you: premarital sex is against our values."

"No." She shook her head. "You're upset because your younger sister had sex before you did."

"*What?*" I took a step back, and her eyes flared, like she'd caught me doing something wrong. "That's ridiculous!" That wasn't why I'd come here tonight, right? *Dammit!* I did worry about becoming a forty-year-old virgin. Had that fear contributed to my angst when Frank told me about Lucia and Dane?

I tried to slow my breathing as I studied her. Her mouth curled up in a smirk, which ticked me off. "This is about my family's beliefs, not some stupid sibling rivalry. You don't understand."

"Why don't I?"

"You're a liberal, right?"

"Why do you think that?"

I gave her an unflinching stare. "Because you're black. Odds are overwhelming that you're a liberal."

Her eyebrows lifted. "Most people aren't so direct about my color."

So she could evade questions just like I did. "Well, most people are terrified of being called racist. Especially white people."

"But you're not white."

"Tell that to the media covering the Simon trial."

She shook her head, seeming to draw a blank.

"You know, the Latino guy who shot a man on his property? The media was up in arms about a white man killing an unarmed black man. They were totally wrong."

"Oh, my brother did tell me about that. It happened in the middle of the season."

She probably missed a lot due to volleyball. "Just admit it—you're a liberal."

She shook her head. "Actually, I couldn't care less about politics."

I exhaled. "How refreshing."

"But my brother cares. He was treasurer of the College Democrats at his school."

I groaned inside. *Of course.* "Which school?"

"Cleveland State."

"Is that where you're from? Cleveland?"

"Yep." She nodded, with a slight smile. "Way different from Houston, Texas."

In a flash, Lucia swooped in next to Maddie. "Sorry I left you alone with my brother for so long." My sister's gaze traveled from Maddie to me, and she stepped back as her smile faded. "Why do I feel like I'm interrupting something?"

My heart pounded, but I tried to play it cool.

"What have you guys been talking about?" she asked.

I glanced at Maddie, who shrugged. "You didn't tell me Alejandro played baseball in college," she said.

"And you didn't tell me Maddie plans to go to med school," I added.

"Oh, phew," Lucia said as she wiped her hand across her forehead. "I thought you might be discussing politics, or s-s-something…" She swallowed and her face reddened.

"Actually," Maddie said, looking straight at me, "we've had quite the conversation about sex."

Her challenging stare was a total turn-on. *Why is sex before marriage so bad, again?* I needed to remind myself to stick to my values. Even when they were growing unpopular with *me*.

"Well, wow. I'm sure that was…uh…" Lucia seemed like she had no idea what to say, and she looked down at the court. "Ooh, guys, Dane's serving!"

19

I turned to the court to watch Dane toss the ball high and execute a screaming jump serve. The ball shimmied so much it landed untouched between two defenders.

"Ace!" Lucia cried. She high-fived Maddie then cupped her hands around her mouth to create a megaphone. "Way to go, Monroe!"

Dane glanced up and gave her a thumbs-up as he returned to the serving line. He bounced the ball, waiting for the ref to blow his whistle.

"He aced them, Maddie!" Lucia did a happy dance.

He sure did, I thought. *Just like he aced my baby sister.*

"Lucia will be okay," Maddie whispered. She clasped my arm, and I looked down at her hand before raising my eyes to hers. "She's just in love."

I grunted.

Her hand lingered on my arm, and I liked it. I breathed deeply, inhaling her calming scent.

"Have you ever been in love, Alejandro?"

As my face warmed again, I kept my mouth shut. My standard position on premarital sex suddenly seemed harder to defend after talking to Maddie, and I hardly wanted to double down on painful disclosures by admitting the truth about this.

Her brown eyes shone up at me. "I'll take your lack of response for a no. Well, it's wonderful. And *horrible*." She flashed me a smile. "You should try it sometime."

3
Maddie
★ ★ ★

Why the bejeebers was I talking about love with Lucia's brother? When his eyes widened, I realized how close he stood.

Lucia tapped my shoulder, breaking the moment. I let go of Alejandro's arm to turn and face her. "Hey, you coming to dinner with Dane and me after the match?" she asked.

"Don't think so, Rez. I'm not suitable company these days."

Lucia's face fell. I didn't like disappointing her. She looked down, and now that she'd finally removed her coat I noticed her hot-pink shirt with yet another volleyball saying: *Don't You Wish Your Girlfriend Could Block Like Me?*

"Nonsense," Alejandro chimed in behind me. "You're great company, and you should join us for dinner. Where're we going?"

Lucia's eyes narrowed, and I stepped back to avoid the heat of her glare at her brother. "You're staying tonight?"

"I don't have a choice," Alejandro said. "The pilot told us when we landed that there's snow headed our way. We can't fly back till tomorrow."

"Ugh."

I wasn't sure if Lucia's disgust was about the snowstorm arriving or the shitstorm staying. I watched their back-and-forth argument like a game of pepper.

"*Where* are you staying, then?" Lucia asked.

"No choice on that one, either." Alejandro's eyes tightened as he studied her.

Lucia's lips pressed together. "So you're crashing my greenhouse without even asking me?"

He sighed. "Would it be okay with you, dear sister, if I stayed at your house tonight?"

"No." She laced her arms together.

Alejandro's hands flew to the sides of his head. "Do you think I *like* this? Being told where to stay, what to do? China and Brad ordered me to stay there tonight, for security." He pointed to Brad, who'd inched closer to us. "Tell her, Brad. I didn't choose this."

The beefy agent's lips puckered in a kiss, which he blew toward Lucia. "C'mon, Luce. You know you miss us. Let your bro stay." He clasped his hands together and lowered his head to blink up at her like a pleading Puss in Boots. The military muscle-head begging for a freshman girl's permission made me giggle.

A small smile relaxed Lucia's mouth. "Okay. Just for you, Braddy Bear." I followed her gaze toward Allison and China, who sat next to each other a few seats down from Frank.

The female agents scrutinized the crowd continually, but I noticed how their shoulders and knees touched. *Yet another happy couple.* My smile faded.

"And I'll agree to it for Allie, too," Lucia added. She turned back to her brother. "But I still don't like it."

"Duly noted." He looked down. "Thanks for making me feel so welcome."

I felt a bit bad for him—Lucia was typically much sweeter than this. He'd done a really good job of pissing her off. When his gaze met mine, I said, "She's just mad because it'll be tougher for Dane to sleep over now."

"Maddie!" Lucia's eyes stabbed my heart. "How could you take his side?"

Whoops. "Didn't mean to do that, Rez." I patted her shoulder. "I'm still on your side. But your brother doesn't visit every day." I looked at him with a hopeful smile. "And maybe he'll let this Dane thing go for now?"

"So Dane never moved out," Alejandro said, his voice strained. "Even though Dad ordered you to live apart."

Or maybe he won't *let it go.* I heard a distant bell ding for round two. Or was this round three of their argument? It was hard to keep track.

"Dane did move out!" Lucia's cheeks flushed. "He moved to a condo in December."

"Humph." Alejandro shook his head. "I still can't believe that green energy shyster Jim Thompson let a Republican keep his house."

"Well, Dane thought one of us should stay while Dr. Thompson's still in DC. It's an awesome house. And since I'm the one stuck with protection, we decided it would be me." She smirked. "Dane said Dr. Thompson's trying to suck up to Dad by letting me stay there."

"Good luck with that." He scowled. "No way Dad will waste money on bogus climate change research."

Bogus? My eyebrows lifted. *Even I know climate change is real.*

Alejandro assessed Lucia. "So how many nights a week does Dane stay over?"

"Not...that many." She shrugged.

A low laugh sounded from Brad, who had drawn even closer to us as the conversation continued. "Bowm chicka bowm bowm..."

Lucia paled.

"Man, do I miss this drama. It made my shifts just fly by last fall." He pointed at Alejandro. "All *you* do is study and exercise."

Sounds like my life, I thought. *Plus Netflix binges. So...no girlfriend for Señor Suave?*

"Sorry to bore you, Agent Jansen," Alejandro muttered.

"Nah, it's cool." Brad stuffed his hands in the pockets of his jacket. "Boring's good in my job. It means the protectee is safe."

A tendril of unease worked its way up my spine at the thought of danger facing the Ramirez family. Lucia often acted like Secret Service was a nuisance, nothing more, but her agents were here for a reason. Rez had become a good friend in a short time, and if anything happened to her...

I swallowed and tried to think about something else as my eyes wandered around the arena. When Dane stepped up to serve again, Lucia gave a giddy, fluttering clap. To my left, Alejandro played with his watch as he too focused on the court. Highbanks already had a two-game lead, and I knew Dane and company would take the third one soon, so I was less interested. Competition got my blood pumping—a shellacking like this was kind of a yawn-fest.

I nudged Alejandro's shoulder with mine. "Brad said all you do is study and work out?"

He frowned. "I know. Lamest guy ever."

"Not at all. I'm stoked to hear you have time for exercise in med school. I was worried about that."

He smirked at me. "Something tells me you'll find a way to fit exercise into your life, no matter what."

"Why do you say that?"

When his gaze floated down my body, my breath caught. He looked back up into my eyes. "You're rather fit." He cleared his throat. "But you already know that."

But I don't mind hearing it from you.

"Some of the second-years claim they don't have time to work out," he added. "But you have to make it a priority. I work out every afternoon after class, and it helps me study better at night. There's a ton of research about exercise improving cognitive function."

"I've heard about that." In fact, my academic advisor had told me most Highbanks athletes earned their best GPAs in season. "Was it tough to find an exercise routine when you retired from baseball?"

He opened his mouth to answer, then shook his head with a smile.

"What?"

"It's good talking to somebody who understands, that's all. None of my classmates get how hard it is to stop playing the sport that consumed you for seventeen years."

I smiled, too. "Why do you think I'm trying out for Team USA? I'm not ready to retire."

"Lucy says you have a good shot."

I glanced to my right, but Lucia appeared absorbed in the game instead of our conversation.

"To answer your question," Alejandro said as I turned back to face him, "at first my workouts didn't feel like enough. I was used to three-hour practices. But then med school started, and now I'm lucky to squeeze in an hour. No matter how busy I am, I make it a point to fit in exercise, though."

It was tough to envision life after Highbanks, and knowing I could work out even at my busiest calmed me. But my anxiety about the rest of life after graduation remained. Would I make the national team? Could I survive med school, if I got in somewhere? And if I did manage to become a physician, how would I find time for family?

I sighed. Having a family seemed like a mirage now. Would I eventually find a man to marry? I'd thought it was Jaylon, but now I had no one. Everything felt uncertain, and I gripped the railing just to have something to hold onto.

"You okay?" Alejandro asked.

"Yeah." When he kept staring at me, I said, "Just thinking about life after school." He nodded, and I tried to brighten my mood. "So, what do you like to do for exercise?"

"Oh, you know, run and lift. But the best workout is pickup basketball with the guys. It's pretty cut-throat."

I'd wondered about a purple mark near his temple. "That's where you got that bruise?"

"Yeah." His eye closed. "Took an elbow to the head. But I freaking snagged that rebound, baby."

I laughed.

Lucia surprised me by piping in. "I didn't know you'd picked up basketball again, Alex." Her voice had lost its edge.

He leaned forward to look at her. "I didn't realize how much I missed it."

"You played in high school?" I asked.

"Yes." He cocked his head. "You too?"

"You can't be six-one and get away with *not* playing. My high school coach would've killed me."

"*My* high school basketball coach guilt-tripped me every day for quitting the team after ninth grade," Lucia said. "But I didn't have time with club volleyball. How'd you find time for two sports, Maddie?"

I'd actually played three sports in high school, including running track, but I didn't want to boast. "I just made it work, I guess. I didn't like the break between high school and club seasons." I glanced at Alejandro to find him looking at me again.

"You love to compete," he said with a hint of admiration. "So does Lucy. Too bad she stopped basketball, because she and Dad made a killer team against Jake and me for two-on-two."

"President Ramirez plays basketball too?" I asked. When Alejandro nodded, I added, "Who's Jake?"

"My high school buddy." His jaw clenched.

He didn't say more, so I looked at Lucia.

"Jake's a marine," she said, then lowered her voice. "He's deployed in Afghanistan. Alex won't admit it, but he's worried about him."

I looked back and noticed him staring over Lucia's shoulder. Frank was approaching.

"Lucia," he said. She tensed next to me. "We'd like you to return to your seat." He gestured to the stands, where Allison patted the seat in front of her. "We don't want you or your brother out in the open like this."

Lucia's hold on the railing tightened. "So you can overhear *more* of my secrets and broadcast them to the world?"

My phone buzzed in my vest pocket, and I looked down to see an incoming call from my brother.

"C'mon, Luce," Brad said. "I was thinking the same thing about exposure—that's why I kept getting closer. Back to the stands, Ramirez *niños*."

To my surprise, Alejandro didn't hesitate. He cupped Lucia's elbow and nudged her toward the stands as he looked over his shoulder at me. "Coming, Maddie?"

Lucia shirked away from his hold. "Get off me, control freak!"

With Alejandro's eye-rolling grin, I stuffed my phone back into my pocket and followed them. It was fun to see that my brother and I weren't the only ones who antagonized each other. And it was too loud in the arena to answer Braxton's call, anyway.

I ended up sitting between the squabbling *niños*. We watched the game in silence for a few points, and I marveled at Dane's perfect set to Josh. Too bad Josh hit the ball into the net. I expected to see Dane explode, but instead he shrugged and bumped fists with his best friend. Then he said something to Josh that made him laugh. *Whoa*. Apparently Dane's counseling had helped him manage his anger. Lucia told me both she and Dane had continued to meet with Dr. Valentine, the school's sport psychologist.

I watched Alejandro scan the crowd, looking more like a protector than a protectee. "You seem to listen to the agents better than Lucia does," I said.

"Probably because it was Brad, not China." He tilted his chin up in her direction. China scowled as she kept watch over her charge.

She was one tough chick. "But I'm not stupid," he said. "There're people out there who want to kill us."

Fear flipped my stomach.

He shook his head. "Especially now that my dad's stepped up counterterrorism efforts."

"Like what?"

He snorted. "Well, it's sure as hell not creating shovel-ready jobs for the terrorists." When my confusion apparently showed on my face, he said, "You really don't watch the news, do you?"

"I'm too busy. And it's too depressing." I wondered if he thought I was an airhead. "I probably should pay more attention."

"Most college students don't follow politics, studies show. So you're not alone in that. But you did vote, right?"

I winced.

"You didn't even *vote?*" His voice rose. "And you call yourself an American?"

Lucia touched my arm as she leaned across me. "Don't give her a hard time, Alex. We had our conference tournament on election day."

His lips pressed together. "Hmm." He patted his thigh. "If you're not following the news, maybe you shouldn't vote, anyway."

Lucia cheered when Highbanks won a long rally, and I leaned closer to Alejandro. "We did have a match that day, but I still could've voted. Honestly, I didn't feel right choosing between Lucia's dad and Dane's mom. They're both my friends."

"Why do you like Dane?"

His tone was more curious than mean. "He's hilarious." I grinned, thinking back to a particularly funny incident last spring. "Jaylon and I were out last April—"

"Who's Jaylon?"

When I paused, he nodded grimly. "The ex."

I tried to block thoughts of him. "We had a few drinks with dinner." When Alejandro's eyebrow dipped, I added, "You know, celebrating the off-season." *Mr. Straight Edge doesn't drink, either?* Then I remembered Dane's public intoxication from last year, and figured out why Alejandro looked so disapproving. I glanced at Lucia, but her attention was focused on an elderly couple standing at the end of the row, likely asking about her father. She couldn't go anywhere without getting stopped. I turned back to Alejandro. "Don't worry, Lucia doesn't drink."

"She better not."

I shook my head. "I think that's for *her* to decide. Anyway, Dane and Nina were there…"

His dark eyes narrowed. "*Nina* was with Dane?"

"You know about Nina?"

"Another reason premarital sex is a bad idea," he grumbled.

Evidently he knew about her abortion, too. My voice rose. "Will you let me tell this story?" I thought I caught a half-smile before it disappeared from his face. "Anyway, it was karaoke night, and all the sudden the MC said, 'Next up's Jaylon Hart, performing *Killing Me Softly*.'" I cracked up, remembering his murderous expression.

Alejandro stared at my mouth when I laughed, which made me feel self-conscious. I swallowed, then continued the story. "When Jaylon figured out it was Dane who set him up, he was ready to kill. But everyone cheered for him to get onstage so he didn't have a choice." Giggles overtook me as I recalled his awkward, tone-deaf performance. "Jaylon was *so* bad. It was the Roberta Flack song, but I guess all he knew was The Fugees' version, so he kept trying to rap. He didn't have a damn clue. The crowd started to boo, and I couldn't wait for the song to end. But then Dane ran up there, grabbed the other microphone, and started singing falsetto. They turned it into a duet and by the end everyone was laughing at these big jocks hamming it up."

"Dane better not ever try that with me," Alejandro said, his voice stern but his eyes smiling.

"I never heard that story," Lucia said, and I realized she'd been listening. "I wonder if I could get Dane to do karaoke—that'd be a riot."

I frowned as the rest of that night replayed in my head. Jaylon had wanted me to spend the night, but I'd left because of an early-morning lab. Now that I thought about it, we'd had quite a few spats about me not spending the night. His injured brown eyes as I left his apartment…hadn't he understood I needed sleep? My throat tightened. Had I turned him away?

"Woohoo!" Lucia yelled as she popped out of her seat. "We won!" I looked behind me to see the agents bolt up as well, their eyes scanning the crowd. When I glanced at the court, the teams were passing each other single file as they shook hands.

Alejandro tilted his head toward me, sending over a waft of spicy aftershave. "So Great Dane leads his team to victory."

I tried to smile at his disdainful tone, but to my horror, my eyes filled with tears. "Sorry." I sniffed.

"You're thinking about Jaylon?"

All I could do was nod.

"Hey." His eyebrows knit together. "Your ex is an idiot." The look of concern on his handsome face made me cry harder. With his thumb, he brushed a tear from my eye. "You're a strong girl, Maddie. You'll get through this."

I took a shaky breath. I hadn't realized Lucia's sweetness was genetic.

Allison and Frank went ahead to scope out the restaurant, and the rest of us waited for Dane to emerge from the locker room. Once I recovered from my emotional freakout, Lucia had convinced me to join them, of course. And maybe I didn't hate the idea of getting to know Alejandro better. I felt my phone buzz again; this time it was a text from my brother:

> **Are you alive?**

What a stupid question. If I wasn't alive, how would texting me help figure it out? Alejandro and Lucia were absorbed in conversation—I'd overheard them say *Mateo*—so I decided to reply.

> **No. There was a plague at Highbanks.**
> **This is Zombie Maddie.**

> **Oh. Don't munch on my brain, Zomdie.**

I grinned.

> **Why'd you disappear on me? You know I hate that.**

My grin vanished. I guess I hadn't wanted to tell anyone about the breakup so it wouldn't seem real. But Lucia and Alejandro had made it less awful to admit the truth.

> **Jaylon broke up with me.**

His return texts showed up instantly.

WHAT?

Want me to come kick his ass?

I rolled my eyes. Braxton was a little taller than me, but he had nowhere near Jay's muscle mass. His next text arrived:

Probably for the best, anyway.

Rude. I knew I shouldn't have expected emotional support from him.

Thanks for the sympathy.

You know what I mean. Nana never liked Jaylon.

Nana never liked ANY of my boyfriends. She thinks they'll mess up my career.

I gulped, deciding not to add the reason for my grandmother's fear: *Just like Mom messed up Dad's career. Messed up his life, really.* Braxton didn't like me to mention our mother. When Mom left us right before my second birthday, Nana had become our true mother, and she'd done an awesome job filling in.

I realized I hadn't asked my brother about himself.

How are your classes?

I'm done with classes, remember?

Whoops. Braxton studied political science, and I tried to remember the next step in the never-ending pursuit of his doctorate.

When are doctoral exams?

February 15. I'll ace them.

I smiled. He never lacked confidence.

How's p-chem?

I groaned. Physical chemistry was my toughest class. *Hmm.* I wondered if Alejandro could help me with it?

I'm surviving.

Call Dad. He's worried about you.

Yes, sir, I wanted to type. I hated how Braxton ordered me around. When Dane emerged from the locker room, I typed a quick *Gotta go, bye!* instead.

Dane's hair was still damp and his face flushed from the shower. He smiled brightly when he saw Lucia.

"Love this coat on you," he said as he lifted her up and kissed her. She squealed. He put her down and clasped my shoulder. "Thanks for being here, Maddie."

"Good match, GD."

"Thanks." He turned to my right. "Well, lookie here, my babysitters are back." Dane reached out to pump Brad's hand.

"Danester," Brad said with a grin.

"Sure missed you, China." Dane wrapped his right arm around her neck and hovered his left fist over her head. "Can I give you a noogie, for old time's sake?"

"Not if you want to keep your balls," she answered.

When Alejandro laughed, Dane's eyes shot to him. The laughter stopped.

"And why are *you* here, Alex?"

4
Alejandro
★ ★ ★

"Just checking in on Lucy," I told Dane. I glanced at Lucia, whose huge eyes and pink cheeks warned me not to say more. I wanted to confront him for sticking it to my baby sister. But everyone else seemed to have other ideas.

"Hey, Dane." Maddie stepped closer to me. "Did you know Alejandro played baseball at TCU?" Her smile disarmed me.

"Yup," he said. "He had a good shot of going pro till he blew out his elbow."

My eyebrows lifted. How'd he know?

"Luz told me," he explained.

Of course. I wondered what else she'd told him. I watched Dane drape his arm over Lucia's shoulders, and she sighed as she tucked into him. They seemed to fit together well—both so tall and strong. When Lucia's eyes continued to plead with me, my resolve to comment grew even weaker. Seeing how happy she was with Dane, I wondered what right I had to interfere with their relationship.

Maddie punched my arm. "You didn't tell me *that*. You could've gone to the bigs?"

I clenched my teeth—I didn't like talking about my injury. Unsuccessful surgery freshman year had squashed my pro baseball dreams, moving me from first-string pitcher to third-string infielder. Dad hadn't said anything, but I knew he'd been disappointed. The hope of playing major league baseball had been my biggest connection to my father, and we'd had less to talk about since my surgery.

"Time to move out," China said. "Brad's got the SUV waiting." She pointed to the exit, but extended her arm to stop Dane from opening the door. "Hold on. Brad's going to escort you two at a time to the vehicle."

Maddie took a step back. "Maybe I should leave? I don't want to make it harder for them to protect you guys."

She can't leave. The sudden thought surprised me. "Don't worry. China's a great agent. She can handle it."

China narrowed her eyes at me, probably trying to figure out why I'd said something nice.

"Yeah, Maddie," Dane said. "Don't go. We'll help you feel better after that dickwad dumped you."

Maddie shook her head, but smiled. "Always the king of tact, Great Dane."

"That's me." He smirked as he gestured to the door. "Okay, you two first. Age before beauty."

It took me a second to realize he meant Maddie and I should go first. *Me old?* I was about to make a crack about his immaturity when Maddie's laugh cut in.

"Wow, Dane. Really boosting my self-esteem here. C'mon, Alex." Her brown eyes shone as she cocked her head toward the door.

Like a mindless idiot, I followed her. I guess Brad walked next to us the short distance to the vehicle; I didn't really notice him because Maddie's exquisite butt captured my full attention. Just like the rest of her, her derriere was lean and muscular, but just curvy enough to make black jeans my new favorite article of clothing.

Once we sat in the private dining room of the city's top seafood spot—the entire restaurant had whispered and pointed as the agents ushered us in—I finally relaxed. We were like normal people having a normal dinner. Well, minus the Secret Service hovering nearby. Most of my meals were hurried affairs, alone in my condo fortress between classes or after workouts, because I didn't want the hassle of security in the public. I hated eating alone in restaurants, too.

Lucia had placed herself across the round table, as far away from me as she could get, leaving Maddie to my left and Dane to my right.

After we ordered, Maddie fidgeted in her chair. She whispered something to Lucia, and their hushed conversation left Dane and me to stare at each other. He gave me a tight smile. *Awkward.*

"So, uh…" I shrugged. "Great match tonight."

His mouth relaxed a bit. "*Gracias.*"

I continued in Spanish. "Lucy told me you learned Spanish on a mission trip to Guatemala?"

Dane nodded and went on to tell me about his experiences there. He made a few grammatical errors, but his accent and fluency impressed me. He'd clearly studied the language for years.

"*No estoy seguro…pero creo que los aldeanos estaban comiéndose con los ojos a Jessica,*" he said, his eyes darkening.

I shuddered. "You thought the villagers were ogling your sister?"

"*Sí.* When I tried to call them out on it, one guy looked offended. So I told him, '*Me echaré un rapidín con tu madre.*'"

"*¿Qué?*" I laughed. "For the love of God, why'd you tell the villager you wanted a quickie with his mother?"

Dane laughed, too. "When my mom and I got there, that's what one of our hosts said to me. I thought it was a way to welcome us, and I wanted to smooth things over with the villagers." He pointed to a scar over his eyebrow. "The *cabrón* welcomed *me* with a busted pipe after that comment."

"I can't believe you said that." I shook my head with a chuckle. I looked up to see Lucia gaping at us, her eyes glowing. A smile spread across her face, replacing her typical look of worry. A brief conversation with Dane could make her that happy? I wanted her to look that way all the time. If giving Dane a chance meant my sister would feel such joy, maybe I could do that. After coming all the way here, I was leaning toward not telling my father about Lucia and Dane now. However, Dad expected me to protect my siblings. I just wasn't sure how to do that.

Maddie had resumed fidgeting.

"Everything okay?" I asked.

Lucia tossed her hair over one shoulder. "I was just telling Maddie how you're picking up the tab tonight."

"I am?" What was my sister up to?

"Rez!" Maddie whispered, looking down. She seemed embarrassed.

Oh. This place was likely too expensive for Maddie. How insensitive of me to insist that she join us.

"I'll get it," Dane said.

"No. I'm the oldest here, as you so kindly pointed out, Dane, so I'll get the tab. My dad can certainly afford it. Maybe he's not as loaded as Dane's grandfather…" I raised my eyebrows at him. "But Dad can pay for this one meal. He gave me a credit card for just this type of situation."

"What?" Lucia's mouth dropped open. "*I* don't have a credit card."

"That's because your scholarship pays for everything. I, however, am totally mooching off Mom and Dad."

Maddie set down her water glass. "Of course your parents are helping you; you're in med school."

I winced. Most of my classmates were incurring heavy debt, but my parents handled the bills for my tuition. They could easily afford it.

"Dude, why feel guilty for being wealthy? Republicans love money." Dane bit off a hunk of bread and smiled as he leaned back in his chair. "Nothing wrong with being rich."

I knew Dane had grown up in wealth. But my family had been middle class until my dad struck it rich with an ingenious oil drilling technique when I was six. "This conversation has taken a strange turn." I nodded at Dane. "Usually *your* party's the one maligning millionaires. 'Pay your fair share' and all that."

"If the millionaires steal from their employees, they should be maligned," Dane said. "But my grandfather earned his money fair and square."

"And our dad did too." I met Lucia's eyes, then looked back at Dane. "I guess what I feel guilty about is not paying my own way. I'm a big believer in self-reliance. I want to take care of myself, not rely on my parents or the government to do it for me. I plan to pay back my parents when I can."

"But you've had some opportunities that most people don't," Dane said. "Sometimes people can't take care of themselves. They need the government."

"Some people do need help to get back on their feet," I admitted. "But not half the population."

Lucia groaned. "Let's not turn this dinner into a political debate."

"Really?" Maddie grinned. "I'm kind of enjoying this. You and Dane never argue like you used to, and I miss it."

"You never argue?" I frowned at Lucia. "Don't tell me you've become a liberal sycophant."

"Alex." She huffed out a breath. "I have no idea what you just said, but give me a break. Dane and I have agreed not to discuss politics, for the most part. We get too mad at each other when we do." She peeked at him and returned his smile.

"Though you are hot when you're mad," he murmured. "*Caliente.*"

TMI. I made a face at Maddie, and she chuckled.

"I don't want to stress you out, Rez, but I do want to hear what the guys think about this," Maddie said. "Alejandro pointed out how ill-informed I am, so I want to change that."

"You don't have to change, Maddie." I shook my head. "I meant what I said. It's refreshing that you're not involved in politics like everyone else I deal with."

"You think it's refreshing because I haven't shot down your views, like Dane does."

As I considered her words, I looked at Dane, who smirked as he chewed more bread.

"For the people who don't have privileges and opportunities, how do you help them?" she asked. "What works to get them back on their feet?"

"We know what works," Dane said, looking smug. "Government programs, job creation, student loan forgiveness. Education's so important."

"Education *is* important for creating a better life, but everything else you said isn't accurate." How could he be so misinformed? "Government programs have only made the poor poorer, because they create a culture of dependency. Making people dependent on the government is *not* compassion."

"But—"

"Secondly," I cut him off. "The government doesn't create jobs; the private sector does. The government only serves to spend the money created by private companies." Dane looked ready to rebut, so I forged ahead. "And thirdly, forgiving student loans? Really, Dane? Who's going to pay for that? My dad inherited twenty trillion in debt! The taxpayers can't afford that."

"Wow." Maddie nodded. "You're pretty passionate about this stuff, huh?"

I looked down at my hands clenched in my lap and felt hotness on my face. I had leaned forward in my seat like I was about to pounce on Dane. As I exhaled, I slouched back a few inches.

"Passionate about bullshit," Dane said. "Republicans only care about rich white men, Wall Street tycoons. The rich get richer, and the poor get poorer."

"That's a nice theory, but wholly unsupported by the evidence. When the Democrats were in charge of the White House, black unemployment was higher than ever. You're not doing black people any favors by giving them handouts."

"Wrong again. Government creates justice by helping those who've faced an uneven playing field, like people of color. By reducing public aid, Republicans prove they don't care about those people." Dane's chin jutted out. "If you cut off government aid, then what?"

"Yes, Alejandro, what do you propose?" Maddie said.

My heart rate sped up, and I tried to be careful in choosing my words. "There aren't easy answers. We need more school choice, so people in poor neighborhoods can attend better schools. But really, it's a systemic problem. It comes down to family values—single-parent homes create poverty and dysfunction. Over seventy percent of black households are fatherless."

When Maddie gasped, my eyes shot to her. Had I said something wrong? *Dios*, had *her* father left her family? Maddie wouldn't look at me, so I glanced at Lucia for answers. But she just pressed her lips together.

"You're so racist," Dane said.

"What?" My heart thundered in my chest. "How's that racist? I'm citing facts."

"Your 'facts' are wrong. But regardless, you're assuming single-parent households are bad. That's not true. One parent can be just as good as two."

As Lucia threaded her fingers through Dane's, he looked at her and took a noticeable deep breath. What was going on between them?

"I disagree," I said. "Look, some single parents do a great job. I couldn't make it work like they do, that's for sure. But to pretend the opportunities are the same as they are with two parents? That's ridiculous. Kids need fathers. I wouldn't be half the man I am today if my father hadn't been there for me."

"Maybe that's your problem," Dane snapped. "He molded you into who you are."

"And I'm proud of it." I glared at him.

"Maddie?" Lucia broke in, gazing at her teammate. "You okay?"

"Yeah." Her voice shook, and she still wouldn't look at me. Why was she so distant? "Did I say something wrong?"

She finally met my gaze, and her eyes glistened. "Dane's right. You're making assumptions about black people. *My father never left us.*"

Thank God. "I'm glad," I said quietly.

She looked like she wanted to say more, but instead she bolted from her seat. I also stood. "I have to go…" She looked at Allison. "I'm going to the bathroom." She booked it out of the private dining room with Allison following her, leaving the rest of us staring after.

"Well done, Alex."

Dane's sarcasm cut into me, and I saw red. "How *dare* you call me racist? You don't know what the hell you're talking about." My jaw clenched as I returned to my seat. "Have you ever been called Spick?" His eyes widened. "How 'bout Cheech? Texican?"

Dane's face paled. "No." He blinked. "And you have?" When I didn't answer, he darted his eyes to Lucia. "Have you been called racist names?"

She looked down. "One time a guy called me a BMW."

I shook my head. *¡Cabrón!*

"What does that mean?" Dane asked.

"Big Mexican Woman."

"What a douchebag!" Dane reached out and tugged her chair closer. "That guy had no fucking clue, Luz. You're beautiful." His arm cradled her shoulders.

"It's okay." She shrugged. "Kids are stupid."

"It's *not* okay," I said. "Racism's serious. That's why I can't stand it when people accuse others of racism just because they disagree with them. It shuts down all conversation. And I don't appreciate it from you, Dane."

He took a deep breath again and mumbled something.

"What?" I prompted.

He looked straight at me. "I'm sorry, Alex."

"Whoa," Lucia said. When we both gave her quizzical looks, she kissed Dane's cheek. "That's a banner moment for you, Monroe: willingly apologizing. I can't wait to tell Dr. Valentine about this."

He breathed out through his nose as he shook his head. "She'll probably take all the credit for it, too." He looked down. "This is classic…the one white person thinking he knows everything about race. That's not cool."

I had to agree with him there.

"But you guys dealing with racism like that is awful. How do we stop that bullshit?"

"We need to keep communicating," I said. "But we're so afraid of saying the wrong thing—of hurting somebody's feelings—that we don't name the elephant in the room."

Dane grinned. "The elephant in the room—you're referring to Republicans?"

I shook my head and fought a smile. "Democrats too. Maybe I should've said the donkey in the room."

"I *want* to keep talking," Dane said. "We need to figure this shit out. Luz, tell me what to do."

She blinked quickly, like she was startled he'd asked her that. "Um…" She looked at me, then back at Dane. "You could start by not calling my brother racist when he says something you don't like?"

"Done." He nodded, then looked at me. "I truly am sorry, dude. I promise not to call you racist—unless you deserve it, that is."

His apology impressed me. But as my eyes fell on Maddie's empty chair, my smile faded. I sensed I had some apologizing to do as well.

The SUV pulled up to what I assumed was Maddie's apartment building. We'd already dropped off Dane, and now it was just the three of us with our agents. Maddie hadn't said much when she'd returned to the table, and she remained aloof as she opened the car door. "Bye, guys."

"Wait." I scooted closer to her. "I'll walk you in."

Brad opened his door, preparing to follow us.

Maddie paused. "No worries," she said. "Don't want to make a big production."

I frowned. "And *I* don't want Secret Service to kill chivalry. C'mon, I'll walk you." When I scooted over again, she sighed.

"Fine."

Her clipped tone made my heart thump. Why was she angry with me? I glanced at Lucia before I climbed out, and she seemed equally perplexed.

I jammed my hands in my coat pockets as I followed Maddie to her building. My breath practically turned to ice crystals as I exhaled, and I wondered why anyone would want to live here. Baltimore was way colder than Houston, but nowhere near as bad as the Midwest. Brad remained a respectful distance behind us.

We went inside and in no time arrived at her door. Maddie almost had her key in the lock when I said, "Wait." She kept looking down. "Please?"

"It was good meeting you." Her voice shook.

"Maddie?" She still wouldn't look at me. "I think I hurt your feelings back there, and I, I'm really sorry."

She looked up at me as a tear slid down her face.

No! "I did. I did hurt your feelings. Oh, Maddie, please forgive me. I don't know what I'm talking about. I'm a total mess—"

"No, you were fine. It's me who's the mess." She swiped the back of her hand across her cheek. "I never cry like this. I don't know what's wrong with me."

I huffed out a breath, disgusted with myself. "I have that effect on women, apparently."

"I should've stayed home. I knew I'd only bring people down tonight."

"You didn't bring *me* down. If anything, I was the one darkening everyone's moods. I shouldn't have said anything about black people—I clearly should've kept my mouth shut."

"You have *no* idea what it's like to be black in this culture," she said sharply. Then her voice softened. "But you're right about growing up in a single-parent household. It's not easy."

My eyebrows drew together. She'd said her dad had stayed, right? "What do you mean? I thought…" My heart seized when a sob escaped her throat.

She clasped her hand over her mouth as tears spilled down her cheeks. "Gotta go." She turned the key and darted inside before I could stop her. "Tell your sister thanks." Then the door closed.

I looked at Brad, who shrugged.

What the hell just happened? I closed my eyes as I exhaled. "Good job, *imbécil.*"

Maddie

It had been three whole weeks now since Jaylon had broken up with me, and I still dissolved into tears every time I thought of him. Feminists everywhere were likely peering down their noses at my pathetic response to a simple breakup. Where was my cheerful disposition? My competitive fire? Those had disappeared along with my dignity.

And how embarrassing that I'd cried in front of Alejandro not once, but twice. I wished I could've been stronger around him, though I wasn't sure why I cared so much about his opinion of me. He'd seen me at my worst two weeks ago, and he must have thought I was a delicate little flower. No wonder he'd questioned whether I could make it as a doctor.

As I stared at the incomplete p-chem lab report on my laptop, I had the same doubts about my abilities. We'd studied phase transitions in the lab yesterday, melting a chemical from solid to liquid, and I couldn't help but compare that little glob of gallium to my own life. If all went as planned, soon I'd transition from student to adult, from college volleyball to the national team. But I'd already phased from coupled to single, and the resulting loneliness felt shaky and ungrounded. I brushed some tears off my cheeks. From solid to liquid.

I yawned and rubbed my bleary eyes. Then I looked at my phone and freaked out at the time. I'd frittered away the entire afternoon, and the lab report wasn't even half done. I shut my laptop and flew into my bedroom to grab my keys. The report was due tomorrow, but I'd have to finish it later. Volleyball practice awaited.

My heart pounded when I walked into an empty locker room. I wasn't *that* late, was I? I stripped off my street clothes and tugged on Spandex shorts, which felt a little looser than normal. I heard balls bouncing on the gym floor, and I prayed warm-up hadn't already begun. As I leaned over to lace up my shoes over my ankle braces, one shoelace snapped. I looked at the frayed piece of string hanging limply in my hand and burst into tears.

"What's your *deal?*"

I looked up to find Nina. *Awesome.* Our cool, blond setter was hardly the best teammate to provide emotional support.

"Just having one of those days," I muttered as I unlaced two eyes so I could tie my shoe with the shorter lace.

Nina continued to stare while I threw a Highbanks T-shirt over my sports bra. "Don't think I've ever seen you cry."

"Yeah?" I sniffed. "Well, stick around. That's all I do these days." I headed for the door. "You coming?"

"Oh!" She jumped. "Forgot I came in to grab my playbook." She lunged for the binder in her locker and jogged to the gym behind me.

"You're leading warm-up today?" I asked over my shoulder. Coach made the team captains take on a leadership role during the winter months.

"Yep." She came up next to me and set the binder down on the bleachers. "Get ready for a tough one today, Brooks." She took off for the net.

I smiled as I stifled a groan. *Not today.* My fake smile vanished as Coach Holter marched toward me with narrowed eyes.

"You're late, Madison."

I glanced at the clock and saw one minute remaining until practice began. That meant I was fourteen minutes late by Coach's standards. "Sorry."

"You know, I don't have to let you practice with us this winter. I'm doing you a favor."

I nodded. I'd gotten this same speech last week when I stunk up the gym with my horrible play, but I wasn't about to point out that he was repeating himself. Nina started the team on a warm-up jog around the gym, and Lucia kept glancing my direction.

"But I do want you here," Coach said, and I noticed his hard gaze had softened a touch. "That is, if you play the way I know you're capable of playing. And the past two weeks—after you missed a whole week of practice—hasn't been it."

"You're right." *Thanks, Jaylon. Thanks for messing up volleyball, too.*

"I've given you some leeway because of all you've done for our program." He rubbed his jaw as he watched the team finish their jog and move to the center of the court. After a moment my teammates shuffled down the net, jumping to block every few feet.

"But if you want to keep practicing with us, and if you want a shot in hell at making Team USA, you have to be all in. No more showing up late. No more missing practice. I want you here—mind, body, and spirit."

My stomach clenched. I didn't know if I had it in me to give him what he wanted. Normally a speech like this would fire me up, but I hadn't slept well last night, or the night before. All I wanted was to go home and take a nap.

"You're still a leader on this team," Coach said.

Nina's screechy voice filled the gym. "You can do better than that, Kaitlyn!" I watched the short, black-haired defense specialist smirk at Nina before she executed a flawless roll—a sideways somersault that propelled her back on her feet after diving for the ball. *Oh, no.* Lucia hated practicing rolls. I looked over to see her long legs emerge from a somersault and thrust her to her feet. *Not bad.* She'd definitely gotten faster at the maneuver over the past few months. Still, Lucia aimed a death stare at Nina, who shouted, "Ten! I want ten perfect rolls!"

Coach's voice lowered. "And a better leader than Nina."

I caught a rare smile from him.

"Maybe we can petition the NCAA to get you one more season?" His eyebrow arched.

"Nina's your captain next year, Coach." She'd be a senior and the starting setter when next season started in the fall. I mustered a sympathetic smile. "No one can save you from that." I jogged to the court to join the warm-up from hell.

About an hour later, we practiced defending cross-court hits. I stood at the center of the net in my typical middle-blocker position with Nina and Lucia on the opposite side of the net. Our assistant coach, Kara, tossed a ball to Nina, who set it to Lucia on my left. I shuffled left to join my teammate Brianna in a double block against Lucia. But somehow her spike careened through our hands yet again.

Typically I loved trying to block Rez's zinger lefty spikes. But today I felt helpless. Even knowing Lucia would hit the ball at an angle across the court, right toward my block, I struggled to reach my spot in time. My timing on jumps also felt messed up.

When Kara tossed the next ball, I cheated a little to my left before Nina launched her set that direction. *I'm getting this one, damn it.* I sensed Brianna at my side and watched Lucia's midsection, leaping when she did with my hands firm over the net. Brianna also jumped for the double block. The play ended all too quickly, and when I came back down I swiveled right to see Lucia's hit zoom to the floor just inside the court. My block hadn't even touched the ball, and her hit had such a vicious angle that Kaitlyn didn't have a chance to dig it. Point to the opponent.

I rested my hands on my knees as I sucked in air. My head felt light and wobbly, and I shook it to get back on track.

"That was one of the worst blocks I've ever seen," Coach said.

I closed my eyes. *He's right.*

"Get in sync, Madison and Brianna. Tighten up that block. Again."

I pulled myself up and returned to the middle of the net. I managed to get my hands on Lucia's next hit, but the ball rolled off my fingertips and flew off court, where Kaitlyn was unable to save it.

"Firm up that block, Madison."

I nodded at Coach as I panted.

"Water break!" he hollered.

Thank God. I realized my legs trembled as I walked toward my Gatorade bottle. What the hell was my problem?

Lucia sidled up to me after I drank some water. "Have you eaten anything today?"

"Of course." As I thought about it, though, I wasn't sure. "I…" I'd skipped breakfast because I hadn't been hungry, but I'd eaten lunch, right? I'd gone to microbiology lecture, then I'd worked on my lab report…

"Maddie." Lucia's voice rose as she blinked. "Have you?"

I winced. "I don't think so."

"I won't stand by and watch you develop an eating disorder."

I laughed. "You don't need to worry about that, Rez." When she didn't crack a smile, I touched her arm. "I just haven't been hungry lately. But you're right, I need to eat. No wonder my blocks sucked today."

"Ask Coach if you can go to the training room. Tina has some protein bars."

"I'll be fine. I'll grab something after practice."

"Go *now*, Maddie." She pointed to the training room in one corner of the arena.

Well, *this* was a role reversal. I'd forced her to visit Tina a few times in the fall when she'd been too scared to eat. I bit back a smile at the stern line of her mouth. It seemed my sweet Rez had grown a backbone. "Yes, ma'am."

Her mouth relaxed. "If *I* have to eat, so do you."

"Paybacks are hell." I smirked.

I approached Coach, who was having a powwow with his assistants. "Uh, Coach?" The three looked at me. "May I go to the training room for a protein bar? Turns out I forgot to eat today." I shrugged.

His shoulders lowered with what looked like relief. "So that's why you played like shit today. Of course you can go."

"Thanks."

I headed to the training room but turned around when he added, "Don't let it happen again."

I nodded.

Tina's eyebrows flew up when I told her why I was there. "*Lucia* sent you to get food?"

I hoisted myself onto one of the padded exam tables. "Ironic, isn't it?"

"How's she doing with her eating?" Tina's dark blond ponytail swayed when she opened a drawer full of bars. I chose peanut butter-chocolate.

"Pretty good, I think." I unwrapped the bar. "I watched her eat salmon, veggies, and rice a couple weeks ago at a restaurant."

My nose wrinkled at the bar's soy-protein smell, but I forced myself to take a bite. Once I chewed and swallowed, I realized how hungry I was. I polished off the bar in about two minutes, swigging water from my bottle between bites.

"So why'd you forget to eat today?" Tina busied herself with arranging the protein bars into neat rows in the drawer, but I knew her eagle eye still assessed me.

"It was stupid. I got caught up doing bio and chem labs."

She shut the drawer and studied me. "You know, loss of appetite could be a symptom of depression."

What? "I'm not depressed. I've just been busy."

"Okay." She patted my knee. "I heard…"

I braced myself.

"I heard you were going through a tough time." She patted my knee again, and I held my breath. "Breakups can be painful."

My nose burned. *Don't cry.* "Who told you about Jaylon?"

"That doesn't matter." She shrugged. "Athletic trainers, we hear things. I know you two dated for a while, so I wondered how you were doing. Want to talk about it?"

I hopped off the table. "No. I'm fine." I rocketed from the room before yet another person witnessed my breakdown over my breakup. "Thanks, Tina," I said from the door. *Time to stink up the gym some more.*

Following a quick shower after practice, I was almost fully clothed when Lucia entered the locker room. She tossed her shoes into her locker as I zipped up my boots. I watched a completely nude Nina saunter to the showers—she'd obviously been hitting the tanning bed. Shaking my head, I grabbed my backpack. "Have a good night, Rez."

"Wait, don't leave." She unlaced her ankle braces. "I wanted to see if you'd come over for dinner. Will you wait for me to get dressed?"

The hopeful look in her eyes made me pause. "I have to write a lab report tonight."

"Please? Dane's playing at Ball State…" As the university's name rolled off her tongue, she started snickering like the freshman she was. "And I don't have anyone to eat with. No one to, you know, support me at mealtime." She tilted her head and peered up at me.

What an obvious ploy to get me to come over. We both knew damn well she was recovering like a champ. My eyes narrowed.

"Please, Maddie?"

My dad's ring tone blasted from my backpack, and I sighed. "Fine. I'll wait for you in the hallway."

"*¡Gracias, amiga!*"

What a manipulator. I jogged to the hallway to the beat of "Superfreak" by Rick James — my dad's favorite artist — and managed to answer the call before it went to voice mail. "Hey, Dad."

"Finally I catch you. Have you been avoiding me?"

I grimaced. "Sorry."

"I thought today's college students relied too *much* on their parents — calling them five times a day, asking them to write papers. But you I never hear from."

My dad taught history at Cuyahoga Community College and often complained about overinvolved parents. "How many calls have you gotten from parents wanting to change their kid's grades?"

"Hmm, about five so far. But it's only February — the semester's still young. Are you going to tell me what's been going on?"

"Stop pretending you don't already know. I'm sure Braxton talked to you."

He paused. "Well, we both know that boy can't keep a secret."

I shook my head, remembering when I was thirteen and got my period. Braxton had overheard me on the phone telling a track teammate about it, and to my horror, he'd ratted me out to Dad. I'd about died. Fortunately, Dad had enlisted Nana's help. My grandmother had been discreet in her delivery of both the feminine products and the lesson on how to use them.

My dad let the line go silent, and I looked around to make sure the hallway was still empty. I backed up against the wall. "So you know Jaylon broke up with me."

"Yeah, uh…sorry about that." Dad's voice hitched, like he was nervous. "You'll be, um, you'll be better off without him."

Would I? It sure didn't feel that way.

"You meet any new men yet?"

"Dad." I exhaled. "You're not helping. I'm nowhere near ready to date another guy." Though I had to admit I'd been thinking about Alejandro, or Jandro, as I'd been referring to him in my head. "You can't make this all go away with the snap of your fingers, you know."

"Sorry. This…this is probably something your mother would handle better."

My face flushed. Why'd he have to bring her up? This was precisely the reason I hadn't called him.

"Sorry," he said again. "I know you don't like me talking about her."

Make it stop. I tried to think of something to distract him. "What did Nana say?"

Dad snorted, and then sounded less anxious. "She said, ''Bout time Maddie dumped that dumbass boy.'"

The image of my feisty grandmother made me grin. She'd never thought Jaylon was my intellectual equal, and she'd been right that school wasn't really his thing. But she'd been wrong about the rest: I hadn't been the dumper. I'd been the dumpee.

"Jaylon's not dumb—he just doesn't care about school. At least he's managed to keep his GPA above two point oh." I pictured his muscular body sprawled out on the bed as he frowned at a textbook. But what he lacked academically, he made up for physically. He was one of the best athletes I'd ever known. He was going places. I frowned as I realized again he wouldn't be taking me with him to said places.

Dad asked another question, but the chime of an incoming text distracted me. I held my phone out from my ear, expecting to see a text alert, but there wasn't one. Huh? The *ding* had sounded so close. Was someone nearby?

"Maddie?" Dad asked.

When I crept around the corner, I froze. Jaylon was backing away, his phone in his hand, staring at me with big eyes. *Busted.*

"You're *eavesdropping?*" I hissed.

He squinted. "You're raggin' on my GPA?"

My mouth popped open. He *had* been listening!

Dad spoke again. "Maddie, everything all right?"

I realized I still held my phone to my ear. "Gotta go, Dad—I'll call you later." Once I ended the call, I glared at Jaylon. "What're you doing here?"

His eyes widened even more as he backed away.

"I told you I never wanted to talk to you again! Didn't you get the message?"

"Got it." He swallowed, drawing my attention to his Adam's apple and smooth, solid neck. He wore the braided gold chain I hated—the one that made him look like a thug. "I'll leave."

Blood rushed in my ears at the thought of him walking out of my life yet again. "No, don't." A line creased his forehead. "How…" I took a shaky breath. "How could you think I didn't love you?"

"Mads." His gentle voice made me want to run to him and curl up in his arms. "Don't put this on me. You didn't let me in." He pushed his lips out as he shook his head. "You don't let anyone in."

As I tried to make sense of his words, a flash of blond streaked past me.

"Jay Jay!" Nina called as she bounded up to him.

My heart stopped. *Nina?* He was here to see Nina? No wonder he'd been tucked around the corner, hiding from me. Had he been sneaking around after other practices, too?

"Aw, fuck," Jaylon muttered.

Nina appraised me. "Thought you'd left already."

My legs shook. This wasn't happening—Nina was dating the star quarterback of the football team, right? I reached for the wall to hold me up. "But, but Nina's with TJ Tinton."

Her nose wrinkled. "We broke up over a month ago."

Oh, God. Jaylon cheated on me with my teammate. I splayed my hand out on the wall as my mind raced. *I'm not good enough. He doesn't want me. I'm not good enough to keep him here.*

Jaylon looked away, and I studied his profile—his strong nose, the ripple of muscle working at the base of his jaw. I'd believed we might get back together, but now I knew that belief was a delusion. Between panicked breaths, I finally spoke. "You're with *her?*" I hated the tremble in my voice, but I hated even more how Jaylon wouldn't look at me. "You cheated on me with Nina?"

"No, girl!" He whipped his head to look at me. "Don't you pin that on me." He took another step back. "We didn't hook up till you and I ended things."

Right. No wonder he'd acted so distant. "You cheated on me with a teammate."

His jaw went slack. "Don't you *listen?* I said—"

"Maddie?"

I turned to see Lucia. She inched toward me and clasped my arm, like she knew I was about to collapse. "What's happening?"

"Maddie thinks Jaylon cheated with me," Nina said. When she leaned into him and rubbed her cheek on his shoulder, I wanted to hurl. "But she's wrong."

Lucia gasped. "You're with Jaylon? You don't waste any time, do you, Nina?"

"This is none of your business." Her blue eyes narrowed.

"Actually, it's none of *yours*," Lucia said. "Maddie and Jaylon dated for three years. They need time to work this out. *Ven acá.*" She curled her fingers toward her open palm, beckoning Nina. "Let's give them some space to talk."

"Hell, no." Nina shook her head. "He's been wanting to leave her for months!" She looked at Jaylon. "Right?"

A sob caught in my throat as I sagged against Lucia's hold. Had he ever loved me?

Lucia launched into a Spanish diatribe—I had no idea what she was saying but her fury was obvious.

Jaylon didn't speak the language, but he was savvy enough to know when he was being insulted. Or when his girlfriend—I felt bile in my throat as I thought of Nina that way—was being disrespected.

He took a step toward Lucia. "Listen, freshman, you don't know jack—"

"Party's over," Allison said, appearing at Lucia's side. I hadn't even seen her, but of course she was there. "Let's go, Lucia." She kept her gaze trained on Jaylon as she pulled Lucia back.

"Not without Maddie!" Lucia tugged my arm. "C'mon. Let me get you out of here."

Weak and numb, I surrendered to being swept off by Secret Service. As I touched wetness on my cheek, I knew why she'd looked so alarmed.

I was crying. Again.

6
Alejandro

I gazed out the tinted window of the SUV. When I saw the Washington Monument, I knew we were close to my parents' house. This would be my first visit to their new residence, and to prepare myself, I'd studied up on the stats: one hundred thirty-two rooms and thirty-five bathrooms centered on eighteen acres of land. The recent exterior paint job had taken three hundred gallons of paint. White paint.

At a stoplight, a woman crossed the street in front of us. She wore tall, black, high-heeled boots, and her swagger said she knew she commanded men's attention. But I knew a girl who looked even sexier in tall boots. A girl whose legs went on for days, not even needing heels since she was over six feet tall.

¡Dios! Maddie had consumed my thoughts again. Two weeks since my visit to Highbanks, and I couldn't get Lucia's teammate out of my head. Not only did Maddie and I have our college athletic experiences in common, we had our futures in medicine. I knew she could reach her lofty goals. She was that kind of talented.

But what I thought of most was how beautiful she was when she cried. She'd seemed embarrassed by her tears, and I still felt like a total cad that I'd caused them. Still, I couldn't deny her alluring softness as beads of glass spilled down her smooth, brown skin. The tenderness in her gaze when I'd brushed them away…

Brad's wolf whistle brought me back to the vehicle. We were still stopped at the light, and I looked to my left to see Miss Long Boots sashay from the crosswalk onto the sidewalk. "*Day-um*," Brad said as he watched her walk away. "You can pin me down with that boot any day, sugar. Rub that heel right into my chest."

I rolled my eyes.

The light changed, and Brad pressed on the accelerator. Next to me in the backseat, China leaned forward. "Gettin' horny as we approach La Casa, Bradley?"

He laughed. "*Sí, mamacita.*"

I pursed my lips. I knew *La Casa* was the agents' code name for the White House now that my family had moved in. But why would Brad feel horny?

We maneuvered around to the back of 1600 Pennsylvania Avenue. I thought we'd enter through one of two heavily guarded gates, but we rolled past them. Marines were everywhere, and I assumed there were many more I couldn't see. Their stony expressions made my stomach clench. I hadn't heard from my buddy Jake in a few weeks; communication was a challenge in Afghanistan. If Jake hadn't needed a Naval ROTC scholarship to afford college, he could've joined me at TCU. But he'd attended Texas A&M and was now a second lieutenant, risking his life overseas.

We rounded the corner of our country's most notorious house, and I braced my hand against the armrest when it appeared Brad was driving us into a brick wall. But then the "wall" slid to the right, revealing the Secret Service entrance. I glanced at China, who smirked at me. I placed my hand back in my lap.

"Officers Jansen and Halloway," Brad told the marine who stopped us.

The guard checked his computer. "Who're you transporting, Jansen?"

"Fernando."

"Proceed." The marine gestured to his left.

But Brad didn't move the vehicle. "I expect my fifty bucks before we leave, Richards."

"Fucking Jets." The marine scowled. "You got lucky this time, jackoff." Then he glanced at me in the backseat, and straightened, resuming his stiff expression. "Sir."

Brad cackled as he rolled up the window and drove us down the ramp to an underground garage. "Can't believe he thought his lame-ass Cowboys would beat my Jets."

Neither team had made the NFL playoffs this year, so Brad must have bet him back in December. "Richards cheers for Dallas?" I asked.

Brad nodded.

"Is he from Texas?"

"Yeah." Brad turned to face me after parking the car. "Why?"

I shrugged. Sometimes I felt homesick for the Lone Star State, especially on a chilly February day in DC.

As we headed into the building, I asked, "Why am I called Fernando?"

"That's on a need-to-know basis," China said.

"Well, I need to know."

"And we need you *not* to know." Her gelled brown hair didn't move an inch as she shook her head.

Oh, China. She lived to antagonize. I understood why Dane had made a break for it last fall. Anything to get away from her for a few hours.

Brad punched in a code for the elevator, which we rode up to the ground floor from deep underground. "Mr. Ramirez." China smiled at me during our ascent, which gave me pause. "We're stopping first at our supervisor's office. She wants to be sure we're taking good care of you."

That's why she was smiling. She didn't want me to complain about her.

Brad was less subtle. "I'm sure you'll put in a good word for us, Fernando." He thumped my shoulder as we stepped out of the elevator and walked down a busy hallway. Several staffers tried to hide their stares when I passed, but they did a piss-poor job of it. The public scrutiny was already getting old, less than one month into my father's presidency.

My agents came to attention on either side of me once we made it to their supervisor's office. When the woman stood and rounded the desk, she was solidly built, though not as muscular as bodybuilder China. "I'm Senior Officer West." She shook my hand. "Thank you for meeting with me, Mr. Ramirez."

Did I have a choice in the matter? I nodded.

"How have officers Halloway and Jansen been treating you, sir?"

China seemed to stiffen next to me, but Brad appeared calm. "It's an adjustment to have protection around the clock, but they've been fine. Thank you for protecting my family. I'd like to see them now, if I could?"

"Of course. I'll leave you to it." She smiled. "Officer Halloway will escort you upstairs. Officer Jansen, please stay." Her eyelids lowered a fraction and something shifted in her smile. "I want to review your performance."

"Yes, ma'am." Brad's voice held a hint of excitement.

I tilted my head on our way out. Brad and his boss weren't about to get it on, were they? I glanced at China, who moved with efficiency as she scanned the hallway. If I asked her about it, I'd likely get another lecture on what I didn't need to know.

We climbed the stairs to the first level and entered an ornate sitting room with mint green walls, fuchsia chairs, and a gleaming chandelier. China dipped her shoulder and opened her palm with a flourish. "May I present the Green Room, sir."

The stiff introduction by a modern bodybuilder in the antiquated setting jarred me. "Knock it off, China. Where's my mom?"

"I *heard* you were here!" My mother entered with her arms extended, and I walked into her hug. I noticed a male agent coming in behind her.

"*Mamá.*" As I patted her back, I felt my shoulders relax for the first time since we'd left my condo in Baltimore. The White House felt strange and formal, but Sylvia Ramirez could turn any house into a home.

She let go and studied me. "Have you been eating enough?"

"Yes."

"I don't want to have to worry about you like I do with Lucia."

"You don't have to. And Lucy's doing fine." *Except for falling into moral turpitude.* I glanced at China. She stood near the wall next to the male agent, but she looked straight ahead.

"Have you been praying? Have you gone to confession?"

I groaned. Mom was always on me about church. "I thought this little interrogation you're conducting would suffice for confession."

Even though I veered to the side, she still managed to cuff my ear, and the smack echoed in my eardrum. I noticed a tiny smirk cracking through China's blank façade. I turned back to my mother and asked, "How's the new house?"

"Overwhelming." She shook her head as she gestured around her. "Stuffy. This entire floor's decorated like the eighteenth century." As she walked over to one of the wingback chairs, I noticed her coiffed black hair and stately red dress. But instead of pumps, she wore fuzzy house shoes over her stockings. I suppressed a smile. How would my family fit into this high-pressure, high-class scene? Instead of the Beverly Hillbillies, would we become the White House Texicans—burping and smoking in the State Dining Room?

"Are you smoking?" I asked.

One eyebrow arched. "No, Dr. Ramirez. I don't want to be remembered as the only first lady to smoke in this historical landmark." She patted the pink chair. "*Ven acá*. Have a seat."

"No, thanks. That chair looks as comfortable as a cactus patch."

She laughed. "Oh, Alejandro. I've missed you. Why haven't you visited us before? You're only an hour away, no?"

"Depends on traffic." I shrugged. "I'm kind of busy with school, you know."

"How are your studies?"

My stomach tensed. I had an exam coming up that I was nowhere near prepared for. But I didn't want to worry my mother. "Great."

"You sure?" Her gaze zeroed in on me.

She read me so well. I nodded with the hope she'd drop it.

"Well, I know you're busy. Thanks for coming down to talk to Mateo."

"Where is he?"

"In his room." She nodded at the agents. "They'll take you there. And your father said he could get away for a few minutes later."

I hadn't seen my dad since his inauguration. I thought his first presidential speech had been heroic, but the press had torn apart his plans to increase border security and national defense spending.

"I need to go pick the menu for a women's luncheon." My mother bounced on her feet. Hosting events was her favorite thing in the world. "We'll catch up later, after you talk to your brother."

I nodded, expecting her to leave. Instead she approached me, and her hand reached up to cradle my cheek. "There's a sadness about you, *hijo*. You're always so serious. You sure you're okay?"

A pang of disquiet reverberated in my chest, but I ignored it. "Just the typical ennui of any med student, I guess." I forced a smile. "Living the dream, you know."

"You're following your dreams?" Her eyes bored into me.

"Of course, *Mamá*." I had to get away from her prying gaze. I leaned in to kiss her cheek, then looked at China. "Will you take me to Mateo's room?"

"Yes, sir."

I followed her out of the room and up a wide staircase to the second floor. As we neared my brother's bedroom, I heard the strum of a guitar. It was a jaunty tune that built in intensity until it sounded like my brother's fingers pounded on the strings. Just before we reached the closed door, Mateo's voice joined the cacophony. When had it gotten so deep? China nodded at the agent outside his door and lifted her fist to knock, but I waved for her to stop. I wanted to hear this song.

Can't go anywhere
Can't do anything
You steal me

They leave me behind
But they don't mind
You steal me

I'm steeling against you
Red reeling and pumping
Your sweetness is murder
Th-Thumping and thumping

You break me
I'm broken
You take me
I'm token
You steal me
You feel me?
You steal me
Fucking steal me

"*Cuidado*," I said as I opened the door and strode into his room. "Let's spare Mom the F-bombs in the White House, shall we?"

Mateo sat with legs crossed on his bed. He swooped the page of printed lyrics behind him and set his guitar on the duvet next to our cat, *Escuincle*. Both of them eyed me with disdain. Mateo's dark hair spiked up on one side of his head and swept over his opposite eyebrow.

"Got a hug for your bro?" I asked.

"Don't you *knock?*" His glare cut into me. "How long have you been listening?"

"Long enough to know what you're singing about."

He cocked his head to one side, looking just like our father as he stroked Squinky's black fur. "Yeah? Tell me what my lyrics mean, then."

"It's about this." I gestured around the foreign bedroom, with only a single poster of my brother's favorite band to indicate he lived there. "You've been through a big change." I pointed to China and the other agent standing outside the door. "Secret Service everywhere, no privacy…"

"What're you talking about?"

"Your song. It's to Dad, right? He's stolen you away from your life in Texas."

He scoffed. "You don't understand *anything*."

Though I hadn't been invited, I sat on one corner of his bed. "Then help me understand. What's your song about?"

"You're too obtuse to even try to explain."

I grinned at his burgeoning vocabulary.

"Don't make fun of me."

"I'm not making fun of you." I exhaled. "Why're you so mad at me?"

"Why are you here, Alex?" He leaned back against the pillows.

"Can't I come visit my only brother?" I smiled, but those wary eyes stayed trained on me. His eyes were lighter than Lucia's and mine, with flecks of green and gold mixed in with brown. I shrugged. Neither of my siblings was ever glad to see me. "I also wanted to tell you about a new insulin pump that'd be perfect for you."

"I *knew* it!" He shot upright. "Mom sent you here, didn't she?"

"Only because she loves you, and she's worried." But despite that valid explanation, he continued to glare. *Now who's being obtuse?* "The pump would allow you to have more freedom, not have to worry about carrying around insulin and syringes—"

"Exactly how would a fucking robo-box attached to my fucking hip give me freedom?"

"Whoa, Matty. Calm down." I glanced to the hallway, wondering what Secret Service thought of this conversation.

"*You* calm down."

I stood and crossed over to the door. I looked at China. "Okay if I close this?"

"No need." Mateo was right behind me. "This conversation's over." He darted around me, and I noticed his faded, frayed jeans hanging off his thin body. He wore only socks, no shoes, which seemed strange in this uptight setting. "I'm sick of you and Mom ganging up on me. I'm gonna go find Dad."

"Even if he's available, which he's probably not, how can he help? He wants you to get the pump, too."

Mateo spun around. "Yeah, but he said it's my choice. He respects my autonomy, unlike some people I know." As he huffed out of the room, I heard a soft thump from behind, and turned to see *Escuincle* stalk toward me. I leaned down to pat his head. He bristled and hissed.

I stepped back. "Still a brat, I see."

"I heard that!" Mateo hollered.

When I emerged from his bedroom, I watched him march down the hall with a male agent, the cat brat prancing behind them both. I opened my mouth to correct his misperception, but then I gave up.

"Quit while you're behind?" China asked.

I blew out a breath. "Do you have siblings?"

She paused. "A younger brother, yeah."

"Is he a petulant pain in the butt like this one?" I pointed down the hall.

She smiled. "Much worse." Then her smile faded. "But *he's* not battling a life-threatening illness."

Fear rose in my throat, but I swallowed it down.

After China took me to the kitchen on the ground floor for a bite to eat, we headed back up to the third floor. The residence alone was huge, and that didn't include the East or West Wings. I knew I'd be lost without my chaperone. Though the solarium on the third floor offered more pale green walls, it was bright and comfortable. I settled onto a tan floral sofa and propped my feet on a striped ottoman.

"Your father's gonna pop up in a few to say hi," China said.

I watched my mother swoop in from an entrance I hadn't noticed. I stood and nodded at the same male agent who'd accompanied her earlier. Was I supposed to know his name?

"Sit, sit," Mom said as she rounded the ottoman to join me on the sofa. "How'd it go with your brother?"

"How do you think it went?"

She sighed. "Stubborn boy. He knows he needs the pump."

"Dad's not backing us up on this?"

"Your father's having a tough time with this situation. He knows what it's like to be bossed around by older siblings."

I smiled as I pictured my assertive aunt Maricela, who wasn't a big fan of my mother. Not that my mother cared two tamales what Mari thought.

"And I think he feels guilty because the diabetes comes from his side of the family."

Tía Mari also had Type I diabetes, though without the many health scares Mateo had endured.

Mom patted my knee. "You were always such a good boy, doing what we asked, following the rules. But Lucia and Mateo—they're more rebellious. What we went through with Lucia in the fall..." Her eyes closed for a moment. "We're still figuring out how to approach her. Her psychologist says Lucy needs to speak her voice."

"What does the psychologist know? Children should respect their parents, no matter what."

She smiled at me. "I agree there should be respect, but I also want my *niños* to have their own minds. To follow their own hearts."

There was a bustle in the hallway, and in walked my dad, followed by Mateo and three agents.

"*¡Mi familia!*" Dad smiled wide as he came over to hug Mom first. He kissed her and murmured, "*Amor.*" Their intimate greeting amid five agents embarrassed me.

Then he hugged me, adding some firm pats to the back. "What do you think, Alejandro?" He gestured to the expansive room.

"You done good, Dad."

He stepped back to sling his arm across Mateo's shoulders. "I'm grateful to Latino voters in California for making it happen. But we're still moving forward with plans to tighten border security. We need to enforce the laws on the books. We were just meeting with *La Raza* to try to iron out our differences."

Some of those same Latino voters were now angry that Dad's policies had curtailed illegal immigration. But he insisted immigration reform couldn't begin before we had border security in place. I agreed.

"I wish Lucia could join us," Mom said. "Then we'd all be together."

"Why didn't you fly her here today?" I asked my father.

"Secret Service says to keep travel to a minimum. There are many trips I have to make, of course, including my flight to Israel next week. But unless it's essential, they told us to cool it."

My stomach tightened. "What're you hearing? Are there specific threats?"

"Don't worry, they'll keep our family safe." Dad exchanged a glance with one of the agents, then looked at me. "Speaking of trips, I heard you visited Lucy?"

I nodded.

Mom asked, "How's she doing?"

"Good." I could see where this conversation was headed, and my heart thudded.

"Why did you visit her?" Dad cocked his head, and now all three members of my family stared at me.

I swallowed. This would be my cue to tell them about Lucy's sexcapades. But Maddie's voice entered my head: *Maybe Rez can take care of herself.* Then I looked at Mateo. He stood away from me, like he was still mad about the insulin-pump discussion—a discussion my mother had begged me to have. I hadn't asked for the responsibility of being the oldest!

"Just wanted to be sure she was eating okay," I answered.

Brad entered the room, all smiles now. *After a quickie with his supervisor?* He nodded at Dad. "It's all set, Mr. President."

"Thank you, Brad." Dad turned to us. "I have a surprise! Follow me."

Mateo looked at me and shrugged. As we filed down the stairs, I patted his shoulder. "I didn't get a chance to tell you how much I liked your song."

His eyes darted to mine.

"Even though apparently I don't know what the lyrics mean," I added, earning a shy smile. "The song's got good energy…good fire."

He continued smiling as we exited the residence.

We entered the East Wing, and the agents led us into a darkened room. When they flipped on the lights, I saw rows of reclining leather seats facing an expansive screen. There was a theater in the White House? I'd missed that one in my research.

"If we could have you four sit in the front row..." The agent I didn't know pointed to those seats.

Was this a private screening of a new movie? As soon as we sat, Lucia's face filled the screen. "Hey, guys." She waved.

My dad grinned at the screen. "*Mija.*" He turned to my mom. "See, Sylvia, we do have the family together—just like you wanted."

Mom cupped her face with both hands as she blinked at Dad with shining eyes. Then she waved back to Lucia, who appeared to be in the TV room of the greenhouse. I wondered if her view was as clear as ours. The screen was surely nowhere near as big. Lucia's black shirt featured rhinestones spelling out *Obsessed,* with a volleyball for the O.

"Lucia, my darling!" Mom gushed. "How are you?"

"I'm good..." Her voice trailed off as she saw me sitting between Dad and Mateo. Our eyes locked, and I knew the question in her wide eyes: *Did you tell Dad about Dane and me?*

"We miss you, *mija*," Dad said. "How're your classes?"

She glanced at me again before looking at Dad, then seemed to exhale. "I got an A on my econ test."

"Great job, honey." Dad smiled. "You're not buying into that awful Keynesian economics they teach, right?"

"Right, Dad." Lucia shifted her gaze. "Hey, Matty. I *loved* that song you sent me." She bit her lip as she looked up. "'Steal Me'? That's the title, right?"

"Yeah." He looked pleased.

"Dane really liked it, too." She sat up after she said that, like she hadn't meant to mention her boyfriend in front of my parents.

My father seemed to tense next to me. "How's volleyball, Lucy?"

I expected that redirection to relax my sister, but the line on her forehead deepened. "Not great. Maddie's struggling, and Coach has been really mean to her."

"What's wrong?" The question left my mouth before I'd even formed the thought.

"Turns out Maddie's ex-boyfriend Jaylon was cheating on her." Lucia grimaced. "With Nina."

"*What?*" I almost jumped out of my seat. Jaylon sounded like a total *pendejo*. And Nina? I couldn't believe Maddie's teammate had betrayed her like that.

I guess my outburst had been kind of loud, because Mateo's eyebrows pulled together as he looked at me. "Chill, dude."

Mom and Dad continued chatting with Lucia, but little of the conversation registered with me. All I could picture were Maddie's wounded eyes as she cried about Jaylon. I wished I could gather her in my arms and tell her not to worry. But I had no right to do that. We barely knew each other.

"Time to go, Mr. President," said one of Dad's agents.

We all waved at Lucia and told her we loved her as we ended the video call. Once the screen went blank, my mother frowned. "She still seems kind of anxious. What do you think, Adolfo?"

Dad turned to me. "How's she eating, Alejandro?"

"Um…" I shrugged. "She ate pretty well when I was there, but it's probably hard for her to be alone. I'd be happy to visit her again—keep my eye on her, if you like."

"And you should visit us more frequently, too," Mom said, giving me the eye.

Dad rubbed his jaw. "I'll talk to Brad, see what he thinks about security risks."

And I'll put a word in with Brad, too. I felt an irrational pull toward Highbanks.

"Time for birthday cake!" Nana clasped her hands together as her shoulders lifted to her ears.

When Nana, Gramps, Dad, and Braxton all stared at me, I lowered my fork and plastered on a smile. "Can't wait."

We sat at my grandparents' cherry-wood table in the dining room of their Cleveland home. I'd driven here the day after learning the truth about why Jaylon had dumped me, but I hadn't told my family about his cheating ass. It was far too embarrassing. At least I wouldn't have to see Nina for two days since Coach had given us a rare weekend off.

Nana pointed at Gramps as she got up from the table. "Dim the lights, Darius." Despite being in her late seventies, she practically flitted into the kitchen.

I hoped I wouldn't disappoint her. I needed to drum up the appropriate excitement when she returned with the cake. My gaze lingered on the chair across the table, and I imagined Jaylon shoveling down Nana's cooking. The chair was empty now.

"Brax, clear your sister's plate," Dad said.

My brother looked up from his phone. "She's got two feet."

Gramps made a grumbling noise in his throat as he dimmed the lights.

Braxton sighed and set down his phone. "Yes, Babu."

I rolled my eyes but did say thank you when my brother took my plate into the kitchen. In college, Braxton had become enthralled by African culture and now spoke Swahili whenever he could. Nana hadn't been impressed the first time he'd called her Bibi. *"What the hell you calling me, boy?"* she'd hollered.

Dad met my eyes. "You're quiet tonight."

"Sorry."

"How's it feel to be twenty-two?"

Terrifying. I shrugged. "'Bout the same as twenty-one, I guess."

"Except one step closer to graduating," he said.

I nodded. One step closer to being nowhere near Jaylon.

"Did you hear about Velasquez?" Gramps asked me.

I shook my head. I'd been too wrapped up in my own drama to follow the fate of the Cleveland Indians' star pitcher in the off-season.

"He threw ninety-nine yesterday." He smiled, and I couldn't help but join him. "Looks like the Tommy John surgery worked."

My mouth returned to its firm line. I knew one pitcher who hadn't recovered from elbow surgery. I wondered what Alex was doing in Baltimore. Probably studying—something I needed to do as well.

"Happy birthday to you…" Nana's vibrato echoed as she entered, and the three men joined her singing. At first I noticed the lively sparkle in her brown eyes as they reflected the candlelight, but then I got a good look at the cake she held, and my jaw dropped. The base of the cake had white fondant with polka dots in maroon and gold—my school colors—but what really grabbed my attention was the volleyball perched on top. It was made out of *cake?* Instead of *Tachikara* printed on the face of the ball, she'd carefully drawn M A D D I E, and little maroon and gold stars extended up from the cake like a halo.

How on earth had she created this masterpiece? I felt a lump in my throat. She'd known how much I needed a pick-me-up after the "dumbass" dropped me. My nose burned, and I fought off tears as my family finished singing. I was so sick of crying.

What if I don't make the national team after she baked me a cake like this? The anxious thought squelched my tears in an instant.

"How'd you make this, Nana?" I was grateful my voice didn't tremble.

She offered a smug smile. "Had a little help from my friends."

Nana's church friend owned a bakery. Braxton and I had benefitted from that friendship over the years with an endless supply of cookies and cakes, though I'd never seen a cake this gorgeous.

"But I did most of it myself." She nodded with satisfaction.

"It's so beautiful." I placed my hand over my heart. "I don't want to eat it."

"*I* do," Braxton said. "Get a move on. Make a wish and blow out your candles."

I scowled at him.

"Go ahead, Maddie." Dad nodded. "Make a wish."

What would I wish for? For three weeks, my biggest wish had been to get Jaylon back. But Nina had stomped on that dream, crushing it with her perfectly painted toes. Maybe I could wish for a spot on the national team? No, I would earn that through hard work—not some magical wish. My throat tightened when I realized what I really wished: *I want my mom to return.*

Why couldn't I stop thinking about her? I'd successfully suppressed Mom from my dreams for twenty years, but now she haunted me, and she didn't deserve a place in my mind or heart. Yet the hollow feeling she'd left burned inside of me like the candles flickering before my eyes.

A sob squeezed my throat, and before tears emerged, I blew out the candles. The cake looked even more spectacular up close, where I could see the careful black lines of icing drawn on the volleyball.

Gramps shook his head. "Neliah, when on earth did you have time to make that?"

"The perks of retirement," Nana said. "You should try it sometime, old man."

Gramps groaned. He was an administrator at the Cleveland Clinic, a renowned hospital where Nana had also worked as a nurse, and he'd refused to retire when she had a few years ago. He claimed he loved his work, but secretly I wondered if he was socking money away for my medical school tuition. *What if I don't get into med school after his sacrifice?* Nana's delicious dinner roiled in my stomach.

I watched Dad look longingly toward the family room. Like me, he probably wanted to avoid hearing the argument about Gramps's retirement again. But that's what he got for living with his parents at age fifty. He'd brought us here after Mom left, and never moved out on his own.

Another birthday Mom's missing. The thought popped into my head unbidden, and I clenched my teeth.

"My boys are waiting for me," Braxton said as he typed a text. "Are we gonna cut this cake, or what?"

"I thought you said you have to study for your doctoral exams," Dad said.

Braxton scoffed. "I've been doing that for four years."

"Wait!" I sat up in my chair. "I want to Instagram this cake first." I retrieved my phone from my backpack in the family room and noticed a text from Lucia, but I would read it later when my family wasn't waiting on me. "Too bad I missed a shot when the candles were lit." I crouched to snap the perfect picture.

"We can light them again?" Nana said.

Braxton growled.

"Just who are these 'boys'?" Dad asked him.

"You know, the brotherhood. We're organizing a protest at the police station later."

"You're wasting your time, Braxton." Gramps shook his head. "The police don't hurt us; they help us."

"Cops are pigs, Babu. Just because you're BFFs with the head of hospital security—"

"Dan Givens is a good man!"

Braxton ignored Gramps. "Doesn't mean I have to sit back and watch my innocent brothers get shot simply for being black."

I exchanged a tense glance with Nana and Dad—an unspoken agreement to stay out of it, knowing Braxton wouldn't shut up until he'd rammed his point into the ground. Nana took the knife and cut a big slice for me. As Braxton and Gramps continued arguing, I wondered what Alejandro would think of this discussion. He'd probably be just as heated as Brax, but I bet he'd be on Gramps's side. Alejandro seemed to like authority.

Feeling the weight of my phone in my hand, I opened Lucia's text.

Happy Birthday, amiga! Glad you got to go home. Cheesecake Factory when you get back—*our treat!*

The mention of my favorite restaurant actually drew out a smile. I couldn't wait to see how much Dane would eat.

"Braxton." Nana's eyebrows lowered. "At least tell me you're going to church with us tomorrow."

He didn't look up from his phone.

A little while later, after Braxton's friend picked him up, I left Dad and Gramps in the family room watching a Cavaliers game. Nana loaded the dishwasher in the kitchen. I came up behind her and squeezed her shoulders. "Thanks for making my birthday special."

She nodded but kept her head down, her silence very unlike her.

"Hey." I came to her side and noticed her eyes tighten the way they did when she was angry. "What's wrong?"

She shook her head. "Just mad about something."

"Am I in trouble?"

Her frown cleared. "Not at all. You're doing so well at Highbanks." She closed the dishwasher. "Your grandfather and I are proud of you." But then her eyes narrowed.

"Okay, so what's making you mad? Are you angry at Braxton for protesting at the police station?"

"I'm more worried than angry. But he has to do what his conscience tells him."

I folded my arms across my chest. "Tell me what's upsetting you, then."

Her voice took on an edge. "Would you bring the butter plate in from the dining room?" She washed her hands.

"Nana." I frowned.

"Did you like your cake?"

"Best cake I've ever had." I steered her to the kitchen table and guided her into a chair. "Stop avoiding my questions. What's wrong?"

She looked down at her hands and twisted her wedding ring. "I'm just so furious…" She sighed. "I'm angry your mother's missing all this. I wish she was here to see you."

I tried to inhale, but couldn't get a breath.

"To see how beautiful and accomplished you are," she added. My devastation must have shown on my face, because her eyes looked sad. "Oh, Maddie…"

She reached to touch my face, but I scrambled from the table and bolted up the stairs to my tiny childhood bedroom. The bed consumed most of the floor space, and I collapsed back into it, grabbing my stuffed koala bear and hugging him to my chest.

Why had I badgered Nana into telling me? As if I wasn't already thinking about my mother nonstop. Even Kiwi Koala reminded me of Mom—he was the one stuffed animal she'd given me, long ago. I stroked his ratty fur as I considered burying him in the backyard for the hundredth time. I could stuff him deep in the ground and never think about him again.

But I knew I'd never let go of my bear. Just like I couldn't let go of Mom.

Nana's anger must have rubbed off on me because I was snorting fire at volleyball practice two days later. I wasn't sure why I was mad instead of sad, but I did know it was awesome not to feel on the verge of crying. Had I ever felt this irritable before? Oh, yeah. At our last regular-season home match in October, I'd been ready to kill someone when Bridgetown blockers had stuffed every hit back into my face. No kills for me that day. After the match, Lucia had told me Nina was to blame for Bridgetown blockers being all over me. She'd refused to set Lucia in retaliation for Dane choosing Lucia over her.

Well, *that* situation felt familiar. The woman Jaylon had chosen over me now came across the court to join me behind the serving line. I studied Nina's blond hair and tanned skin but said nothing. We hadn't spoken to each other all practice long. My hands itched to scoop up her Barbie body and slam it into the rolling ball cart, just like Jaylon did when he took down an opponent.

"What're *you* looking at?" Nina huffed.

I spoke under my breath. "Skanky ho."

She did a double take. "What'd you say?"

"Gotta keep these serves low." I smiled at her.

My smile must have looked as evil as I felt because she gave me a wide berth as she circled around the ball cart.

"Ladies!" Coach said. "Might we expect a serve today?"

"You got it, Coach." I glanced at my assistant coach, Kara, who held up a clipboard with the number five written on it, indicating the area of the court to aim for. *Easy enough*, I thought. I looked across the net to find Lynette crouched in the back right corner, where I wanted my topspin jump serve to land. In front of Lynette, Lucia stood at the net, her eyes darting back and forth between Nina and me.

Don't worry, Rez. I'll show that ho what a real serve looks like. I tossed the ball in the air, executed my approach, then leaped. But my hand snapped through the ball too high in its trajectory, and the serve soared. Kaitlyn bellowed, "Out!" and Lynette wisely let it go as the ball landed far out of bounds.

Shit. My jaw clenched.

"Way to keep it low," Nina cooed.

What a bitch. Acid churned my stomach.

Nina stepped up to serve next, but Coach said, "I want another from Madison."

Nina pouted as she moved to the side.

This time it was the number four on Kara's clipboard, and my nerves jangled. Serving toward Lucia in the front row was more challenging. *Picture Nina's hideous face on the ball.* This time my toss wasn't high enough, and it didn't surprise me when the ball zoomed into the net.

Nina snickered. "Not *that* low, Maddie."

"You know all about getting low, don't you, Nina? Like, on your knees?"

Her eyes narrowed. Evidently I said that louder than I'd intended, because Coach snapped, "Hey! Do we have a problem here?"

"Yes," I said.

"No," Nina countered. "Can I serve, Coach? That way the team can actually *play*." She smiled at me, and I wanted to punch her. She scooped a ball from the cart but Coach interrupted.

"Madison's serving."

Nina exhaled as she smacked the ball back into the cart. But my thrill at her comeuppance lasted only seconds as the reality of my situation set in. I knew Coach was giving me one of his little tests to see what I was made of. Testing my mental toughness. Could I serve the ball in play after two errors in a row?

71

I heard a noise in the stands and gripped the ball tighter when I saw who'd just walked in: Alejandro! What was *he* doing here? Damn, he looked hot, with dark jeans and a navy suit jacket over a white shirt. He and his agents went to sit with Frank and Allison, and the butterflies in my stomach batted their wings like hummingbirds on amphetamine.

I looked at Lucia, who seemed equally surprised by her brother's entrance. Then she looked back at me. "Don't forget your pre-serve routine, Maddie. You didn't do it before the last two."

Air left my lungs in a whoosh. Hot damn—she was right!

Nina snickered again. "How could you forget something so basic?"

I'd let her get into my head. She'd thrown me off my game. *Ho-bag bitch*. I glared at her. She'd stolen my boyfriend, but I wouldn't let her steal my game, too. I took a deep breath.

I looked at Kara's clipboard, but instead of a number, she'd written *Anywhere you want*. God love my assistant coach; she was trying to help me.

Bounce, bounce, bounce went the ball, and I told myself, *Steady toss*. Then I launched the ball in the air with a prayer. I followed through with a strong swing, and exhaled as I watched the serve travel in bounds. The ball made a beeline for Kaitlyn, who passed it in a perfect arch to Murphy, who set it to Lucia. With no blockers to stop her, Rez slammed the ball cross-court.

"Good job, guys," I called across the net.

Nina arched a sculpted eyebrow. "*Monkeys* could've scored off that easy serve."

"Fuck. You."

"Madison!" Coach yelled, and I gulped.

Nina shook her head. "Classy. I have no idea why they invited *you* to the camp."

She was still ticked off that USA Volleyball hadn't invited her to the national team selection camp in April. At least I had *that* over her.

Lucia ducked under the net and marched toward us. "Maddie got invited because she's a top-three hitter in the NCAA." She glared at Nina. "Despite having *you* as her setter."

"Lucia, get your ass back over here," Coach commanded, but she stayed put.

Though I adored Lucia for going to bat for me, she should've known it would draw Nina's wrath.

"Easy, big girl." Nina spoke so quietly that I prayed Lucia hadn't heard her, but her flinch backward told me otherwise. Rez's face crumpled.

My heart and mind competed to see which could race faster, and I stalked toward Nina with the intent to put her on the ground. Her fake tan paled as I neared, and her eyes widened.

I heard Coach yell, "Madison, you're done. Get out of my gym!" but it didn't stop me. I just wanted to hurt Nina. But when Alejandro shouted too, I stopped.

"What the hell kind of program are you running?"

I spun around to see Alejandro lean over the railing, pointing at Coach, his face red. "You're throwing *Maddie* out of practice? Do you have any idea what Nina did to her?"

I whirled to find Lucia. She'd told him about Nina and Jaylon? Her eyes were glued on her brother as she stood there with her mouth agape.

Coach frowned. "You're Lucia's brother, right? Who let you in here?"

"I have every right to protect my sister from the likes of *you!*" Alejandro emphasized the last word by thrusting his pointed finger again. Brad hovered behind him, shifting from one foot to another. The other three agents looked equally unsure of how to handle the situation. How could they protect the protectee from himself?

"You need to leave." Coach shook his head. "My practices are closed."

"So no one can witness your intimidation, *¿sí?*"

Coach glared at his assistant. "Brian, get him out of here."

Brian nodded and jogged toward one end of the court, where a ramp led up to the stands. But Alejandro didn't appear to be finished.

"I don't know how your teams win with you bullying them at every turn."

"*Out* of here!" Coach pointed to the door.

"You think you're such a big man, Holter."

"Ay, Dios mío," Lucia cried softly.

Coach yelled something back at Alejandro, but Kara's appearance by my side distracted me from hearing it. "Hey, Maddie." She cradled my elbow. "Coach asked you to leave. How 'bout you go now? Let Coach cool down a bit?"

I gasped. "Am I kicked off the team? But how will I train for camp?"

"I'm sure you're not kicked off forever," she said. I started breathing again. "But for now he's about to blow, and I don't want you here when he does."

I glanced at Nina to make sure she wouldn't gloat about my departure, but she was absorbed in the Coach-Alejandro soap opera like everyone else on the team. I looked back at Kara. "Okay, I'll go." As I walked on unsteady legs to the locker room, Lucia joined me.

"Oh my God. Alex has lost it."

I looked up as Alejandro's agents pushed him to the exit with Brian trailing behind. He kept yelling at Coach but had shifted to Spanish.

"Wow, your brother's awesome. He's really letting Coach have it."

"Good thing Coach doesn't speak Spanish. But I'm a dead woman. I bet Coach will boot me out next."

"Don't you get ejected on my behalf."

She clutched my arm. "I can't believe he's making you leave instead of Nina. Why didn't you cry? You told me Coach freaks out when we cry. It would've stopped him in his tracks, and he probably would've let you stay at practice."

"I think I'm all cried out, Rez." I frowned. "By the way, don't let Nina get to you. She *wishes* she could be as strong as you. And she's still jealous about Dane."

Abruptly, Rez giggled. "Dane will be so mad he missed this!"

"Lucia!" Coach barked.

She jumped, then sprinted back to the court.

As I headed to the locker room, I noticed Tina standing by a wall with her arms folded across her chest. *Uh-oh.* I knew that appraising look; she'd obviously witnessed my meltdown. Her index finger curled toward her chest. Could I ignore her? I sighed. I knew she would hunt me down if I didn't talk to her now. I changed course to follow her into the training room.

"What's going on with you?" she asked.

The adrenaline from the altercation began to fade, replaced by shock. *I just got kicked out of practice the first time in my life. My serves have never sucked so bad. I told a teammate to fuck off, and then I almost punched her.* Fatigue weighed down my shoulders. "I'm—"

"And don't tell me you're fine, 'cause you're so *not* fine, Maddie. I've never seen you act that way."

I swallowed.

"Here." She handed me a business card. "Call her."

Carly Valentine, PhD, the card read. *Highbanks Sport Psychologist.* "But it's just a breakup." My voice trembled, and my throat burned. *Don't cry.*

"It's more than that. You're a hot mess."

I wasn't sure if the burst of air from my mouth was a laugh or a cry, but it certainly wasn't a happy sound.

Tina patted my shoulder as she looked up into my eyes. "Talk to her, Maddie. Figure out what's going on with you, okay? I miss your smile."

I blinked quickly. I missed my smile, too.

8 Alejandro

"What did I just do?" I ran my hands through my hair as I crumpled back against the wall. The dim lighting of the arena hallway hopefully hid my embarrassment.

Frank approached and cupped my shoulder. "You got a little heated back there."

"Oo-rah," Brad said. He raised his palm for a high-five, and I gave it to him. Though I didn't want to celebrate my eruption, I couldn't leave him hanging.

China grinned. "I've been dying to castrate that jerk for how he treats these women."

"I just kept thinking about how he told Lucia to lose weight last fall — and he dared to eject Maddie from practice? But I should never disrespect a coach like that." I shook my head.

Allison's eyebrows pulled together. "Coach Holter hasn't exactly earned our respect. Maybe you could've been more tactful…"

"You *think?*" I clasped my head in my hands again.

"But he's had that coming for a long time, like you said." Allison smiled. "We're just jealous you got to say it, not us." She glanced at China. "We should head back up for Lucia. You coming?"

China's smile actually looked shy. She pushed off the wall and walked to the stairs, drawing close to Allison's side.

Watching two women together still jarred me. When I'd fallen under China and Brad's protection the day after the election, Lucia had told me about China's secret relationship with Allison. *"It was different for me at first,"* she'd said, *"just because I didn't know any lesbian couples. But now I think they're cute together."*

Cute together? Nothing about China was cute. I still felt uncomfortable around her, and not just due to her overbearing nature. It was strange to me that she had zero use for men in her life. She certainly didn't need a man's protection, nor did she need a man for sex. And how did sex actually work without…? *Chin.* I sounded as naïve as Mateo.

Would *Maddie* want to be protected by a man? I sure hoped so, because I felt drawn to do just that. I couldn't get the image of her facing off against Nina out of my mind. She'd stormed toward Nina like she'd wanted to flatten her, but I'd worried Maddie would be the one to get hurt. We'd both lost our cool.

I wondered how Maddie felt about me yelling at her coach. She probably wouldn't want anything to do with a hothead like me.

"Alejandro," Brad said, and I looked up. "Want to wait here at the gym for Luce, or head to the greenhouse?"

I glanced at my watch. "She has a half hour left of practice?"

"About that," Frank said.

"Uh, how about…" My voice faded when Maddie rounded the corner. She stopped short once she saw me, and her rapid blinks couldn't hide her tears. *Damn, she's beautiful.*

She threw her hand in the air as she shook her head. "Great! You catch me crying once again. You must think that's all I do."

I wished she didn't feel embarrassed. Her tears didn't make me judge her — they made me want her. The contrast between her emotional softness and her athletic toughness allured me.

I noticed Frank and Brad slinking away, giving us some privacy. I looked back at Maddie. "Of course you're crying — that was a rough one out there. It's not every day you get thrown out of practice."

She winced. "That's my first time ever."

I took that in and considered all the practices of my baseball career. "Me too, actually."

A smile appeared, then a giggle leaked out. "What the hell got into you, boy?"

"I bought a one-way ticket to loco, I guess." Her smirk captivated me, and pretty soon I laughed too. "I don't know what came over me." I straightened. "Are you upset with me?"

"*What?* You're like the team's hero now. Everyone loved how you went off on Coach." She tensed, then turned to look down the hallway, but all was clear. "Everyone besides Nina, that is."

"That girl's got problems." My vision narrowed. "What did she say to my sister? Lucy looked really hurt."

Maddie bit her full bottom lip. "Definitely not worth repeating." Her hand fluttered away from her body like she was nervous.

I noticed she clutched a business card in that hand. "What's that?"

"Nothing." She swept the card inside her Spandex shorts. I saw a patch of toned abs when she hiked up her shirt, and I kept staring at the rectangular outline pressing against her Spandex. I wouldn't mind being that business card.

"What a great birthday this turned out to be." She sighed.

I inhaled. "It's your birthday?"

"Yesterday."

"Happy belated twenty-second, then."

She smiled, seeming pleased.

"I hope you have a celebration lined up—something better than that awful practice."

"I celebrated with my family at home this weekend." Her smile faded as she looked down. "But Rez and Dane are taking me to dinner tonight."

"Oh." I felt deflated—I'd hoped to spend some time with her. "I know you'll have a great time."

"You're not coming with?"

I shook my head. "I shouldn't crash another dinner with your friends. Besides, Lucy didn't know I was visiting. She'll launch a protest if I try to tag along."

"Why *are* you visiting?"

Because I can't stop thinking about you. "Dad wanted me to check in on Lucy. And our professor canceled class tomorrow, so I figured this was a good time."

"Well, I bet Rez will let you go with us to dinner."

"She isn't furious with me for screaming at your coach?"

Maddie grinned. "She said she was glad Coach doesn't speak Spanish. What exactly did you say?"

My mouth closed. "Shouldn't repeat it around a lady."

"Oh Lord, you think I'm a lady?" She chuckled.

I think you're exquisite.

"Keep talking like that, and I'll be sure to get you to come to dinner with us." Her eyes glimmered, but she'd stopped crying a while ago. "In fact, I insist you join us. It's *my* birthday—I get to do what I want." She gave a definitive nod.

"Well, okay then," I said. "I'll go, if you insist." I pretended I was reluctant.

"Good. But first, the lady has to shower." She curtsied in her Spandex.

How freaking cute is that?

"*Señor*." She bowed her head before peeking up at me with a grin.

"*Señorita bonita*." I swept my gaze up her long legs to her lean torso, then up to her radiant face.

Her grin faded as she watched me. A spark lit in her eyes, then began to smolder as she stared at me.

I felt myself growing hard, and my chest tightened as I struggled for air. I looked from her eyes to her lips. When she licked her lower lip, my heart seized. God, I wanted to kiss that pretty mouth!

When she started, I jerked back. I could see she'd felt it, too. The connection. The turn-on.

She swallowed. "Gotta shower."

When she darted past me, I almost lunged to grab her, to press her to me so I could maul her with kisses. But she was too fast. She left me with just the sight of her lithe body disappearing into the locker room.

I closed my eyes and noticed my galloping heartbeat. I felt like I'd just hit a single and sprinted to first base. But we hadn't made it to first base…yet. Would she want me to kiss her? Touch her soft skin? Do things to her body I'd only imagined before?

"Damn it!" Dane thumped his fist on the table when we finished telling him about Coach ejecting Maddie and me from practice. "Why'd I have to miss it? So unfair. I've wanted to go bitchcakes on Holter's ass for over a year."

Lucia grinned as she leaned closer to Dane. Over a black turtleneck she wore a black T-shirt with two cartoon hot peppers wearing sombreros and tossing volleyballs in the air. The caption read *Wanna Pepper?*

My sister hadn't seemed so jovial after practice. On her way to the locker room, she'd found me in the hallway. As expected, she'd scowled with her hands on her hips when I mentioned dinner plans, even after I explained that Maddie had invited me. When I promised not to spy on her or boss her around, she'd finally relented. Maddie hadn't emerged from the locker room yet, so I'd shared my birthday gift idea with my sister. Lucy's demeanor had changed in an instant: she'd actually clapped and grinned.

Later, when Lucy had pranced out of the locker room with Maddie following her, she'd said, "C'mon, we're picking up Dane at Josh's."

Maddie had shrugged and given me a smile.

Now that we were tucked into a booth in the corner of the restaurant, I glanced over at Maddie next to me. She stared at the thick menu in her hands, and her delicate eyelashes cast tiny shadows on her cheeks. When she turned the page, she must have felt my stare, because she looked right at me.

"So many choices," she said as she shook her head. "Do you know what you want, Alex?"

Yes. The light blue eye shadow she'd used made her eyes sparkle. *You.*

When I didn't respond, she cleared her throat. "Have you been to The Cheesecake Factory before?"

"A few times. There's one in Houston…at a mall called The Galleria."

"The fifth largest mall in the country," Lucia added.

"Really?" Dane's straw gurgled as he polished off his coke. "Who knew Texas could be so civilized."

Lucia elbowed him.

The waitress approached. "Another Fresca, sir?"

Dane nodded.

"And are we ready to order?"

Once she'd taken our orders and disappeared into the bustling restaurant, Lucia looked at Dane. "I can't believe you've never been to Texas. We should go."

"Want to show me cows? Rodeos? Your old house?"

"Well, there's another governor living in the mansion now," Lucia said. "But I could show you the house we lived in before that. And there's more to Texas than cows and rodeos."

"Oh, right. There're lots of guns, too." Dane rolled his eyes. "Figures Texas elected *another* Republican governor."

"I'm proud of my home state," I said.

"And I'm proud *my* state put a Democrat in charge." Dane smiled.

"It's too bad for your economy, then."

Lucia glared at me for riling up her boyfriend, but I couldn't help myself.

Dane's mouth tightened. "It's great for human rights to have Democrats in charge. We're not letting the police take target practice on African-Americans just for the fun of it. Right, Maddie?"

She looked up from peeling oats off a slice of pumpernickel bread. "Huh?"

"Braxton texted me about what he's been doing." Dane leaned closer to the table. "I think it's awesome."

Maddie seemed to freeze, then her eyes darted to mine.

"Your brother?" I asked. "What *has* he been doing?" If Dane thought it was awesome, I probably wouldn't like it.

"Uh…He, um—"

"He's been protesting at that Cleveland police station about the shooting last month," Dane supplied.

Lucia placed her hand on her chest. "That sounds dangerous."

And idiotic. "But the trial's still going on," I said. "The officer hasn't been convicted. Justice hasn't been served. What happened to innocent until proven guilty?"

"Justice can't be served when the system's stacked against you," Dane said.

Maddie remained quiet, and I asked her, "Is that what you believe? Do you think the system's unjust?" She squirmed. "Do you agree with your brother?"

"I think I see both sides?"

"Jeez, Alex." Lucia frowned at me. "It's her birthday. Give her a break."

I blew out a breath. "You're right." I looked at Maddie. "Sorry." Why did it matter what her brother did? It wasn't like Maddie and I were dating or anything. "I seem to commit countless peccadillos in your presence."

Dane snorted. "Feeling nervous, Alex?"

"Why do you say that?"

"You've got your defenses up."

"I don't know what you mean. I'm having a good time at Maddie's birthday dinner." I raised my glass of water with lime and nodded at her.

"Defense mechanisms, I mean," Dane said. "We've all got 'em."

I studied him. What was the psychologist's son up to? "So what is my supposed defense mechanism, then?"

"Intellectualization." Dane smiled. "When you have an uncomfortable emotion, you unleash a big vocab word."

Lucia's mouth popped open. "He *does* do that!"

"Shut up, Lucy," I warned.

Dane smirked. "Don't you mean, cease your chicanery and verbosity, sister Lucia?"

When Lucia chortled, he laughed. It wasn't long before Maddie joined in, and her giggles lit up her face—the way she should have looked at her birthday dinner. I couldn't watch the three of them laughing without my own smile breaking through.

"Okay, Mr. Psych Major," Maddie said. "What's *your* defense mechanism?"

"Isn't it obvious?" Dane held out his arms, revealing an impressive wingspan. "Regression. I regress to adolescence often."

Lucia and Maddie laughed.

I marveled at how my anger toward Dane lessened with his self-deprecating comment.

"Oh." He raised his finger. "And sublimation. That's another defense mechanism I use."

"What's that?" Lucia asked.

"It's when you channel difficult impulses into more acceptable behavior. Like when you have sexual fantasies that you can't act on, so you exercise like crazy."

Or throw yourself into school. *Mierda*. I used that one, too.

Dane brushed strands of hair off Lucia's face, then cradled her chin. Her cheeks burned crimson as she looked at me.

And...the anger returns. I muttered under my breath, "Guess he doesn't have to use sublimation anymore."

When Maddie vibrated next to me in the booth, I turned to find her shaking with suppressed laughter. I scowled, and she shook harder—her lips glued together, her eyes alight with mirth. And then her hand clasped mine. In an instant I stopped thinking about Lucia and focused only on the feel of Maddie's warm, soft fingers. I squeezed back.

"Here we are." The waitress swooped in to place huge plates in front of us.

An hour later, Dane collapsed back into the booth. "Food baby," he moaned as he cradled his belly.

"You didn't have to eat the whole plate of pasta *and* the whole piece of cheesecake," Maddie chided.

"But it was so *good*."

Dane hadn't eaten the entire piece—Lucia had taken a couple of bites. But I wasn't going to point that out since Mom had told me not to comment on what Lucia ate. Other than Dane helping her order when she'd seemed mired in indecision, my sister had managed the meal without much evident anxiety. I was proud of her.

"So you liked my peanut butter cup cheesecake?" Maddie asked me.

I smiled and nodded. The few bites I'd stolen were tasty, though I wasn't a big fan of desserts. I *had* enjoyed watching Maddie eat the sweet treat. Not only was her mouth the sexiest damn thing I'd ever seen, it was good to see her eat. She looked thinner than when I'd met her in January, and that was only three weeks ago.

Lucia glanced at me before she dug in her backpack and extracted an envelope. "Time to give you your present, Maddie."

"Rez!" Maddie's lips parted. "I told you not to get me anything. This dinner's present enough."

Dane's eyebrows lifted. "Did you get her the T-shirt, Luz?"

"No, I told you that was in poor taste."

"What shirt?" Maddie asked.

Dane stopped pouting long enough to answer. "I wanted to get you a T-shirt that said *I'm Not With Stupid Anymore*."

Stillness settled over the table, and I braced myself for more of Maddie's tears. But then she giggled. "Nana would love that shirt."

"You see?" Dane railed. "I should've ordered it."

Lucia shook her head at Dane. She looked back at Maddie. "I know you said you didn't want a gift, but I got you a card to tell you what a great friend you are."

"Oh." Maddie nodded. "I guess that's okay."

Lucia fidgeted before she handed over the envelope. "And Alejandro came up with a gift idea that sounded perfect. So that's inside the card, too. It's from both of us."

"But you didn't know it was my birthday until an hour ago," Maddie said, eyeing me.

I shrugged. My breath caught in my throat, wondering how she would react.

"Let me see this," Maddie grumbled as she reached for the card and tore it open. She said "Aww" as she read what Lucia had written, then her mouth opened. "You guys got me an MCAT study book?" She looked at me. "And you're offering to help me study?"

Does she like it? "You said it's been tough to concentrate lately, so I thought a team approach would help."

Maddie still didn't speak.

"Sorry for the nerdy gift," Lucia said. "Alex thought you'd like it."

"No, it's perfect." She looked up. "I *am* a nerd."

Dane chuckled.

Maddie's voice trembled. "But it's too much. I don't deserve this."

"Nonsense." I leaned closer. "I'd be happy to help."

She kept looking down, and I exchanged a nervous glance with Lucia. Maddie's voice was soft. "But what if my score doesn't improve?"

And I thought *I* put a lot of pressure on myself. "Then we'll buy you an MCAT prep course."

Maddie's head shot up. "You will not! Those are, like, over two thousand dollars." She exhaled. "I think you Ramirez *niños* went overboard...but okay. Thank you. I really appreciate it."

I let out a breath. When I looked at Dane, though, I tensed. He cocked his head like he was trying to figure me out. Could he see my affection for Maddie? Could Lucia tell? I looked at my sister, but she was wrapped up in her teammate. Seeing both of them happy relaxed my shoulders.

I didn't stay relaxed for long, however. Once our agents led us out of the restaurant into the freezing night air, camera flashes blinded me. Someone had tipped off the paparazzi.

"Lucia!" one reporter said. "Do you still have your eating disorder? What did you order for dinner?"

I gasped.

"Not one word," China warned.

Dane pivoted toward one of the cameras, showing me the hard set of his jaw. I was jealous he didn't have to listen to Secret Service anymore.

Before he could speak, Lucia whispered, "Don't give them the satisfaction."

"How do you feel about your mother losing the election, Dane?" another reporter asked.

He still looked pissed off, but his mouth closed, and he started walking again.

Reporters jostled closer, and one almost tripped Maddie. I reached out for her hand to steady her. We weren't quite to the SUVs when one reporter asked, "Who's your date, Alejandro?"

Maddie's eyes widened.

Lucia giggled. "She's not his date!" Frank tucked her and Dane into the backseat of their vehicle, while China got my "date" and me into our SUV. We sped away.

"Sorry to drag you into the national spotlight." I rolled my eyes.

"That was intense." She laughed. "No worries. I had a great *date*." When her thumb stroked my palm, I realized we were still holding hands.

9
Mads
* ★ *

I can't believe he wants to tutor me. Sure, Lucia said the present was from them both, but I had the sense it was all Alejandro's idea. Only he had survived the ferocious, slashing claws of the MCAT. I looked over in the backseat of the SUV to find him watching me. The passing streetlights glittered in his dark eyes, sending a shiver up my spine. Was I hot for teacher?

When we arrived at my apartment building, I didn't protest his exit from the vehicle along with me. I was getting to know his gentlemanly ways. It also wasn't a surprise when China joined us on our brisk walk inside.

But I *was* surprised to find two hundred fifty-five pounds of chocolate muscle and cheating hustle waiting at my apartment door.

Jaylon's eyebrows drew together when he saw my companions.

"What're you doing here?" My throat constricted when I spoke. I felt Alejandro step closer behind me, and China didn't appear to be leaving either.

Jaylon's glare lingered on Alejandro before landing on me. "I got to talk to you."

"I think your actions have said far too much already." My heart pounded with heated indignation, which flared up my neck into my face.

"You got this all wrong!" He pointed at me as he neared. "I *told* you nothing happened with Nina—"

"Back off, Mr. Hart." China wedged her way between us.

Jaylon's eyes stormed. "Who the fuck are you?"

I patted China's hard bicep. "It's okay." She kept her focus trained on Jaylon as she stepped to the side. I glanced over my shoulder at Alejandro, and he looked even more suspicious of Jaylon than China did. Turning back to my ex, I said, "This is Lucia's brother Alejandro and his Secret Service agent."

"Everything copacetic here?" Brad asked as he climbed the last few steps.

"And this is his other agent." I dipped my hand toward Brad, who winked at me. China must have summoned him via the bat signal.

Jaylon inched back. "Why're they with you?"

"Lucia and Dane took me out for a birthday dinner. Alejandro, too."

"Aw, damn!" Jaylon knocked his forehead with the heel of his hand. "I forgot. February twelfth, right?"

I shook my head. "Why do *you* care? You broke up with me. You don't get to care about my birthday."

"Mads…"

I would've thought hearing my old nickname would pierce my heart, but all it did was make me angry. *Mads.*

"…I still care."

Alejandro stepped into my shadow, and his spicy scent wafted over me. "You have an interesting way of showing it."

"Man, pig *off.*" Jaylon shook his head. "This don't involve you."

The anger in Jaylon's features quickened my breathing, but Alejandro didn't seem fazed. "Maddie's had a long day. How 'bout you save this for another time? You can leave now."

"You don't tell me what to do." Jaylon's eyes blazed. "You the one needs to leave."

The hallway crackled with tension, and I was glad my neighbors hadn't emerged. I wanted to suggest that Jaylon and I go somewhere to talk, but I knew Alejandro wouldn't go for that. Neither would his agents. They'd inserted themselves into my little relationship drama, and it didn't look like they would leave anytime soon. Too bad for them.

"Jaylon." I sighed. "How about you tell me whatever you need to say so we can all go home."

"Just me and you, inside. You owe me that at least."

I don't owe you a crumb from my cheesecake. "No." The harshness of my voice surprised me, and seemingly Jaylon, too. I aimed for a more measured tone. "Look, Alex is right—I'm tired. It's been a long day. Either you tell me right now what's on your mind, or we talk later. You decide."

As he chewed the corner of his lip, I noticed the wrinkles in his jeans. He'd probably grabbed them off the floor when he'd gotten home from practice. He didn't have me to tidy up his place anymore. "You gotta believe me, Mads," he said. "I didn't cheat on you. That's not me."

My heart clenched.

"Nina threw herself at me, I swear. Don't even like that girl."

My stomach churned, and I wished I'd eaten fewer bites of my cheesecake. To picture Nina in Jaylon's bed…I could puke all over his gold high-top shoes.

"You believe me, right? You know I'm no dog like that."

It wasn't until Alejandro touched my shoulder that I realized how frozen I'd become. I sucked in a breath as I wondered how to respond. He sure seemed like a dog to me.

When I didn't say anything, Alejandro spoke up. "This is between you and Maddie, and I don't mean to interfere. I'm just here as a friend, making sure she gets home safely."

Alejandro's warm hand cupped my shoulder in a more-than-friendly way, and I had to admit I liked it. Especially when my romantic failure stared me in the face. His touch bolstered me to speak. "So, Jay, you want to talk about the timeline?" I clenched my teeth. "The timeline for when you *fucked* my teammate?"

Jaylon flinched and Alejandro inhaled. Brad was behind me, but I could see China nodding, propelling me to continue. "You want to be the good guy in this scenario. But you're not. Regardless of when things started with Nina, it's not cool to hook up with my teammate. Don't you see that?"

Jaylon's eyebrows pulled together in a scowl. "What was I s'posed to do?" He shrugged. "I gotta focus on wrestling, man, but the girl went up and macked on me."

Macked on him? *Ew.* I craved the satisfaction of smashing an entire cheesecake in Nina's face. I could see it now: creamy goo framing her startled blue eyes and button nose, her pursed lips opening with a wail of protest, chunks of melted chocolate clinging to her platinum hair…

That delicious image must have distracted me for some time because I noticed how quiet it had gotten when Alejandro cleared his throat. The pressure of his hand on my shoulder disappeared, and I watched him stroke his chin as he sized up Jaylon.

"Okay, so after you broke up with Maddie, what if one of your wrestling teammates had swooped in to seduce her? What if he'd started dating her, his hands all over her in public? How would *you* feel?"

Jaylon's face fell in a crash, and a rush of gratification washed over me. He got it. He finally got how much he'd hurt me. And Alejandro had been the one to show him.

"Preach." Jaylon nodded at Alejandro, then looked at me. "Any teammate who did that would be in for a beatin'."

So Jaylon would feel jealous of me with another man? Was he telling the truth when he said he still cared about me? Then why did he break up with me? And why wouldn't he just leave me alone in my breakup misery?

"Gotta go," Jaylon said as he tugged up the low waistline of his jeans. "But I'll be back. I'm taking you out for your birthday. Belated and shit."

What? I exchanged a confused look with Alejandro. Before I could protest that insane idea, though, Jaylon had hustled down the stairs. "Hasta la vista, Mads!" he hollered.

Brad followed Jaylon down the stairs, and China backed up to give us some space. I blinked at Alejandro, and he arched an eyebrow in response.

"So." I exhaled. "*That* just happened."

"He's, uh…interesting."

"Thanks for stepping in, making him see the light." I felt myself unwind now that Jaylon was gone. "You made him think about someone besides himself for a second. Impressive."

"*You're* the one who was impressive, standing up for yourself like that. You started off so well." A frown crept over his face. "But then you seemed to lose steam. Did he frighten you?"

"No. He's not like that. It's just that every time I think of him and Nina…" I shivered in disgust.

"It causes emesis?"

I smiled as I extracted my keys from my coat pocket. "Thank you for dinner, and the gift. You made me feel special." I didn't really want him to go, but he'd done far too much for me already. "Maybe I'll see you tomorrow?"

"Oh, no. I'm not leaving."

"What?" I lowered my key from the doorknob.

"You think I'd leave you alone when Mr. Heavyweight Wrestler plans to return? He doesn't seem the type to take no for an answer."

So this was the overprotective behavior Lucia had mentioned. "Thanks for your concern, but I'll be okay. Jaylon wouldn't hurt me."

"Physically, maybe not. But emotionally? You want him to hang around uninvited, dredging up images of Nina 'macking' on him?"

I shuddered.

"Mr. Ramirez." China came forward. "We planned to house you at the greenhouse tonight."

"Then re-plan to house me here. I can sleep on the sofa." He looked at me. "You have a sofa?"

The turn of events revved my heart. Hot Jandro would sleep at my place? The idea excited me, but I didn't want to seem too eager, lest he think I had men over all the time. "I don't recall inviting you for a sleepover?"

"Oh, come on, Maddie." He smiled boyishly, and I caught a glimpse of the charm that had won his father the election. "You need to study, right? I can help you. Start paying up on my birthday gift — mine and Lucia's, I mean."

A door clicked shut down the hall, and I saw my neighbor, an elderly woman crazy enough or poor enough to live in off-campus housing. She had her Yorkie, Charles, on a leash, and he gave the cutest little bark when he noticed us loitering at my door. His barks weren't so cute on the rare mornings I got to sleep in.

"Hi, Mrs. Marshall," I said.

She scowled at me through her glasses. Once she noticed China, then Alejandro, she paused. "You're the president's son."

"Yes, ma'am." Alejandro smiled down at her and stooped to let Charles sniff his hand.

"I didn't vote for that man." She tugged the dog's leash and shuffled to the stairwell. "He's going to ruin the country!"

Instead of looking offended, Alejandro's eyes shone with amusement. He glided behind her. "Would you like some help down the stairs, ma'am?"

"Back off!" She flung her hand in a dismissive wave as she descended.

He returned to me with a grin. "Great apartment complex. Real friendly neighbors."

"Yeah?" I studied him. "You should meet three C; he loves eighties hair bands, plays them at full blast. And the Korean woman below me. Kimchi does *not* smell good in the mornings." I shook my head. "But Mrs. Marshall's the worst. Does it bother you to hear stuff like that about your dad?"

He shrugged. "I hear it all the time. The press excoriates Dad on a daily basis."

I suppressed a giggle. "Feeling anxious, Alex?"

"Why?"

"*Excoriate?*"

"Damn that Dane!" He skimmed his hands through his thick hair. "I can't wait for my psychiatry block. I'll learn some psychobabble to defend myself against him."

Psychiatry would be fascinating to study. I wondered which defense mechanisms I used. I'd definitely been in denial about my breakup, though Nina's sudden surfacing had squashed that. Then Jaylon had shown up tonight claiming he still cared for me—more than he did for Nina anyway. I supposed that meant he thought we had a chance of reuniting. Did I think that too? Did I *want* that? The graceful lines of Alejandro's body captured my attention instead.

"So what do you think?" He leaned against the wall, his scent hovering between us, his intelligent eyes on mine.

"About what?"

He smirked. "About me staying here. If not to protect you against Jaylon, then to save you from your unpleasant neighbors."

"Well…"

"Got your bags here, Alex," Brad said as he lumbered up the stairs clutching a backpack and duffel bag.

"Oh!" Alejandro straightened. "But Maddie hasn't said yes yet…"

"Huh." Brad looked between us. "China told me to bring the bags."

I looked at her, but her face revealed nothing. I thought she'd said changing housing plans would be difficult.

Alejandro stepped back. "If you'd rather be alone, I totally understand—"

"If Brad already brought up your bags, I won't make him drag them back downstairs." My hand trembled as I unlocked my door. Could I deny the thrill that zipped through me?

"Gotta do a sweep of your apartment first," Brad said.

I cringed. "It's kind of a mess…" I led the two men inside, picking up wayward pieces of clothing off the floor and furniture as I went. I tossed them into a corner behind my sofa.

As Brad snooped around my tiny kitchen and headed into my bedroom—oh no, there weren't bras lying around, were there?—Alejandro stood just inside the entrance. His sharp clothing highlighted my shabby décor. I nodded at the beat-up sofa. "It's kind of a dump."

But he didn't seem repulsed at all. "You get to live by yourself as an undergrad? No roommates? That's like paradise. How'd you swing that?"

"My dad got me a tutoring job at his school last summer."

"His school?"

"He teaches history at Cuyahoga Community College."

"All righty then," Brad said as he swept back into the room. "All clear. One of us will be in the hallway tonight, the other in the SUV."

Alejandro looked stricken. "I'm sorry; I didn't mean to make you do that. Maybe I should—"

"Hey." Brad held up his hand. "*Es bueno.* The protectee needs to live his life, right? *I* wouldn't turn down a night in a pretty lady's home." He grinned wolfishly at me.

"*Bye*, Brad," I said.

He laughed on his way out.

I removed my coat. "Um, can I get you anything to drink? Something to eat?"

"You must be joking." Alejandro took off his coat as well and hung it near the door. "Like Dane, I've still got a food baby going over here."

Yet his navy jacket and dark jeans were a sleek fit over his lean frame. I thumped the sofa's sagging cushion. "Want to sit on Shitty?"

"You named your sofa?" He grinned as he joined me on the monstrosity that would be his bed tonight. Beneath the armrest, stuffing bulged from a rip in the upholstery. Alejandro eyed the clouds of fluff gaping from the wound. "Looks like something our cat would do. He trashes everything."

"Oh, right—you and Lucia have a cat. He has an unusual name, as I recall…" I looked at him for help, but he frowned.

"Damn cat hates me."

"Did your family take him to the White House?" When he nodded, my eyes bugged. "Will he destroy all the furniture?"

Alejandro snorted. "Probably. It's too stuffy, anyway. Time for some new décor, new blood in that place."

It was so bizarre that his parents lived there.

"You said your dad teaches college history. Does he have a doctorate?"

My throat tightened at his change of subject. Dad had been in his third year of a doctorate program when Mom left, and he'd never finished. "No."

Thankfully Alejandro moved on to a different line of questioning. "So you worked in Cleveland for the summer. Didn't you have to train?"

"I was in Colorado Springs for a developmental camp in May, and I worked the Highbanks volleyball camps in July, but I got to go home for June."

"I can't believe Holter gave you a whole month off."

"Oh, it was a negotiation. Believe me."

"He's intense."

"He's helped me have a shot at the national team, so I guess I like intense." I shrugged.

He hesitated for a moment. "Like Jaylon?"

"Mmmmm…If you think that was intense, you should see him wrestle."

"I wouldn't mind seeing him wrestle China." We laughed at that image. After a beat, he added, "Jaylon's had unparalleled success in college."

My eyebrows arched, and I noticed a slight blush on Alejandro's cheeks.

"I may have looked up his stats on the Highbanks website."

That made my heart flutter. Had he been scoping out the competition?

He glanced away, toward the corner, and I hoped he couldn't see the pile of dirty clothes I'd flung there.

"Jaylon's a much better athlete than I was," he noted.

"Jaylon's never had a serious injury like you did, though."

He was quiet for a moment, seeming to think that over. "So that's what drew you to him? His athletic success?"

"I…" I pursed my lips. "Yes, I guess. My dad and brother, they're all into school and grades—they've really supported my dream to become a doctor. But they don't understand my athletic side. They told me not to delay med school for a shot at the national team. They think I'm wasting my talent."

"But you're talented at volleyball, too. Can't they see that?"

"Nana says volleyball won't pay the bills, and she's right. They're just looking out for me. But Jaylon's different. He's such a motivated athlete—he trains like a mad man, and he always pushes me in the weight room. He may not be the best student, but he's the only one who really gets my competitive side."

"Why can't you have both?" His gaze lingered over me. "Someone to support both your academic and athletic sides?"

Because you weren't here three years ago.

I stared back at him, not knowing what to say. As the silence stretched between us, I blurted, "Do you have 'intense' exes?"

That was definitely a blush, and I tried not to grin at his discomfort. "I dated a tennis player at TCU. Not long—a few months."

My amusement vanished. Just who was this girl? "What…happened?" When he looked down, I winced. "I mean, if you don't mind me asking."

"She didn't like the attention that came with dating me, my dad being governor and everything."

The reporters mobbing us outside the restaurant had jarred me a bit, though hanging out with Lucia and Dane had already exposed me to the media maelstrom.

"And, she…" He blew out a breath, but didn't finish the sentence.

I watched the muscle working at the corner of his jaw and longed to smooth my hand along his five-o'clock shadow. How would he react if I did? Would it turn into something more?

With a start, I knew how to finish his unspoken thought. "She…wanted to have sex with you?"

When his eyes widened, I knew I'd hit pay dirt.

"It must be tough to live with such strong values," I said.

"It wasn't that tough." He looked at me. "Before."

Before? His eyes scorched me, flushing my face with heat. I found myself inching toward him on the sofa.

"So, uh, you and Jaylon."

I leaned back. Why'd he have to bring *him* up?

"Forgive me if this sounds truculent." When he scowled, I wondered if he'd caught himself spouting a big vocab word. "Uh, *offensive*, I mean. But Jaylon seems different from you." He paused. "His background. His priorities."

I swallowed as my heart juddered. Alejandro was being direct, so I should be honest with him, even though it hurt to say the truth. "Jaylon thinks I don't act black." My stomach flipped. "He used to tell me I talk white."

Alejandro blanched. "He didn't."

"He did." My stomach tightened. "But he didn't say anything I haven't heard before."

"That's despicable." His eyes flared. "And untrue. There are all types of black people. And all kinds of ways to speak. To speak articulately doesn't mean you're white. You can be black, Filipino, Mexican…"

"Wait a minute—have *you* ever been told you talk white?"

He pinched the bridge of his nose as his gaze shifted away. "Some guys in high school." He closed his eyes. "They called me a potato."

"Potato?"

"Potato," he confirmed. "Brown on the outside, white on the inside."

A laugh bubbled up my throat, but I stifled it, as he didn't seem amused. "That's awful." When his eyes opened and he looked back at me, I lost it. Laughter spilled forth like volleyballs from a ripped burlap bag. My hands flew to my mouth to stop the carnage. "S-S-Sorry," I stuttered through my fingers.

He barked out a laugh as well. "You think that's funny, calling me a potato?"

"Yeah, I do." I giggled. "Tater."

"You better stop laughing, White Talker."

That made my giggles multiply.

"Unbelievable. Never thought I'd laugh about that." His eyes crinkled as he scooted closer to me. "But I have to know, Maddie. Do you like potatoes?"

My heart raced. "Maybe." He tilted his head as he studied me. "They do go great with salsa."

His grin faded as his eyes smoldered. He clasped my hands and stroked my palms with his thumbs. I looked down at our joined hands, our skin a contrast in shades of brown. His skin lighter, his fingers longer, his touch solid and warm. He'd cut his fingernails in neat squares.

When he lifted my hand to his face, my breath caught in my throat. His warm breath tickled my palm, then his lips burned kisses along my lifeline. Heat flooded my core. I felt this alive from a kiss to my hand; what if he kissed my mouth?

The ding of an incoming text startled me, and I stole my hands back like I'd touched a hot stove. I glanced at my coat on the floor. Had Jaylon texted? "I better get that."

Alejandro just nodded.

My hands were on fire, and I fumbled through both pockets before I found my phone. It was a text from Braxton:

You're on CNN.
Why the hell are you with that right winger?

When I inhaled, Alejandro said, "Everything okay?"

"My brother." I looked up from my phone. "He said we're on CNN."

"Oh, no." He rested the back of his head on the sofa. "I didn't mean to drag you into my world."

As I fired up my laptop, my hands shook. Maybe I wanted to be part of his world.

10
Alejandro
* * *

Thoughts bounced inside my skull as I tried to sleep.

"*My dad and brother don't understand…*" Single-parent homes. Her soft hands in mine. Polyelectrolytes. "*It's not easy being raised by a single parent.*" You're so obtuse. "*Just who is this mystery girlfriend with Alejandro Ramirez?*" The atomic mass of lithium is… "*Yeah, I do, tater.*" Defense mechanisms. MCAT. "*Nana said volleyball won't pay the bills.*" A tear on her cheek. Single-parent homes create poverty and dysfunction.

"Could I be more stupid?" The fleece blanket tumbled off me as I sat straight up in the dark. How long had I been thrashing around? In the dim light from the kitchen stove, I could barely make out the time on my watch: 1:47. I tried to quiet my groan so as not to wake up Maddie in her bedroom.

Somewhere in the preceding hours, I'd realized she'd never mentioned her mother. That must mean her mother had died, and stupidly, I hadn't known. I'd probably stuck my foot in my *boca* about a hundred times, going on about single parents neglecting their children, my own mother annoying me, black families needing more stability. What a *cabrón*. But why hadn't Maddie told Lucia her mother was dead?

"I *thought* I heard you up."

I glanced toward the bedroom door to see her emerge from the darkness. She clicked on a floor lamp. Her curly hair shot up and out from her headband, framing her sleepy face like a halo.

"Sorry for waking you," I said.

She shook her head as she sat on the other end of the sofa. "Not your fault. I never got to sleep."

"I hope you weren't replaying that news clip in your head." I held my breath. We'd watched video footage on her laptop of our hounded dash to the SUV.

"No." When she smiled faintly, I exhaled. "It's kind of fun being the 'mystery girlfriend.'"

"You won't be a mystery for long, I'm afraid."

She nodded, but didn't seem distressed by my prediction. "I'm surprised they haven't figured it out yet since I'm Rez's teammate."

"They're probably too busy with the Mexican gang story." She cocked her head. "Apparently there's been an increase in gang activity not too far from Highbanks."

"Oh." Her shoulder lifted in apology. "The news and I don't chill together, as you know."

"Don't worry about it. I wish I'd never heard the story either." She watched me rub my stubbly jaw. "So if it wasn't your television debut that kept you up, what was it?"

She sighed. "I've had trouble sleeping for a while now."

"That sounds frustrating."

When she yawned and curled her neck against the sofa cushion, I noticed her zebra-print pajama top tightening across her chest. She looked warm and fuzzy; I wanted to pull her on top of me, drape her over me like a blanket.

She stared at her lap, seeming weighed down. I had a sense she was about to tell me something, but it took her a while to speak. "That business card I had, back at the arena?" She tracked me from the corner of one eye, and I nodded. "It's for the sport psychologist. My trainer wants me to see her—thinks it's a good idea." She grimaced. "She's probably right."

I couldn't believe she was opening up to me.

"Tina told me I'm a hot mess. She thinks I'm crazy."

"I doubt she thinks that…Med school fun fact: Do you know what percentage of primary-care office visits relate to behavioral health problems like stress, overeating, and lack of exercise?"

She shook her head.

"Over seventy percent. So as future physicians, we should know this stuff. We should know what therapy's like."

She turned to face me. "Have you ever seen a sport psychologist?"

"We didn't have one at TCU." I shook my head. "But even if we had, I wouldn't have gone. Machismo and all that."

"What's machismo?"

"Ah, masculinity, masculine pride. Being brave, taking care of the family." I hesitated. "It's about being strong and virile."

She blinked up at me with a smirk. "Virile, huh?"

My face flushed. I was hardly virile. "Anyway, not only did machismo hold me back, but the whole athlete mentality prevented me from even considering therapy."

"I get it." She nodded. "Never ask for help."

"Never show vulnerability," I added. I remembered the tears she'd cried and felt grateful she had the strength to be vulnerable with me. "But I probably could've benefitted from therapy, especially after my surgery." I'd been one miserable bastard then. "I'm glad they made Lucy go to therapy—the psychologist has definitely helped her."

"That's true. Dane too."

"And if you have trouble sleeping, it's a good idea to see her."

"I guess." She stifled a yawn. "So enough about my insomnia. What kept *you* up?" She patted the sofa. "Besides the luxurious pillow-soft bed I gave you."

"Hey, I was the one who invited myself over." I looked down at my black pajama pants and started to play with my watch.

"Or maybe you can't stop thinking about the applications of conjugated polyelectrolytes," she teased. When I smiled, she added, "Thanks for taking the time to help me tonight."

She had no idea how our geek-out over physical chemistry had been a highlight of the evening. "Not sure how helpful I was. You're very bright. You'll do fine on the test."

She stilled, like she wasn't sure how to respond. "I work hard, but I'm not that smart."

"Well, you're smarter than me."

Her mouth popped open. "What're you talking about?"

My heartbeat kicked up a notch. "I realized…" I swallowed. "I was lying here, kicking myself for the stupid things I've said."

She pulled her feet up on the sofa, her knees below her chin. "What do you mean?"

"About single-parent homes. Here I am, railing against fathers who leave their families—"

She drew in a sharp breath, but I continued. "When I think you were trying to tell me about your mother."

Maddie quailed, blinking as she looked straight ahead.

"I'm so sorry your mom died."

She looked up at me, eyes blazing. "What makes you think she died?"

"She didn't?" I leaned back, surprised by the heat of her glare.

"Of course you thought that. That's the only thing that makes sense." She spat the words at me. "Because what mother would ever *leave* her family? Unless her ch—" Her hand flew to cover her mouth, and before I could reach out to comfort her, she'd raced back into her bedroom and slammed the door.

What the hell just happened? My phone buzzed, and in a daze, I picked it up to see a text from China.

You okay?

No. Maddie's mother had abandoned her family? Who would do that? My phone buzzed again.

I'm coming in.

I typed a swift reply:

No need. Todo está bien.

Everything's great. I collapsed back on the worn sofa. The image of Maddie covering her mouth before she'd absconded to her room played on repeat in my head. I'd known the specter of Jaylon still lingered in her life, but I thought I'd have a chance with her once she healed. She seemed drawn to me the way I felt attracted to her. But part of her was clearly shut off—a piece I couldn't touch. I closed my eyes, knowing neither of us would get much sleep tonight.

A rustling sound woke me, and my eyes scanned the darkened apartment. *Where am I?* A light flipped on, illuminating the galley kitchen. *Maddie's apartment.* I must have fallen asleep at some point.

I heard a cabinet close, then liquid pour into a container. I heaved myself to sitting. "What time is it?"

Noise from the kitchen ceased. "Five thirty." Maddie's voice was husky, and she cleared her throat. "Sorry. Had to get some coffee so I don't fall asleep at weights."

She continued bustling around as I pressed the heels of my hands against my closed eyes. How could she drag herself to practice after a night like that?

She came out of the kitchen and managed a smile. "You can stay if you want." Smudges darkened the skin beneath her eyes, but she still looked lovely in her hoodie and yoga pants. "Sleep in if you like. Brad has my extra key, so you can lock up on your way out."

"No. We can take you to practice." I stood and folded the blanket she'd given me.

"That's okay. I can drive."

"You look too tired to drive. Really, it's the least I can do after…" I swallowed. "After crashing your place."

Her eyes narrowed. "After hearing about my mother, you mean? I don't need your pity, Alex."

"I, I don't pity you." My heart galloped. "Did I say something wrong? I thought we had a nice night, but now you're mad at me."

She threw her hands in the air. "It's not you! It's me. I'm a hot mess, remember?"

"You're not."

The front door flew open, and Brad stuck his head in. "I heard shouts. Everything okay?"

"We're fine." I met Maddie's eyes. "Can you drive us to the arena in five minutes?"

"No problemo." He wrinkled his nose. "What in tarnation is that smell?"

Maddie grimaced. "My neighbor's cooking downstairs."

"Ugh." Brad waved his hand in front of his nose. "'Bout to pass out from the fumes here." He closed the door.

Maddie's lip trembled, and I wondered if she was about to cry. To give her some privacy, I slung the strap of my duffel bag over my shoulder. "Okay if I use your bathroom?"

She nodded and turned back to the kitchen.

After I brushed my teeth and threw on some clothes, I emerged to find her waiting for me by the door with her coat on. She offered me a large Styrofoam cup of coffee.

"Beautiful," I said as I accepted it.

"I have some hazelnut creamer, but I left yours black. I wasn't sure how you take it."

"Black is perfect." I locked my eyes on hers as I took a sip.

Her hand flitted along the zipper of her coat. "Well, black's not for me."

The cup hid my smile. "I figure I won't have time to add cream and sugar when I'm on rotations next year, so I trained myself to drink it black."

She nodded. "You're good at that. Training yourself, being self-disciplined."

"And you're not? I can't imagine going to practice on so little sleep."

She shrugged. "I'm used to it."

"You sure Holter will let you back?"

"He won't be in the weight room, but I'll try to talk to him later. This morning it'll be Coach B, the strength coach. And she gets pissy if we're late." She clasped my left wrist, turning it to see my watch. "We still have a couple minutes, though."

"Good. Let's get you something to eat." I looked toward the kitchen. "You shouldn't practice on an empty stomach."

She dropped my wrist, to my dismay. "With the smell of kimchi in the air? Gag." Her nose wrinkled. "Besides, I don't have anything. I need to go to the store."

"Just when will you have time to do that?"

"I'll figure something out." She pointed to the door. "We better go."

In the heated SUV, Brad turned up the Top 40 station. *"February fourteenth,"* the DJ said. *"Happy Valentine's Day to all you nauseatingly sweet couples."*

My stomach clenched—I hated Valentine's Day. I glanced at Maddie to see her reaction, but she gazed out the window. Thinking of Jaylon, perhaps?

"Singles Awareness Day, more like it," Brad grumbled as he turned into the arena parking lot.

I smirked. I'd never been in a relationship on February fourteenth, and this year would be no different.

"You know the acronym for that, Brad?" Maddie asked. "S.A.D."

Brad laughed. "Good one, darlin'. Now go show 'em how it's done in the weight room, okay?" He put the car in park.

"Okay." She looked at me for a long moment, then skimmed her fingertips over my stubbly jaw. "So *that's* how that feels."

It was hard to get a full breath. "I need to shave."

She nodded, but the pressure of her fingers pulsed hotter, like she enjoyed my whiskers. "Sorry for my freakout back there," she whispered.

"No problemo." My imitation of Brad's Mexican accent made her smile.

When she lifted her hand, I trapped her wrist. Damn, I wanted to kiss her. But I wasn't sure if she wanted that, too. And my brain was too addled to go for it.

Aware of my agents in the front seat, I stroked her hand, then let it go. "Hope you don't have a *sad* day, Maddie."

The leather cushions of the greenhouse sofa molded around me like pillows. Though it was ten times more comfortable than Maddie's, it lacked something: her warmth.

I'd studied for a few hours now, but I doubted much information would stick with me, given my sleepiness. The oppressive silence didn't help, either. Lucia was at class, and Brad and China were probably catching some shut-eye after our monster workout and trip to the grocery store. The well-stocked basement gym had impressed me, and I had to admit I was glad Lucia had such a safe, lavish home at Highbanks.

"Studying hard, I see."

Lucia's voice started me awake. I watched her plop down next to me, cradling a plate of salad, and groaned as I wiggled up to sitting. My watch indicated an hour had gone by. An inelegant yawn stretched my mouth.

"Up all night having sex with Maddie?"

My eyes flew open as I watched her shovel a bite into her mouth. "Funny, Lucy."

She laughed. "*Tranquilo*. I know you just slept on her sofa." Her smile vanished. "Allison told me Jaylon showed up?"

I sighed. Privacy was a thing of the past, evidently. I moved my laptop to the side so I could stretch my back. "He's some piece of work."

"Yeah." She chewed, and my stomach growled. "Can't believe he'd get with Nina. I thought he was cooler than that."

"He said Nina threw herself at him."

Lucia huffed. "That I *can* believe. Nina's got issues. Dane thinks she was invalidated as a child. Still his choice to reciprocate, though."

I shook my head. "Dane psychoanalyzes everyone. Is it possible Nina doesn't have some childhood trauma? Maybe she's just a bitch."

Lucia cackled, covering her mouth. After a few chews, she said, "I like your analysis better."

She chomped on her salad for a few minutes more as I opened my browser. "Oh!" She sat up. "How rude of me—Mamá would not be proud. Can I get you some lunch?"

"Sure. I'm starving after that workout."

I closed my laptop and followed her into the expansive kitchen. She glanced at me as she retrieved some salad fixings from the fridge. "You worked out with China?"

"*Sí*. I'm getting closer to her bench press."

Lucia giggled. "She lifts way more than me, too. Nobody beats her in the weight room except for Brad."

I watched Lucia slice cucumbers and filled two glasses with ice water. "How about Dane?"

"Right. His max is higher than hers—I forgot." Then she snickered, like she was remembering something.

I loved seeing my sister so happy. Was Dane responsible for that? "What's funny?"

"Not sure I should tell you this." She scooped cucumber onto a pile of romaine lettuce. "What the hell? Dane told me that one time China physically restrained him. I'm sure he was exaggerating, but he said she almost snapped his arm off."

"*That's* not good for the machismo. He probably deserved it, though." She shrugged. "Probably. Want some tuna? Hard-boiled egg? Cheese?" When I nodded, she added all three. "Was Maddie upset when Jaylon showed up?"

I frowned, remembering the feel of her shoulder muscles contracting beneath my hand. "Of course."

"Poor Maddie. Why doesn't he leave her alone?"

I had the same question. "Apparently he needed to convince her he didn't start up with Nina till after the breakup."

"Whatever." She eyed our salads. "I should probably add some carbs to this. How 'bout a banana?"

"Is that what your dietitian would tell you to eat?"

She groaned. "No. She'd tell me to get some bread, maybe a bagel."

"Sounds great." I opened a bag of bagels on the counter and headed to the toaster.

After she poured on dressing, she asked, "So did Maddie believe him?"

You fucked my teammate. The memory of her fury tightened my body like a coil. I buttered the hot sesame bagels. "Not sure. But she stood up for herself."

"*Excelente.* Let's eat in the TV room."

I picked up both loaded plates as she took the water glasses, and we headed back to the sofa. After we munched for a while, Lucia looked at me. "So then did Jaylon leave?"

"Finally. But when he promised to return, I couldn't leave her alone. We worked on her lab report for a while."

Lucia stared at me. *Does she suspect my attraction?* I put my fork down. "What?"

"Thank you, Alex. Thanks for being there for Maddie. She's been acting weird lately, but last night she seemed more like herself. I think you helped."

I let out a breath. That was all I wanted—to make things better for Maddie. The click of the DVR drew my attention to the TV. "Someone's recording a show at one in the afternoon?"

She looked at her salad, and I leaned in, intrigued by her blush. "Lucy? What's the show?"

Giggles spilled forth. "Dane's gonna kill me!"

"It's Dane's show? What is it? *Dime.*" She kept laughing so I scooped up the remote. "Tell me, or I'm turning on the TV."

She grabbed the remote. "Okay, okay." She sighed. "It's *Days of Our Lives.*"

"A *telenovela?*"

"It's actually good."

"Don't tell me you watch that garbage too." When she hid her face, I laughed. "What has Dane done to my smart sister?"

"Hey, he's smart." She tossed her hair over one shoulder. "He has a four point oh GPA."

No wonder he was so good at arguing politics.

"But I must confess, we're hooked on *Days*. Mom said she used to watch it, too."

I shook my head. What respectable first lady would watch a soap opera? I finished my salad and started in on the bagel. "Mom's been on my case to go to confession."

"Mine too." She rolled her eyes.

I thought about Maddie's full, soft lips. "Do you go? I mean, have you found a church here?"

Lucia nodded. "My AIA group meets at the Newman Center on campus—"

"You're part of Athletes in Action?"

"Yeah, I forgot you did that at TCU. It's great, isn't it? Anyway, Allison took me to confession there, and the priest was pretty cool. Father Jacob."

"Hmm." I hadn't really found a church I liked in Baltimore, though I hadn't spent much time looking. School and the election had stolen most of my weekends. But Mom was right—I did need to confess my sins.

Lucia had thanked me for helping Maddie, but she didn't know my true feelings. If Lucia knew how much I craved seeing what was beneath Maddie's hoodie and yoga pants, she wouldn't be so grateful.

"Thanks for lunch," I said. "*Delicioso.*" When she nodded, I added, "Do you cook for Dane?"

She shrugged. "Sometimes. But tonight he's cooking for me, for Valentine's Day."

"Oh." I'd thought they'd go out, but maybe they didn't like the public scrutiny any more than I did. "I'll make myself scarce, then." I opened my laptop and resumed studying. From the corner of my eye, I watched her type on her phone for a few minutes.

"Alex?" Her big, brown eyes blinked at me. "Dane wants to invite you to dinner, too."

I stared at her, waiting for the punch line. When none came, I frowned. "That's sweet of you, but I don't want to be the third wheel."

"You won't be. We're inviting Maddie, too. Valentine's Day is probably really tough for her, so we want to distract her."

I'd see Maddie again? "Okay, then. Sounds good."

"Welcome, Madison." Dr. Valentine's eyes gleamed as she smiled at me. "I'm glad I had an opening today. I'd like to review a few things with you before we get started."

I braced myself against her sofa cushions. Why had I agreed to be shrinkified? Maybe fatigue had lowered my defenses. Or maybe it was Alejandro's gentle nudge last night about pursuing counseling. Lucia and Dane had said good things about the sport psychologist, but Braxton would tell me not to trust anyone trying to get inside my head.

"I'll just highlight some info on this consent you signed." She held up the document. "What we discuss in here is private and won't go beyond this office unless you give me written permission to speak to others. There are some rare exceptions…"

My gaze wandered around her office as she continued. Translucent white flowers shot up from a deep-green houseplant tucked in the corner, reminding me of the same plant in Nana's house. Nana had said the Gerber daisy was quite resilient — even she couldn't kill it. I, on the other hand, was not feeling so resilient.

"Is there anyone you *want* me to talk to?" Dr. Valentine asked.

"Um…"

"You said Tina referred you. Is it okay if I let her know you met with me?"

"Yes." Hopefully that would get her off my back. I signed the release form.

"Would you like me to speak to any of your coaches?"

My headshake was immediate. I'd mustered the courage to stop by Coach Holter's office this morning after macrobiology class, and the memory of that encounter caused squeezing in my lungs. Though he'd allowed me to return to practice, starting later this afternoon, I'd never seen him so disappointed in me. My eyes burned.

Dr. Valentine smiled gently. "When I saw a therapist, I cried the whole time."

I'd been here less than two minutes, and I was already sniveling.

"Crying's really normal in here. I have tissues on either end of the sofa for that reason."

Her assurance eased the tight ball in my chest, and I leaned to my left to pluck a few from the box.

She typed on a small laptop. "What brings you in today, Madison?"

I sniffed as I wiped tears off my cheeks. "My friends call me Maddie."

"Gotcha. Have you been crying more than normal?"

"Definitely." I sighed. "Tina says I need to get my smile back."

"I see." She typed some more. "You've been feeling down and blue?"

I nodded.

"When did the crying and blue mood start?"

My hand skimmed my cheeks as I considered her question. My skin was smooth, in contrast to the roughness of Alex's stubbles. His square jaw had felt so solid beneath my touch this morning. Not much felt solid these days. "About a month ago, I guess."

"Around the start of spring semester, then. What was going on in your life at that time?"

I glanced at the bookshelf and noticed a framed photo of an obese cat. The gray beast glared at me, and I wondered what color the Ramirez cat was. "It's rather cliché, I'm afraid." I turned back to her. "My boyfriend broke up with me."

"Oh, dear." She typed away. "So, on a scale of one to Adele, how bad was this breakup?"

I laughed as I sank back into the sofa.

"I can see why Tina wants you to get your smile back. It's beautiful."

I felt myself blush. Dad always said the same thing. "I guess the breakup was pretty damn close to Adele."

"'Rolling in the Deep' or 'Turning Tables'?"

I shrugged. "I'm more partial to Rihanna's 'Take a Bow.'"

"Oh." She nodded. "So the bastard cheated on you?"

I nodded, impressed in spite of myself. "He claims he didn't get with her till we were done."

"But you don't believe him?"

I exhaled. "I don't know. It's…messy. The other woman's my teammate."

"No shit. That's horrible." She shook her head. After a beat, she asked, "Is your ex a student-athlete as well?"

"Only the most successful wrestler in school history."

"Yikes." She sighed. "You must hear about him all the time. Painful reminders of your relationship."

"You have no idea. He keeps showing up, too."

Her eyes narrowed. "Is he stalking you?"

"No!" My back straightened. "I…I don't think so. I just don't get it. He's the one who broke up with me, yet he won't let sleeping dogs lie."

She observed me for a few moments. "How long were you dating?"

"Three years."

"Wow. Must be tough for both of you to move on after sharing so much together. Did he say why he broke up?"

I looked down. "He said…" My throat constricted, making my voice tremble. "He said I didn't let him in. He told me I didn't love him."

"That sounds quite painful to hear."

I nodded.

She leaned forward. "*Did* you love him?"

"Of course! We were perfect together. I did everything for him." A sob pulsed up my throat, pressing for release. "But I wasn't good enough. I screwed it up somehow—I made him leave." A tear leaked out.

Dr. Valentine opened a file cabinet to extract a piece of paper. I accepted the handout and read the heading: *Irrational Beliefs After Breakups.* I looked up at her. "You think my beliefs are irrational?"

"Read them and see. People who hold these beliefs suffer more after breakups, and it sounds like you've been suffering a lot."

I glanced at the paper. "Number one: The breakup is all my fault." *Whoops.* I'd just said that. "But how is that belief irrational? It's certainly not Jaylon's fault. He told me he left because I was closed off to him."

"I'm not saying the breakup is entirely his fault, either," she said. "But you both had a part in this. Relationships take two. You probably made some mistakes, and he made some mistakes."

"Like hooking up with that skank, Nina," I grumbled. I covered my mouth with my hand. "Sorry for using her name."

She seemed unfazed. "Like I said, our discussion in here is private. Keep reading."

I looked back down at the page. "Number two: I'm not good enough." The words stabbed my heart. That wasn't irrational thinking. That was fact. Jaylon had discarded me because I wasn't good enough, and Alejandro would soon discover that truth as well. To my horror, shameful tears spilled down my cheeks. The paper shook in my hand, and I reached for more tissues to hide the tremor. *She must think I'm a nutcase.*

Dr. Valentine gave me a moment, and I wondered if I'd deplete her entire supply of tissues.

"Do you believe that, Maddie? That you're not good enough?" she asked.

I stilled. Could I admit that to her? I barely knew her. But when I detected warmth in her eyes, I nodded.

"That's odd coming from one of the most successful student-athletes at Highbanks. Won't you be up for the conference medal of honor this spring?"

I shrugged as I sniffed. Awards like that didn't matter if I couldn't even hold on to the people I loved.

"Where does the inadequacy come from, do you think?"

My head lowered. "I'm not sure. It's just what I've always felt."

"Perhaps we can explore that some more. *I* believe you're good enough." She waited until I met her eyes. "You. Are. Enough. And we'll work together to get you to believe that, too. Now." She pointed at the paper. "Keep reading."

I took a shaky breath. "Number three: I'll never find someone else. Well, damn, I've had that thought, too." But I hadn't felt quite as hopeless since meeting Alejandro. Could he be my someone else?

"How could you challenge that belief when it comes up?" She gazed at me.

"Uh." My heart thumped. "I definitely *will* find someone else?"

She dipped her head to one side. "Well, there's no evidence for that either." She chuckled when I scowled. "No guarantees in life, my friend. But to believe you'll never find romance is wrong. You still have a chance of finding love even after one hundred men break up with you."

I gasped. "That would be awful!"

"You could handle it, though; especially if you don't accept these irrational beliefs as truth. They're just thoughts."

I closed my eyes as I let out a breath. This conversation exhausted me.

"How have you been sleeping, Maddie?"

My eyes opened. "It's been rough."

"Trouble falling asleep? Trouble staying asleep?"

"Yes and yes." Last night I'd been thinking about Alejandro sleeping on my couch, his spicy scent invading my little apartment. The video of him grabbing my hand as we hustled to the SUV outside the restaurant had played in my mind, bringing a smile to my face, but every time I'd almost drifted off, the image changed. He would let go of my hand, his dark eyes clouding with disgust. Then he'd walk away from me.

My chest hurt thinking about it now. "My mind won't shut off."

"How frustrating. At the end of our session, I'll share a technique to help you sleep. I'm guessing your energy been low?" I nodded. "Concentration too?"

"Studying's near impossible these days." My cheeks flamed. "My grades are horrible."

"You have a stellar GPA as a biochemistry major, according to your paperwork. So by 'horrible,' I'm guessing you mean Bs?"

She seemed to know me well already. "*Low* Bs. Maybe even a C in p-chem."

"That must be upsetting, especially with med school applications looming."

She had me pegged.

"Has your athletic performance declined as well?"

I nodded, remembering my serves zooming into the net. I hadn't served an ace in ages. The more questions she asked, the more impaired I sounded.

"How's your appetite?"

"Ugh." I scrunched my nose. "Food's gross. But I did eat lunch today, don't worry. Lucia's been on my case to eat something."

I thought I detected a faint smile before she asked her next question. "Have you had less desire to do activities you normally enjoy, like hang out with friends?"

I frowned. "Lucia asked me to join her and Dane for dinner tonight. She's so sweet—I bet she asked because she knows Valentine's Day's hard for me. But I don't want her pity." Heaviness weighed down my eyelids. "And I'm so tired that I don't know if I can make it."

"Do you feel that way often? Too tired to be social?"

"I have a couple friends on the basketball team, but I haven't gone out with them since December." A pang of guilt hit me. *I should call Tamisha.*

"Have you thought about death or suicide?"

I froze. I hadn't told anyone about that night.

"Sometimes people who feel depressed also have thoughts about killing themselves," she continued. "Have you had any of those thoughts?"

"I would never do it—it'd destroy my dad. But the night Jaylon broke up with me...I thought about taking pills. I had some pain meds left over from an injury sophomore year. Probably not enough to do the job. But then I realized how stupid it was to let a guy end my life. Jaylon wouldn't care, anyway."

"You were brave to face the pain. Feelings are temporary, but suicide is permanent. You've seen for yourself that your pain has decreased since that night." She typed on her laptop, then looked straight at me. "And that sounds like more irrational thinking. Jaylon *would* have cared, as well as your family. They'd be devastated to lose you."

That night had scared me, and my shoulders slumped in relief after telling her about it. Dr. Valentine said other people had suicidal thoughts, too. She made it seem like I wasn't totally off my rocker.

"So you've been feeling down for a while now. What led you to come in today?"

"It's Valentine's Day. I figured it was a sign that I should see you."

She smirked. "Yes, it is my day, isn't it?"

"You should take the day off to celebrate."

"But then I wouldn't get to meet *you*." Her smile lingered.

I thought about her question some more. "I guess the real reason I bit the bullet and scheduled this appointment is…I kind of like this other guy now, and I don't want to mess it up. I don't want it to end like it did with Jaylon."

"Interesting. Are you ready for another relationship?"

"I have no idea." I tossed my hands in the air. "Isn't that your area of expertise?"

She grinned. "I don't give advice in here. It's more like helping you find your own wisdom. What do your heart and mind say about your readiness to love again?"

I pursed my lips. "My heart says 'He's hot. He makes you feel good. Go for it.'"

She laughed. "And your mind?"

"My mind says 'Girl, Jaylon destroyed you. You'll *never* be ready to love again.'"

"Hmm." She pointed to the list of irrational thoughts. "I don't think that's your logical mind talking. Sounds more like fear. Jaylon could've broken up with you after twenty years together, and there's still no evidence that you couldn't have another relationship. You're hurting, and you're trying to protect yourself from more pain. Of course you're scared of getting hurt again."

She was right. I wasn't destroyed…just a little damaged.

"But we all need connection. A life without love is barren and bereft."

I frowned.

"One of life's most poignant dilemmas," she mused. "To embrace love, we risk heartbreak. To resist love, we risk emptiness."

I leaned back on the sofa. I didn't want emptiness, and my life sure had felt empty since Jaylon dumped me. Alejandro had begun to fill that void, however. With his sharp intellect, sleek physique, and self-assured approach, he'd set up his place inside of me. He'd moved in and infused a sense of hope for the future. But what if that future held more pain? More abandonment? Could I risk it?

"Let's talk about your family. You mentioned your father earlier. What about your mother? Are your parents married?"

My stomach flipped. "Divorced." My dad had received divorce papers after my fourth birthday, and we hadn't heard from my mother since.

"How old were you when they divorced?"

"Four. I mean two."

She squinted at me.

I took a deep breath. "Let's just save some time here. My mother left us when I was two." *Damn it!* I started to cry again.

"Whoa." Her fingers paused on the keyboard as she studied me. "And she didn't return?"

I swallowed the lump in my throat. "Divorce papers arrived when I was four, apparently, but she hasn't sent one letter since. Hasn't called once." My mouth trembled. "I don't even know if she's still alive."

"That's shattering."

Her response hit me like a volleyball to the gut. My mother's abandonment *had* been shattering. I was shattered. But I didn't want to be shattered! I held my head up as I blinked away tears. "It hasn't been that bad." *Liar.* "My dad's been there for me and my brother, and Nana and Gramps too."

She stopped typing. "Hmm…"

"What does *that* mean?" My face felt hot as I brushed away tears.

"Could this relate to this mistaken belief that you're not good enough?" Her eyes held a note of tenderness. "Any child whose parent leaves might conclude that."

Sobs bubbled up from a place deep inside of me. I *knew* I wasn't good enough. My mother had proven it to me the day she'd walked out of my life.

"You think you weren't good enough to make your mother stay. You think you're unlovable."

How'd she know that? I felt my eyes widen as I stared at her.

She continued, "And you're afraid this new guy will find that out. He'll figure out you're unlovable, and he'll abandon you, too."

I gripped the edge of the cushion, and stiffness from my fists radiated up my arms. No matter how tense my body was, though, the tears kept coming.

"But you're wrong, Maddie." Her soft voice somehow soothed me. "Children are egocentric—they think the world revolves around them. When good things happen, they take full credit. When bad things happen, they blame themselves. Naturally you thought your badness caused your mother to leave, because that's what children think. But you aren't responsible for your mother's adult choices. *She's* the one who left."

I struggled to take that in.

"You don't know why she left, and each day that goes by without knowing makes you doubt yourself more, makes that hole inside of you bigger."

I nodded as tears spilled down my cheeks.

"I don't know why your mother left—only that it's not your fault. But if she's alive, I bet she regrets leaving you. I'm sad she doesn't know what a strong, beautiful woman you are."

I shook my head. "I'm not beautiful or strong. I'm weak."

"That's not what I believe. Give yourself a chance, Maddie. Give yourself a chance to write a new story."

I grabbed more tissues, surprised there were still any left in the box. She typed for a while as I mopped myself up. Thank God nobody else could see me like this. Alejandro had seen me cry enough already.

I sniffed. "So the new guy…"

She looked up from her laptop.

"He won't abandon me, then?"

She shook her head with a sad smile. "Asking for more guarantees, I see."

I exhaled. When had I become so needy?

"You're tying yourself in knots by tying your mother and this guy together. This potential relationship has nothing to do with your mother. She left, and you felt abandoned, but that's over. What happened with your mother has no bearing on whether it works out with this new guy. And whatever future this relationship holds, he can't make you whole. Only you can. That's why you're here."

Overloaded. I let out a long breath. Maybe she spoke the truth. Alejandro deserved more than being compared to a woman who abandoned her own children.

"I see we're almost out of time." Dr. Valentine set aside her laptop. "Here's what I think: you meet the criteria for major depressive disorder, also known as clinical depression."

Tina was right, damn her.

"Depression is not simply feeling sad. It's not something you can just snap out of, no matter how hard you try. It's a clinical syndrome with a neurobiological basis. Sometimes depression runs in families. Is there anyone in your family who's been diagnosed with depression?"

Dad seemed down sometimes, but not to the depths of the dark morass I'd tumbled into. "I don't think so."

She nodded. "The good news is that your depression will resolve over time, no matter what you do. But you can speed up your recovery with counseling and medication." She smiled at me. "How does this feel between us? Would you like to continue to meet?"

I hesitated. She seemed cool, but would I become a blubbering mess every time I met with her? "What would it be like?"

"Similar to today's session, though fewer questions from me. Today I needed to gather some information, and I still want to ask you about substance use and your spiritual beliefs, but in the future it will be more like teamwork. You'll discuss what's going on in your life, and I'll teach a few skills for coping with stress. Many student-athletes find it helpful to talk it out, see things from a different perspective. Sound good?"

I needed to cope with stress better—that was obvious. "Okay."

After we scheduled an appointment for the following week, she asked, "Would you like to try antidepressant medication? I can set something up with your team physician."

She thought I needed medication? What would Nana think of that?

"There's no pressure," Dr. Valentine said. "Why don't you think about it until we meet again? You could research SSRI medication to learn more."

"Why do you think I need it?"

"Your depression sounds rather severe, with the suicidal thinking, sleep and appetite changes, and impaired function. Medication's an option to address imbalances in your brain and help get your smile back more quickly. But there are some downsides, like possible side effects and having to wait two to four weeks for the meds to kick in."

I hadn't cried for a few minutes, but my burning eyes indicated the cry-fest was about to return. I just needed to get out of here. "I'll think about it."

"Okay. I'm giving you some homework." When I scowled, she laughed. "Have you heard of TED talks?"

I nodded. "They're presentations by experts you can watch online."

"Exactly. I want you to watch a TED talk by Brené Brown, titled 'The Power of Vulnerability.' It may help you learn self-compassion. And when you have trouble falling asleep, I want you to try a counting technique to derail the nonstop worries in your head. Count one to ten, ten times. The first time through, pause after one. The second time through, pause after two. And so on."

How is that supposed to help? My skepticism must have shown.

"Try it," she said. "It works for me every time. I drift off at round six or seven, but if you're still awake after ten rounds, start over. You can't worry about all the crap in your life and count at the same time."

I nodded. It was worth a try—anything to get some sleep.

"Any questions?"

I shook my head and stood on wobbly legs to toss my used tissues into her garbage can.

She stood as well. "Wonderful to meet you, Maddie, and I'll see you next week." The laugh-lines at the corners of her eyes deepened as she smiled. "Remember. You are enough."

12
Alejandro
* ★ *

You owe me, Mom.

The tall buildings of the Highbanks campus flew by the car window on our way to church, where Father Jacob awaited my confession. After Frank had driven Lucia to practice, I'd watched a recorded lecture on gastrointestinal disorders so many times that I'd begun to feel sick to my stomach. I hadn't exactly killed it with my typical laser-beam focus, either. All I'd been able to think about was Maddie.

I considered visiting practice to see her before I realized Coach Holter wouldn't let me anywhere near that place. So instead I caved to Mom's request. Check that — Mom's *demand*. Allison had agreed to drive me to church since Brad and China were still sleeping after their night of guarding me at Maddie's.

From the back seat of the SUV, I watched Agent Largent twirl a strand of her curly, blond hair at a stoplight. Her gentleness stood in stark contrast to my agents' tougher vibes.

"How do you like being an agent, Allison?"

She met my eyes in the rearview mirror and smiled. "It's got its pros and cons, but for the most part I enjoy it."

Interesting. "What pros and cons?"

"I love protecting your sister. I've grown quite attached to her."

I smiled as well. I knew the feeling.

"But I worry I'm *too* attached to her. We need objectivity to do our jobs. We can't let our feelings interfere with our mission."

I could also relate to that. When I'd rebuked Lucia about her sex life, I'd probably made it harder to protect her by alienating her. But I worried about her, and I wanted to obey my dad. As we pulled into the church parking lot, I studied the simple brick building. With lustful feelings toward Maddie pulsing through me, I had to admit I worried about myself, too.

Allison held the car door open and followed me inside. We stomped clumps of snow off our shoes onto the mat by the door. I followed her down a brick hall lined with wood furniture straight out of the seventies. I knew most university Catholic centers were rather plain, but this one made our church in Houston look ornate.

"Lucia meets with Father Jacob in there." Allison pointed to a door at the rear of the sanctuary. She led me inside the small room with two chairs facing each other. "I called Father Jacob to get you an appointment for confession, like I do with Lucia. He told me he'd be in his office. Stay put, and I'll get him."

I eyed the seating arrangement. My church in Houston had a screen between priest and parishioner, and avoiding eye contact when confessing ugly sins was a definite bonus. This setup put everything out in the open, and I squirmed at the impending exposure. No wonder Maddie had avoided therapy.

You owe me, Mom. I draped my coat over a wooden chair and took a seat.

"Ah." A man dressed in jeans and a Highbanks sweatshirt entered. A janitor? He had salt-and-pepper hair and thin wire glasses. "When Secret Service came to get me, I expected Lucia."

Wait — this was the *priest?*

"Father Jacob." He held out his hand, and I bolted out of the chair to shake it. "You must be Lucia's brother, Alejandro."

"Yes, sir. Uh, yes, Father."

He let go of my hand and tugged down his sweatshirt to reveal the clerical collar beneath it. "It gets drafty."

I nodded. "It's freezing up here."

He was a good deal shorter than me and stared up with a placid expression.

What do I do now? "Uh, I'm visiting Lucy, and I thought I'd go to confession, but if this isn't a good time—"

"It's an ideal time." He gestured to the chairs. "Shall we begin?"

Once I sat, the routine rushed back to me. I made the sign of the cross as I said, "In the name of the Father, the Son, and the Holy Spirit." I shifted in my chair. "Bless me Father, for I have sinned. It's been…" I swallowed. "…over a year since my last confession." His watchful gaze unnerved me.

"Welcome back. I'm pleased you found your way here."

I exhaled. There seemed to be calm in his eyes, and it steadied me, too. Maybe it wasn't so bad to face the priest. Although now came the time to list my sins. It would probably be best to start with my immodest desire for Maddie, but my lack of control over my feelings embarrassed me. There were quite a few other sins I could begin with, unfortunately.

"I haven't attended mass regularly." Dad's campaign schedule and school had interfered with church attendance—hardly an excuse.

"We hold mass almost every night," he said.

"But I don't live here. I live in Baltimore."

He nodded. Thankfully he didn't respond with the obvious: *And there are no churches in Baltimore?*

"I've tried to control things instead of seeking God's will." My head lowered. I needed to squelch my control-freak tendencies. When he looked at me expectantly, I continued. "I've done unnecessary work on the Sabbath." This was a constant sin for me, between baseball games in undergrad and Monday exams in medical school.

Father Jacob hadn't seemed disturbed by any of my sins up to this point.

I took a deep breath. "I disrespected an authority figure—Lucia's coach. I yelled at him and swore at him." My face got hot. "I lost my temper." My fists clenched. "I want to be better. I want to be more loving."

He nodded. "Remember, Jesus tells us to be quick to hear but slow to anger. Our anger does not produce the righteousness of God." His unfaltering scrutiny somehow urged me to keep spewing my mistakes.

"I didn't obey my father. He expects me to protect my sister and brother, but I've failed." I grimaced.

"Protecting your sister—was that what you were trying to do when you yelled at her coach?"

I considered that. Dad wouldn't approve of me going ballistic, though he would want me to stand up for Lucy. "Yes, I suppose. But I *didn't* protect her when I withheld some important information from my father. I'd planned to tell him, but it didn't seem right when I had the chance."

"Hmm." Father Jacob crossed one leg over the other. "Does your father need to know the information to keep your sister safe?"

"Yes." I remembered Maddie telling me Lucia could take care of herself. "No." I breathed out. "I don't know." I eyed Father Jacob. Did he know Lucia had broken the sixth commandment? "I guess what it comes down to: do I obey my father, or do I respect my sister?"

"That sounds like a tricky moral dilemma. Pray to the Holy Spirit, and you'll receive guidance."

I nodded. I did need to pray more. But I wished he'd answered my question. "I've been prideful and judgmental. Someone…a, a friend…" If only Maddie were more than that to me. "She told me I shouldn't judge Lucy. And I know it's not my place, but I'm concerned about my sister. Maybe my father should know what she's done."

He blinked at me. "It appears you're also thinking about your father's judgment."

"Yes." I didn't want Dad to be disappointed by me or Lucia.

"And judging yourself as well."

I shrugged. How else was I to keep myself in line?

He opened his arms, his palms facing up. "In confession, there is no judgment. There is only mercy."

Cierto. Truth. I was here to receive God's mercy. I closed my eyes and tried to open my heart. I needed to end the caginess and deceit and put it all out there, ask for His mercy. "You know, it's ridiculous that I'm judging others for the very sin I'm committing." My hands tingled with the yearning to stroke Maddie's skin. I couldn't stop thinking about her even in the confessional. *God, help me.*

"And what sin is that, my son?"

"I have impure thoughts. I have lust in my heart." My chest tightened. *Tell him.* "I want to make love to a girl who's not my wife."

He sat back in his chair as he nodded slowly. Did he think I was hopeless to receive God's grace?

"*Have* you had sex outside of marriage?"

"No, Father." I sighed. "It was my full intent to wait for the sacrament of marriage, no matter what happened around me, until…"

"Until?" He prompted.

"Until I met Maddie." Her enticing scent and smooth skin flooded my senses. "She's so intelligent. So accomplished. She's kind. She's giving." I pictured tears rolling down her face and frowned. "She's hurting. When she hurts, I hurt, too. I want to help her." My heart skipped a beat. "I, I've never felt this for any girl before."

His mouth twitched. Was that the beginning of a smile?

"Truth is, she's consumed me." When blood rushed to my groin, I crossed my wrists in my lap. My face flamed. "She arouses me, and I know that's not right, but I can't control—"

"Has God brought love into your life, Alejandro?"

Startled, I looked up. Did I love Maddie? I didn't know her well enough to determine that, right? I knew I cared deeply for her, though. That was indisputable.

Father Jacob tilted his head. "You confessed to trying to control things instead of seeking God's will. And the depth of emotion you have for this woman feels out of your control."

"Very much so."

"You said you seek more love in your life, and He wants that for you as well. Perhaps your growing attachment to this woman is God's will. Perhaps opening yourself to her is a way to honor our Lord, not diminish Him."

Increíble. Was he saying it was okay to have sex with Maddie?

Father Jacob patted my knee. "This is about you and your relationship with God. Feel His love for you. Let His strength replace your fear. Pray for His guidance. Pray for His grace."

I sat still as his words settled over me like a silky altar cloth. I'd always been the responsible one in my family. I'd tried to set a good example for my siblings by working hard in school and baseball. I'd followed the dictates of my parents and parish without question. But my baseball dreams had died under the surgeon's knife. And my utter compliance with authority had left me detached and lonely. Were these the just rewards of a godly life?

Maddie had assuaged my lonely heart. Spending time with her was a salve to my solitary existence. Could it be wrong to want her like I did? *Guide me, Father. Bring me love, if that's Your will.* An unfamiliar burning sensation climbed up my throat, and I realized I wanted to cry.

"Do you have other sins to confess?"

I clenched my teeth against the threatening tears, and shook my head. I'd probably taken up too much of his time already. "I'm truly sorry for my sins."

"In response to God's mercy, pray three Hail Marys."

I nodded. Father Jacob seemed different from my priest in Houston—less intimidating, more accepting—but the penance he gave me was standard fare.

"And I suggest daily prayer to let go of your fear, bring you closer to God's love."

I paused. That penance seemed more unusual, but also more needed. "Yes, Father."

He waited for me to continue.

I cleared my throat. "Dear God, I'm sorry for my sins with all my heart. You are deserving of all my love, but I've sinned against You, my God. I resolve, with the help of Your grace, to confess my sins, do penance, and amend my life."

Father Jacob took my hands in his. "God, the Father of Mercies, through the death and resurrection of his Son, has sent the Holy Spirit among us for the forgiveness of sins. May God grant you pardon and peace. I absolve you from your sins in the name of the Father, and of the Son, and of the Holy Spirit. Amen."

"Amen."

He looked into my eyes. "God has freed you from your sin. Go in peace."

I nodded. I craved peace. "Thanks be to God."

I walked out of the room and found Allison sitting in a pew toward the back of the empty sanctuary. I pointed to another pew and raised my eyebrows to ask if I could stay and do my penance. She nodded and smiled; Lucia probably did the same thing. I slid into a pew a few rows ahead of her and leaned down to pull out a kneeler.

As I knelt and set my elbows on the wood pew in front of me, a familiar twinge of pain shot up my right arm. I glared at my elbow, which hadn't been right since the surgery. *Goddamn baseball injury.*

My head popped up with a guilty glance around me. *Whoops.* Here I was, sinning again, not yet two minutes since my confession. I definitely needed to pray. I lowered my forehead to my clasped knuckles.

Hail Mary, full of grace, the Lord is with thee; blessed art thou among women, and blessed is the fruit of thy womb Jesus. Holy Mary, mother of God, pray for us sinners...

Hail Mary, full of grace... My mind wandered as I repeated the silent prayer. *Bring me closer to Your love, God. Let me not be controlling or prideful. Guide me to honor my parents, my sister, and my brother. Show me how to proceed with Maddie.*

I would see her tonight. Would she still be angry with me? Would she let me kiss her? Was it okay to kiss her when I wanted even more?

Hail Mary, full of grace...Help me get an A on my next exam. No, I shouldn't ask for that. Help me be worthy of your love, God. Guide me to do the right thing.

Allison studied me as I stood and approached her. "Ready?"

"Yes."

She kept glancing at me on our way to the car.

"What?"

"Oh. Sorry." She blushed. "I was checking to see if you were crying."

"Why?" I suddenly felt exposed.

Allison scanned the parking lot as she held the door open for me. "Lucia cries when she prays. She says the spirit moves her, that she feels God's love at church."

My sister. She was a precious gem, a sensitive soul. Dad had worried about her attending school so far away from Texas, but she'd made a home here. I was proud of her.

As we drove back to the greenhouse, I remembered my phone had buzzed during confession. I took it out of my jacket pocket and saw a text from Jake. We tried to talk at least once a week, but it had been a while since I'd heard from him. I looked at the time — it had to be almost midnight in Afghanistan. Hoping he hadn't gone to sleep already, I typed out a reply.

Sorry, was in confession. You still up?

Just finished patrol.
What the fuck has choirboy got to confess?

I grinned. I missed his insults.

We're all sinners. Even heroes like you sin sometimes.

It took him a while to reply.

Cut it with the hero stuff. I'm no fucking hero.

My grin faded. Jake always deflected my praise, but tonight he had an edge.

What happened on patrol?

Can't discuss it.

C'mon, you know my security clearance is stellar.

That's right, El Niño.

I relaxed a little when he joked again. Ever since my father had become governor, Jake had referred to Dad as *El Presidente* and me as *El Niño*. Somehow Jake had known my father would become president before my family figured it out. He also knew how much I lost when my father won. Jake was the only person I'd confided in about my disdain for public scrutiny. Before Maddie, he'd been the only one to know Charlotte had left me because of my family's fame and my values. Jake had been there for me, and I wanted to be there for him.

It gets rough out there. But El Niño knows your heart, knows you want to make things better. Keep fighting.

I had a long wait for his reply.

Maybe I need confession too.

What had happened out there? God, I hoped he hadn't been forced to take a life.

You definitely need confession, Marine. You're messed in the head.

Pot, meet the fucking kettle. You prob ruined that priest. So you found a church you like?

I'm at Highbanks.

Have you punched Douchebag yet?

I smirked. Jake had gotten an earful after the first time I met Dane. And I hoped Lucy wouldn't find out I'd told Jake about Dane getting to know her in the biblical sense. I'd been so angry when Frank had called me I hadn't known what to do. So I'd texted my best friend. Jake had been against me confronting Lucy, and I should've listened to him. But when did I act rationally when I was ticked off?

Hail Mary, full of grace...

Not yet.

You okay? Why'd you go to confession?

I played with my watch. Should I tell him about Maddie? He'd give me hell, I knew. But that meant he cared.

I met a girl.

Holy FUCK! So you want to boink her bones, but your stupid religion holds you back?

You're a Neanderthal.

I knew it. El Niño's finally growing up. *wipes a tear*

I hate you.

Get some for me, ok? It's a desert out here. The only action I get? Cleaning my rifle.

I rolled my eyes. He texted again.

Bopping my baloney. Polishing the banister.

Thanks, I get it.

No really, you like this girl, huh?

Yes. Not sure how she feels about me.

She must be damn special.

She is. I smiled. But enough about me; he was the one who'd texted.

Enough about me. You ok?

Your lameass life's the perfect distraction. Ow. Benson just threw his boot at me. Gotta turn off the phone.

Be safe, Jake.

You too, El Niño. Hey, ask El Presidente to send some chicks over for me and my boyz.

I laughed.

I'll get right on that.

Maddie

As I climbed the last stair to my floor, I let out a long breath. Jaylon was not waiting at my door. *Praise God.* After the day I'd had—weights, class, Coach chewing me out, class again, mind-shrinking therapy, practice—I couldn't handle him on top of it. Mrs. Marshall's Yorkie started his high-pitched yaps when I unlocked my door and walked inside.

Bed. I peeled off my coat and left it pooled at my feet. I wanted my bed. And that little fucker had better shut his pie-hole by the time I got there. But when I turned toward my bedroom, my stomach growling stopped me.

Is that you, hunger? I haven't heard from you in a while. Maybe I'd actually worked up an appetite at practice. I somehow hadn't been the worst athlete out there today. Perhaps I should've accepted Rez's Valentine dinner invitation. She'd looked so sad when I turned her down in the locker room.

I changed direction and entered my little kitchen. Then I realized I didn't have anything to eat. My road trip to Cleveland had interfered with my usual weekend grocery store run. With a groan, I sagged against the wall. I was way too exhausted to venture out into the cold for food.

Maybe there was *something* left to eat. An old piece of bread? I opened the fridge and jumped back. It was fully stocked! I gasped as I sorted through apples, oranges, and salad fixings in the produce drawer. Deli-sliced turkey and cheese sat on one shelf next to Greek yogurt and a tub of salsa. And there was fresh milk and a new container of hazelnut coffee creamer on the top shelf. Who had bought these groceries for me?

Then I noticed a brown clump on my countertop: a basket of potatoes. I howled with laughter. Brad hadn't given my spare key back. My potato must have gone grocery shopping.

I held my belly as my shoulders shook, and I laughed so hard that tears came to my eyes. I didn't mind *these* tears. A long sigh left my lungs when I finally gathered myself back together. I didn't feel quite so tired anymore.

Ten minutes later, I turned onto Rez's street and hit the brakes when I saw media vans outside the greenhouse. I'd thrown my hair into a ponytail after my locker room shower, and had hastily applied mascara and lip gloss on my drive. Was I up for dealing with paparazzi?

Brown eyes, dark and deep, filled my mind. Eyes that studied me with interest and knowing, that crinkled when their owner smiled. *Yes.* I was up for it. My eleven-year-old Hyundai and I inched toward the Barbarian horde.

I tensed when the reporters erupted into action. I locked my gaze on the keypad near the gate like it was my target for a volleyball spike.

"Madison!" a reporter yelled as she hustled to my car.

So the girlfriend mystery had been solved. I wondered how Braxton would react to my name on the news. Cameras rolled and bulbs flashed. A blast of frigid air assailed me when I rolled down my window.

"Dane Monroe's inside with Lucia and Alejandro," the reporter panted. "Is this a double date for Valentine's Day?"

Here's hoping. I weaved my arm around reporters to press the buzzer. "Speaking of Valentine's Day…" I glanced at them. "Don't you guys have dates tonight?"

"I'll take *you* out, sugar," one cameraman said, and the reporters laughed.

C'mon Rez, let me in. Questions zinged my way as I waited for a response from inside the greenhouse.

"Why is Alejandro visiting Highbanks?"

None of your business, I thought.

"Will President Ramirez be here?"

Not likely. But whoa, what'd it be like to meet him?

"What will Lucia and Dane do tonight?"

Each other. I couldn't believe that answer popped into my mind—Alejandro would not be pleased. Thank heavens I hadn't said that aloud.

Another reporter: "What will you and Alejandro do tonight?"

Each other? I gasped at the thought. My girly bits tingled with the realization I wanted to get naked with him. I craved a peek at the long, sleek muscles I knew hid under his stylish suits. But then I remembered Alejandro's moratorium on sexy times before marriage. Why'd he have to be so strict?

The gate opened at the same time Frank jogged out of the house. He shooed reporters away from the driver's side and frowned down at me through the open window. "Scoot over, Ms. Brooks."

I scrambled over the center console as he slid into the driver's seat and put the car in drive. "Stay outside the gates," he barked to the throng of media before rolling up the window.

"You should've let us know you were coming," he said as he pulled my car up in front of the house.

"Sorry."

His scowl faded. "It's hard dealing with publicity when you're not used to it." He parked and bounded around to open my door. "Lucia will be thrilled you're here."

She waited for me right inside the door. "You came!" She wrapped me in a boisterous hug. Over her shoulder, I noticed Alejandro watching me. There was a tightening in my belly.

"Sorry those vultures attacked you," he said when Lucia let me go.

"It's okay." I shrugged. "By the way, they know my name now."

His eyes closed as his mouth tensed into a hard line.

Frank turned the corner and disappeared.

"Luz!" Dane bellowed from inside the house. "Fuck. Need your help in here!"

She giggled. "He's helpless without his sous chef. Be right back." I read the saying on her long-sleeve T-shirt on her way out:

You Know I'm All About That Ace, 'Bout That Ace

Once she left the foyer, Alejandro and I stared at each other.

"Lucy said you couldn't make it," he murmured. "But you're here."

"*Somebody* stocked up my fridge." I cocked an eyebrow.

He started to smile, but then stopped. "Was that okay?"

"Oh my God, yes. Thank you so much."

"You're welcome. I knew you wouldn't have time for shopping with your schedule. So…" He smirked. "Did the chips and salsa give me away?"

I laughed and gave his chest a playful push; he inhaled sharply. Did he feel it too? The frisson of energy when we touched?

"It was the potatoes, of course." My body vibrated as I looked into his dark eyes.

He swallowed. We stared at each other like we were meeting for the first time. He wore navy dress pants with a zippered dark-gray cardigan over a plaid button-down. Suave and well-heeled, like usual.

"May I take the lady's coat?"

I nodded. He circled behind me and grasped the collar of my coat as I shrugged out of the sleeves. When his fingers brushed my neck, a shiver crept up my back. His hands stilled—he must have noticed—and I froze too.

He leaned over my shoulder, my coat collar still in his hands and the sleeves halfway off. His bright eyes burned into me. "Cold out there, hmm?"

I took a deep breath to steady my racing pulse, and his spicy scent wafted over me. He stood so close that I could feel his warmth. His presence overwhelmed me, sent trembles down my spine into my legs. Without thinking, I lunged for his sweater and pulled him to me. I noticed the shock in his eyes just before I tilted up to press my lips to his.

His mouth was firm at first—hard like the rest of him—but I coaxed his lips open with persistent kisses. As I molded my lips to his, I knew the moment he yielded to me. His mouth softened, then pressed back with a heated urgency, building a bonfire inside of me.

Once he fully engaged, *he* directed the show. One hand cradled the back of my head while the other slid down my spine, tracing a line of fire as it descended to the small of my back. My breasts pushed against his chest, drawing a soft moan from somewhere deep inside of me. His mouth was hot and frantic on mine.

The kiss was rushed, desperate, and inelegant. It was perfect. At some point my coat crumpled to the floor. And I couldn't care less.

I relished our contact as his kiss slowed to a sensual burn. He smelled so good and felt so real. But I knew good things didn't last.

With a sigh, he unlatched his mouth from mine and looked down at me. I couldn't tell what he was thinking. Then he pressed me flat against him, his hands clasping my head and back, tucking me into his chest. I melted into his firm body. He was taller than me, which I liked, and we fit together seamlessly. I listened to his heartbeat, a galloping pulse that matched my own. The fine knit of his sweater felt soft against my cheek, and damn, I loved his aftershave. My breathing evened out as he held me. He was someone to hold onto, someone to steady me. I needed that.

When Lucia's laugh echoed from the kitchen, we broke apart. His eyes darted around the foyer, flashing alarm. Lucia hadn't wanted her brother to interfere in her life, and her best friend mauling him with kisses portended major interference. My cheeks flushed.

"Was that okay?" My voice came out in a whisper, and I cleared my throat. "What I just did?"

"Are you *kidding* me? I've been fantasizing about kissing you for a month now."

Relief and joy filled me.

He picked up my wrinkled coat and draped it over his arm. "I just don't know what Lucy will think of this."

We were a *this?* I hoped so. I already knew how *my* sibling would react. Braxton would be pissed. But Nana would probably like Alejandro's smarts and his gentlemanly ways. Wait—I was already thinking how my family would like him, after one kiss? That had been some kiss. My body still thrummed.

"Well, dessert's a disaster, but—"

Lucia stopped short after rounding the corner. She gave us a curious look. "Everything okay?"

"Sure, Rez." *More than okay.*

"But...?" Alejandro asked.

Lucia stared at him.

"What were you about to say?" he prompted.

"Oh!" She smiled. "Dinner's ready."

"Good, 'cause I'm starved." I turned to Alejandro, whose eyes flared.

"I'm hungry too," he said.

Lord, have mercy.

"Guys, listen..." Lucia began.

I glanced at her. "What?"

"Dane's trying some new dishes tonight, and he's not very confident about them. Go easy on him, okay?" She grabbed my hand and led me into the house. I felt Alejandro's quiet presence behind me.

As we entered the kitchen, Dane hovered by the oven. "Fucking shit," he muttered.

"Happy Valentine's Day to you too, GD," I said.

He spun around. "Glad you made it, Maddie. But *you* might not be so glad once you taste this."

"Aw, c'mon," Alejandro said. "Lucy told me you make a mean fajita."

"Yeah, but tonight I wanted to make *my* family's dishes." Dane lifted his chin. "White people have culture too, you know."

I laughed. "This should be good. What're you serving—McDonald's cheeseburgers?"

"Don't be a hater." He scowled at me. "Sit your ass down and get ready for a cultural experience."

I smirked at Alejandro, who slid into the chair next to me at the round kitchen table. "Those are beautiful flowers," I said, admiring the centerpiece of orange and red tiger lilies.

"Dane got them for me today." Lucia sat across from her brother. "*¡Qué bonitas!*"

I nodded, and noticed Alejandro's frown. Was he still upset about Lucia's relationship with Dane? He'd seemed more accepting.

"Okay." Dane removed the vase of flowers and replaced it with an oval plate filled with a mélange of pink and green. His hands clasped together like a little boy's. "To represent my maternal grandmother's Danish heritage, I made a smoked salmon appetizer." He gestured to the plate as he sat. "Our guests, please begin."

"So we'll die first, then?" Alejandro asked with a gleam in his eye.

"Alex!" Lucia chided.

Alejandro nodded for me to go first, and I slid a cucumber slice topped with cream cheese, smoked salmon, and a sprig of dill onto my plate. I took a tentative bite, and crisp flavor flooded my mouth. "This is actually kind of good."

"I *told* you!" Lucia shoved Dane's shoulder. They both helped themselves.

When I reached for another one, my hand collided with Alejandro's. He yanked his back and smiled at me. "*Really* good," he said.

"I tried to recreate an appetizer we had in Copenhagen," Dane said. He popped a cucumber slice in his mouth.

For the entrée, he served us plates with two dark red balls atop asparagus and turnip greens, with a side of mashed potatoes. What the hell was this? "Allow me," Dane said, and he cut open one of the balls on my plate to reveal a white circle with a yellow middle… maybe an egg?

"Scotch eggs?" Alejandro guessed.

"To represent Grandpa Monroe, from Scotland." Dane sat up a little taller.

I leaned toward Alejandro and whispered, "What's around the egg?"

"Sausage." He chuckled. "Try it, you'll like it. We had these at the governor's mansion once."

The first bite was interesting, and not my favorite. Still, I managed to finish one of the balls and all of the potatoes and vegetables. When Lucia stood to help Dane clear the plates, Alejandro's foot brushed mine. He leaned closer and scooped up my hand under the table.

"Thank God Lucy didn't tell Dane how much she liked his balls," he whispered.

I laughed, which earned me a questioning look from Lucia. But Dane's swearing soon drew her attention back to him. Alejandro's stroking my hand and the talk about balls had me on edge, hot and bothered.

Dane brought over ramekins filled with some sort of chocolate topped with raspberries. "Soufflé fail," he muttered. "To represent my father's French heritage."

"Patrick DuPont," Lucia supplied.

"The berries are supposed to surround the peak of the soufflé," Dane explained. "Not fall into the crater."

"An ambitious dessert," Alejandro said.

Dane looked at him. "I'm an ambitious guy."

"That you are."

Alejandro was ambitious, too. His ambition was one of many traits that drew me to him.

Lucia took a bite. "*I* think it's delicious."

"My egg whites didn't get stiff enough," Dane complained.

Stiff? God, this dinner was torture. My hand squeezed Alejandro's, and a little smile broke over his face.

Dane shook his head. "Figures I'd screw up the part of the meal representing my dad."

"Why's that?" I asked him.

"I'm not that close to my dad. He has his jerkoff moments." He sighed. "My mom deserves better."

I hadn't known that—I felt sad for Dane. But at least he had a good relationship with his mother. Braxton thought Senator Monroe would've made an awesome president, and she seemed like a strong, admirable woman the few times I'd seen her on TV.

"Well, maybe your soufflé needs more practice, but I'm impressed by this entire meal," Alejandro said. Dane seemed surprised, but smiled.

"I agree!" I added. "Thanks for inviting us to dinner."

Alejandro nodded. "Maddie and I will do the dishes, of course."

We will? He winked at me as he stood and picked up my plate. My legs squeezed together.

"But we want to play euchre," Lucia said. "Let's wait to do the dish—"

Dane cut her off when he grabbed her hand and tugged her to her feet. He whispered something in her ear—I thought I heard the word *stiff*—and she giggled.

"You guys do the dishes, yeah," he said, pulling her close. "Luz had something to show me." He whispered again, and her cheeks turned pink. Then he laughed and led her out of the kitchen.

I looked at Alejandro, who held our plates aloft near the sink, a grim look on his face. I gathered he was imagining exactly what Lucia planned to "show" Dane.

"How 'bout some cleaning music?" I asked to distract him.

He blinked. "Huh?" He set the plates in the sink.

"Nana says music makes cleaning go faster. I'll get my phone—it's in the other room."

"Or do you want to hear my brother's songs? I coaxed him to send me a few."

I paused. "Oh, right, Mateo plays guitar."

"Yep, and he writes his own songs. Kid's got mad talent." He pulled his phone out of his pocket and aimed it at the wall. "Lucia showed me the sweet sound system in this place. Check this out."

A thumping salsa beat filled the kitchen, reminding me of Pitbull's latest single. My body began moving of its own accord to the infectious drums. Alejandro grinned as I bounced my head from one side to the other. He shimmied his shoulders on his way to the table. I'd never seen him so at ease. His dancing wasn't flashy, but his moves were smooth, fluid, and intimately connected to the music.

He danced some glasses over to the sink, and I grabbed Lucia's and Dane's plates to follow him. His shoulder plunged to the beat as he lowered the dishwasher door, and Mateo's voice rang out, strong and full of pep.

Hey, chica! Where did you go?
Don't wanna do this thing solo
But you're running away like a track star
Leaving me all alone in my black car

Your pace is fast; it's so blazing
Can't keep up, girl; you're amazing
I'd follow you to the end of the state
If only my life didn't always frustrate

"Wow," I said when the drums kicked up again. "He can really sing."

"You think so?" Alejandro shrugged but I could see him hiding a smile. I retrieved a fork from the table as Mateo started his third verse.

Hey, chica! Come conmigo
And baby, why don't we go
Down under the bridge to the water
With you it can only get hotter

Alejandro placed a plate in the dishwasher. When I handed him a fork, he clasped his hand around mine. My skin tingled as he guided our hands higher. "Hey, chica, come conmigo," he sang into the fork-turned-microphone. "Come with me, Maddie," he said softly. His dark eyes glimmered.

"Where we going, chico?"

"Down under the bridge to the water."

My heart thumped faster than the pulsing drumbeat. "With you it can only get hotter."

The fork dropped to the floor with a clang, and he grabbed my hips, drawing me into him. His scorching mouth landed on mine, searching and insistent. My lips devoured him as I clutched the back of his head, massaging my hands through his thick black hair. He tasted like chocolate and smelled like spice, and my body burned for him.

Damn, he was hot. *Hot Jandro.* "Hotajandro," I murmured against his mouth. A giggle bubbled up my throat. That *had* to be his new nickname.

"Ready for euchre, guys?"

Oh, shit! I jumped out of his arms as Lucia came around the corner.

14
Hotajandro

Maddie's abrupt departure from my arms left a cold vacancy, but Lucia's fiery glare soon filled that space. I grabbed my phone to pause Mateo's song, and uneasy silence hung between us.

"How could you *kiss* her?" Lucia hissed. "She's *my* friend."

Maddie blanched. "That upsets you?"

"Of course it does!" She glowered at me. "You take over everything in my life—just like at St. John's."

I cringed hearing the name of our private high school in Houston. Mateo had already complained about how my "spotless legacy" there had led to exhaustive comparisons.

"Oh, you're *Alejandro's* sister." Lucia mocked one of our teachers. "No wonder you're such a good athlete. But why don't you excel in science? You must not study very much. Or maybe you're not as smart, hmm?"

"Lucy." My voice was stern, but she kept going.

"Why can't you be like *him?* Alejandro was a National Merit Finalist. Alejandro was all state in two sports. Alejandro stayed in Texas for college. Blah, blah, blah, gag."

Dane frowned as he entered the kitchen. "What's got you all riled up, Luz?"

"You were right. I just caught them kissing!" She gestured at us with a disgusted wave of her hand.

He started laughing.

I tilted my head toward Dane. "You knew?"

"I've suspected for a while now. You've been totally jonesing for Maddie, dude." He shook his head with a chuckle.

"It's not funny!" Lucia said.

"Sorry." Dane wrapped his arm around her. I looked at Maddie, wishing to do the same. I wanted to pull her to me, smell her fresh, beguiling scent. But Lucia's narrowed eyes stopped me.

Maddie stared at Lucia. "I thought you were off, ah, showing something to Dane."

"I was." My sister squirmed. "But hearing your baby brother sing about lust kind of kills the mood."

"I thought I only played that in the kitchen," I said.

"Try the whole house," Dane said. "Your agents are now singing 'Hey, Chica!'"

Oh, no. Would China and Brad tease me about Maddie? Thankfully they'd stayed in their rooms during our little discussion. "Look, Lucy…" I crossed my arms. "I'm sorry you're upset. I didn't mean to cause problems for you at St. John's, or anywhere for that matter." I looked into Maddie's eyes and melted a little. "We didn't plan this."

Maddie beamed at me. "It just happened; I promise."

"C'mon, Luz," Dane said as he tucked her in closer. "Don't you want your teammate and your brother to be happy?"

"That's not fair. Of course I do. It's just…" She frowned. "It's a lot to take in."

"Well, take it in while we school them in euchre," Dane said. He looked at Maddie and me. "You two are going down." He led Lucia out of the kitchen.

Maddie squeezed my hand. "Have you ever played euchre, Texas?"

"You and your nicknames." I stroked her warm skin with my thumb. "I thought I was Tater."

She reached out to straighten my collar with her free hand, bringing her chest flush with mine. "How do you like *Hotajandro?*"

A jolt to my groin. I couldn't stop staring at her sexy mouth. "It'll do."

Her hand trailed down my sternum to rest on my belt. I inhaled a shallow breath—would she go lower? Did she know how hard I was, just from her presence?

She looked up at me with a faint smile. Her body angled closer, thinning the air I tried to breathe.

Dane hollered from the family room. "We're waiting. Get in here so we can kick your asses!"

Maddie shook her head. "He's a little competitive."

"And I've never played."

"I think a National Merit Finalist like you can figure it out." She smirked.

"I'm going to kill my sister for telling you that." Her smile widened. "So what's *your* SAT score?"

"I'm a nerd just like you."

A very sexy nerd.

"We'll be Team Nerd tonight," she added.

"We'll beat those dumb jocks in there." I inclined my head toward the other room as I kissed her knuckles. "Let's do this."

A little while later Lucia and Dane had won the first game—and Dane gloated—but Maddie and I were ahead four-two in the second. I could see the appeal of this swift card game. We kept the deals moving quickly by using two decks.

Lucia kept eyeing Maddie and me. But now she turned to look at Dane, holding the cards in her hand instead of dealing. "You're sure you're okay with them being together? Maddie's your friend, too, and I didn't think you were crazy about my brother."

Ouch.

I met Dane's eyes before he looked away. "I admit he rubbed me the wrong way the first time I met him."

I hadn't been Dane's biggest fan then, either.

"But Alex isn't so bad now." He smirked. "As long as he's not spouting tea party rhetoric."

I shook my head.

Lucia's hand found her hip. "Yeah, well, Alex threatened to tell my dad we're having sex."

Dane's eyes grew big as he leaned back in his chair. *Good.* At least he seemed contrite for sticking it to my little sister.

"But obviously he hasn't told your dad," Dane said, seeming to recover quickly.

"How do you know?" Lucia asked.

"He would've crashed this house in a hot minute if he knew. I'd be lucky to still have my dick."

I loved the throaty sound of Maddie's laugh. She had encouraged me not to tell on Lucy, and I was grateful for her wisdom. Unable to resist her touch any longer—no matter what my sister thought—I reached for Maddie's hand across the table. She smiled at me, and I closed my eyes and breathed her in. This was undoubtedly the best Valentine's Day of my life.

"You said yourself Alex is good for Maddie," Dane told Lucia. I opened my eyes to find them watching us. "What's your exact concern about them being together?"

"Maybe I shouldn't feel this way," Lucia said. "Maybe I'm being jealous…" Her mouth trembled as she blinked at Maddie. "But you were my friend first, and I don't want to lose you. What if you spend all your time with Alex, and don't hang out with me? What if you ditch me for him? I already don't know how I'll make it next year without you."

Maddie let go of my hand and gave Lucia a sideways hug. "Oh, Rez, I'll always love you; don't you know that?" She patted her back. "You're such a good friend. You've really helped me get through this depression."

"You're depressed?" Dane asked.

Maddie slipped back into her seat and nodded. She looked down. "That's what Dr. Valentine said."

"You went." I was proud of her.

"This afternoon." She swallowed.

Dane snorted. "Well, that makes three of us." His eyes danced. "You need a shrink, Alex? You're the only one who isn't seeing her."

"Heck no. I'm not crazy-town like you three."

Maddie kicked my shin under the table. "Don't worry, Rez. I won't be spending *any* time with your brother."

Lucia actually managed to grin at me, and I smiled back.

Lucia dealt us each five cards. Across the table, Dane studied his. "Pick it up," he told her, and she slid an ace of spades into her hand.

Glancing down at all the spade trump cards in my hand, I tried to hide my excitement. Surely Maddie and I could win three out of five tricks to earn two points with the euchre.

Once Lucia discarded, Maddie was about to lead when Dane said, "Wait. I'm going alone."

What? We were definitely taking Dane down now, without his partner to help him. Lucia smiled smugly as she placed her five cards on the table, face down, since she wouldn't play this hand. Dane would have a big payoff if this worked—and Lucia seemed convinced it would. But I was determined not to let that happen.

Maddie led an ace of diamonds, which Dane trumped with the nine of spades. *Chin.* He then led the jack of spades, the most powerful card, and I followed suit by playing my ten of spades. Maddie didn't have trump, so she played a nine of hearts. Dane had already won two tricks and needed one more to earn a point; if he won three more tricks, he'd earn four points.

When I proceeded to take the next three tricks, Dane scowled. "Fuckin' a!"

Maddie grinned as she added two points to our total. "*Euchre,*" she taunted in a singsong voice, "that's the name of the game."

"Shut it, Brooks," Dane growled, and Maddie's eyes shone.

"You went alone with only two trump?" asked Lucia, wide-eyed.

"Sorry, partner." He shrugged. "But you gotta take risks to get ahead in life."

Lucia shook her head. "Calculated risks, you mean. Going alone with only two trump was way too risky." It was a relief to have her anger directed at someone else this time. When I'd beaten her at childhood games, she'd often become so incensed she burst into tears.

"You didn't seem to mind me taking a risk the first time I kissed you," Dane said.

Lucia turned bright red. Just like that, her anger vanished. "But it was only my cheek," she pouted.

Dane laughed. "You're insatiable."

"I'm right here," I reminded them as I scooped up the cards to shuffle.

Maddie began to deal the next hand.

I pondered Dane's comment about risk-taking. He could be impulsive, but he was also good at going after things he wanted.

Sometimes I wished I could be less inhibited. I was certainly grateful Maddie had kissed me tonight.

"I think those cards are shuffled, dude."

I looked at Dane, then realized everyone was staring at me, waiting for me to pick up my hand. How long had I been replaying that kiss? I placed the shuffled deck in front of him and cleared my throat.

"He's very thorough," Maddie said with a smirk.

I hid a smile. How the hell was I supposed to focus on cards when she sat right across from me, her sweet mouth enticing me with every word she spoke?

Somehow I played the right cards despite her distracting presence, and Maddie and I won the second game.

"Okay, rubber game, baby," Dane said. "Whoever wins the next game is the supreme champion of the universe."

I just shook my head.

"Team Nerd will conquer all," Maddie said.

China materialized by our table. "Just an FYI, the media's showing video of Maddie arriving tonight."

Maddie stiffened.

"Do you want to watch it?" Lucia asked.

She chewed on her lip. "I don't know, do I?"

Please, don't, I thought. *Publicity and girlfriends don't mix.* Our first night together might be our only night together.

"Face the music," Dane said. "Better to know what they're saying about you so you can defend yourself."

Maddie nodded and stood to follow China. My consternation must have been apparent because Lucia patted my arm.

"I know. It sucks being famous." She gestured to the TV room. "C'mon, let's go watch."

"Here's a sweet story for Valentine's Day," the reporter said as I entered. *"Looks like the president's kids have themselves a double date."*

Maddie perched next to Dane on the sofa. Lucia circled around to plop down next to him, but I was too nervous to sit by Maddie. I wouldn't blame her for wanting to ditch me. My hands balled into fists as I paced near China and Allison behind the sofa.

"Earlier tonight, Senator Monroe's son, Dane, arrived at his former residence, where President Ramirez's daughter, Lucia, currently lives."

Video rolled of Dane jogging from the SUV to the greenhouse, with Frank following him in.

"Looks like the bipartisan romance between Lucia Ramirez and Dane Monroe is still sizzling."

"Whatever." Dane grunted. Then he groaned as the broadcast cut to footage of him and Lucia from election night four months ago.

We watched as Dane stared at the camera and proclaimed, "I love Lucia Ramirez."

The Lucia on the screen gasped as she looked up at him. "And I love Dane Monroe." Her smile reddened her pink cheeks as she smothered Dane with a kiss.

I noticed her squirming on the sofa now, her current blush much deeper than the one on the screen.

Allison sighed as her hand covered her heart. "That kiss gets me every time."

"Maybe there's another romance in progress tonight." The reporter's voice drew my attention back to the TV, where Maddie pulled up to the greenhouse in a small silver car.

When I watched the media mob her vehicle, my teeth clenched. *Get away from her, ¡cabrones!*

"Madison Brooks is a senior at Highbanks University. She's a star volleyball player whose four-fifty hitting percentage ranked third in the NCAA last season. Ms. Brooks is teammate to Lucia Ramirez, but who is she to Alejandro Ramirez?"

I glared at the TV. *She's none of your damn business.*

Maddie's lips parted as she watched, spellbound. I knew the sickening feeling of witnessing your life played out on screen, with no idea how deep the excavation would dig. My world was spinning out of control, and there was nothing I could do about it.

They cut away from Maddie's luminous face inside her car at the gate to a shot of us heading for the SUV outside the restaurant. The camera zoomed in on my hand grasping hers as we weaved through pesky reporters.

"Is there love in the air, heating up this cold February night?"

"Hello, cheesy," Dane scoffed.

Then an image of a modest white, two-story home flashed on the screen, and Maddie sat up straight.

"Madison Brooks grew up in this Cleveland Heights home owned by her grandparents, Darius and Neliah Brooks."

"Oh my God," she said. "Nana and Gramps…"

Now her grandparents were in the public eye, too. What an invasion of privacy! She hadn't asked for this.

I suddenly remembered my ex-girlfriend Charlotte marching over to me after baseball practice at TCU, her eyes flaring. She'd thrust her phone in my face.

"Look what they're saying about me!"

The headline read *Ramirez Dates a Party Girl*. "Nobody reads this. It's just a local Ft. Worth magazine," I'd said.

"That's all you have to say?" she'd screeched.

I'd scanned down the article; the reporter had discovered an Instagram photo of Charlotte drinking beer at a party.

"You're not twenty-one," I'd said. "Why were you drinking?"

"Everybody does it! But not everyone has the freaking media breathing down their necks. Now I'm in trouble with my coach, thanks to you."

"I'm sorry, Char—" But she'd already stormed away.

She'd broken up with me the next day.

"Madison's father and brother also live in the home," the reporter continued. My stomach flipped. I had a sense where this story headed. *"Friends of the family report that Madison's mother abandoned them when she was only two years old."*

Dios, no. Maddie's mouth quivered as she looked down into her lap.

Lucia leaned across Dane. "That's not true, right, Maddie?" When she didn't answer, Lucia pressed on. "How dare they make up lies? I'll get my dad's people to retract that."

"Don't, Rez." Maddie's voice was soft.

"But why?" Lucia asked. "Don't let them make up stuff about you."

I didn't want my sister to keep badgering her. "Lucia!" I said sharply. "Leave it alone."

Lucia gawked at me over her shoulder. After a moment her face changed. "Oh…I didn't know." She looked at Maddie. "I'm so sorry."

Dane glanced back at me and dipped his head toward Maddie to tell me I should comfort her. I knew he was right. But I was glued to the floor. She would never sign up for this now. We'd only shared two kisses, so why did the end of our relationship depress me so much?

"That's awful, Maddie." Dane draped his arm over her shoulders when I didn't move. She kept her eyes on the floor.

I'd missed the end of that dreadful story, and now the reporter blabbed on about yet another state legalizing marijuana. Maybe that's what I needed: a big, fat blunt. Not that I'd know how to smoke it. Let the media get ahold of that story: *President's Son Caught Toking it Up.*

Maddie raised her head and looked at me.

No.

Tears glistened in her eyes, and for the first time, she didn't look beautiful when she cried. I just saw pain—pain that I'd caused. I did this. I'd made her life worse by bringing her into mine.

Thoughts ping-ponged in my mind, racing faster than my heartbeat, and I had no idea what to do. I needed to get the hell out of there. My feet swept me away from the TV room, and I found myself in the guest bedroom before I realized I'd left. My breaths came shallow and quick as I looked around.

Now what? It was probably time to pack my duffle bag. We were scheduled to fly back to Baltimore early tomorrow for my class, but I wondered if Brad and China could find a way for us to leave tonight. Lucy was fine—much better than myself at the moment, anyway. So now there was nothing for me here.

Dane filled the doorway. "Hey. Luz is talking to Maddie, but she sent me in to check on you."

I hid my shaking hands behind my back.

He stepped forward. "You okay, man?"

"I'm good." *Breathe. Help me, God. Help Maddie.*

He studied me for a moment, then looked around the bedroom. "This used to be my room." He brushed his hand across the sage green duvet. "Before the election."

I waited for a snide comment, but none came. Actually, Dane hadn't said one word to me about his mother losing in November. The more I thought about it, the more I marveled. "How do you do it?"

"What?"

I slid my hands into my pockets. "You're handling the election results a lot better than I would've, had the shoe been on the other foot."

Dane smirked. "I kind of surprise myself, actually. It's probably that damn therapy." He closed his eyes and held his hands out to the side like a praying Buddha. He breathed in. "Everything is…" He exhaled. "As it should be." He grinned at me. "My mom losing isn't all bad. At least I don't have Secret Service up my ass, or the media in my face."

"True that."

Dane assessed me for a long moment. His hand skimmed his jaw. "And it gave me my parents back."

My confusion showed on my face.

"You don't know what went down in my family?" he asked.

I shrugged. "Don't know what you're talking about."

"I love that girl." He smiled fondly. "I love Luz for keeping things secret." He crossed the room in two strides and fiddled with a book on the shelf. A few moments passed. "My dad had an affair last year."

I wasn't sure how to reply.

"And my parents were considering divorce." He looked over his shoulder at me, probably trying to gauge my reaction.

"That sounds horrible."

He frowned as he turned. He pressed his hands against the desk chair, his long arms bent at the elbow as he leaned back. "But now they're going to couples counseling, trying to save their marriage. No way that would've happened with the pressures of the White House."

I nodded. "I'm glad for you and your sister then."

"Yeah." He blew out a breath. "It would kill Jessica if they split." After a moment he tapped his fingers on the chair. "That sure sucks about Maddie's mom leaving."

My mouth pressed in a grim line. It seemed my parents' happy marriage was an anomaly.

"You knew about her mom, huh?" Dane asked.

"I sort of figured it out, and Maddie confirmed it." I ran my hands through my hair. "It rips her up inside, and she didn't want anyone to know. But now everyone knows." My shoulders slumped. "They really violated her, and just because she was seen with me. She won't want any part of being with me."

"She trusted you," Dane said. "That means something."

I paused.

"I think Luz is bummed that Maddie never told her," he continued. "She thought Maddie's mom just didn't like coming to volleyball games or something. But I get it. Maddie kept it quiet because she probably blames herself for her mom leaving."

"What?" I recoiled. "That's ridiculous."

Dane shrugged. "My mom says kids blame themselves when things go wrong in their families."

Interesting.

"Mom won't shut up about how her problems with my dad aren't my fault." He rolled his eyes. "But I know it's my dad's issues, mostly. He's got that crazy narcissist artist thing going on."

I liked this open, introspective side of Dane. *Wait a minute*—were we *bonding*? I'd never expected to have such a deep conversation with him, let alone on the heels of a tumultuous evening with Maddie. Maybe my sister hadn't been as foolish as I thought when she'd fallen for Dane.

"Thanks for your help with Lucy earlier—after she discovered Maddie and me together," I said.

"No problem. She'll be fine with it once she realizes Maddie will still be there for her. It's just been hard for her to find friends, you know, with Secret Service and all."

I could relate to that. Jake was far away, and it was tough to get close to med school classmates with two agents shadowing my every move. I tossed my running shoes into my duffle bag, then pressed them into the sides to make room for my clothes. "I hope Maddie will stay close to Lucy, even if she doesn't want to be with me."

Dane's eyebrows pulled together. "What're you smoking, man?"

My hands stilled.

"Maddie's into you, and one crappy news story isn't going to change that. You've got this sophisticated Latin vibe going on. Drives all the ladies crazy, right?"

"I'd hardly say that."

"Aw, come on. I bet you've got lots of notches on your bedpost."

My chest seized. Was he mocking me? Had Lucia told him I was a virgin? But he kept smiling like he believed I was some ladies' man. Maybe Lucia had kept my secret too.

"Maddie's not talking about ditching you." Dane gestured to the door. "She thinks *you're* leaving *her* because you're embarrassed to be with her or some nonsense. Luz is trying to convince her she's wrong."

I bolted out the door.

Dane followed me back to the TV room where Lucia huddled next to Maddie on the sofa. They looked up when we arrived, and I let out a breath when I saw Maddie had stopped crying.

Lucia patted Maddie's arm, then stood and nodded at me. An awkward silence stretched between us.

"Luz, weren't you going to show me something in your room?" Dane asked.

"Umm…" Her gaze bounced from Maddie to me to Dane. "Oh! Yeah, I was." She walked around the sofa.

"*Oye.*" I touched her shoulder as she passed. "Did I ever tell you you're a great sister?"

Her eyes widened. That surprise told me I should praise her more often. Then she smirked. "You don't have to. I already know I'm an awesome sister."

I shook my head and gave her a hug. When she and Dane disappeared down the hallway, I looked at Maddie. Despite her height, she seemed small on the expansive sofa. I took a risk to sit down next to her and pointed at the now-silent TV. "I'm sorry."

She sighed. "It's not your fault."

"It's not yours, either." I looked into her eyes. "You know that, right? It's not your fault your mom left."

She bit her bottom lip for a moment, leaving it full, wet, and pouty. *Kissable.* It would be awful never to kiss her again, but I had to know if she could deal with this. "You don't have to sign up for this, you know. The spotlight. I don't have a choice, but you do."

"Hey." She sat up. "I'm not the TCU tennis player, okay? I won't leave just because of stupid reporters. I can take it. I'm stronger than her."

Happiness warmed my chest. She was definitely a strong woman. I exhaled. "Okay." We kept looking at each other. I wanted to ask her more about her mother and the rest of her family, but she seemed overwhelmed as it was. Not knowing what else to say, I asked, "How are you?"

"Tired," she said, falling back into the cushions. "It's been a long night."

I nodded. I felt exhausted.

"I can hear my phone buzzing all the way over here." She pointed at her backpack across the room. "My family's probably freaking out. But I'm too tired to answer."

"Do you want me to bring you your phone?"

"No." She closed her eyes. "I just want to sleep."

She smelled so good—a heady combination of mint and outdoors. "Then sleep," I said. I scooted forward to bring the back of my neck flush with the cushion and extended my legs on the ottoman. My heart hammered as I lifted my arms to the side. Would she accept my offer to be her pillow?

A slow smile spread across her face, and she snuggled down into me, her head on my chest and her long legs lengthened next to mine. I wrapped my arms around her and rested my palms on her back. I felt her lean muscles shift beneath me, and heard her sigh. Over time, her soft breaths began to even out. There was no insomnia for Maddie Brooks tonight.

My heart about burst with tenderness as she slept in my arms.

15
Maddie

W ow, that was one tough practice — the third in a row that had kicked my butt since Alejandro went back to Baltimore. My quads quivered as I climbed the last stair. For my next apartment, I'd be sure to choose the first floor.

A delivery notice from a florist was stuck on my door. *Squee!* Next to a checkmark by the box *Sorry We Missed You*, the delivery person had scrawled, *Left in 3E*.

My excitement vanished. That was Mrs. Marshall's apartment. The second I knocked on her door, Charles went apeshit. For my next apartment, I'd be sure not to live on the same hall as a yippy dog.

"Charles, hush!" Mrs. Marshall admonished. An eternity passed before the door swung open.

As soon as he could, the little dog rushed my feet, weaving between them. He was actually adorable when he wasn't barking, and I reached down to souse his ears. I looked up to find his owner frowning at me.

"You shouldn't go out in this cold with wet hair."

"I wore my hood." I lifted it off my shoulders to show her.

"Humph." She pursed her lips. "I suppose you want your flowers."

Nah, I just really enjoy you berating me like you're my mother or something. I paused. Had she seen the news report about my mother? "That would be great."

With a flare of her faded turquoise housecoat, she turned back into her apartment, leaving Charles and me to stare at each other. Was I supposed to follow her?

"You coming?" she hollered. "I can't lift this heavy vase myself."

Heavy vase? The smell of menthol assaulted me when I stepped inside. Charles bounded ahead and vaulted onto the floral print sofa next to Mrs. Marshall. Her apartment floor plan was the mirror of mine, and I soon found her dining room and the enormous flower arrangement spilling over her small table.

"Whoa." I circled it, taking in the pinks, reds, and deep purples. I didn't know the names of all the flowers, but their lush beauty stunned me.

"Some boy's got it bad for you," she said. She scooped Charles into her lap and stroked his wiry fur as she watched the local news on TV.

I pulled a card out of the small envelope embedded in the arrangement.

Happy Valentine's Day
~Your Hot Potato

My grin stretched from ear to ear.

Mrs. Marshall said, "It's that Ramirez boy, isn't it?"

My smile faded as I turned to her and nodded. Why wouldn't she assume the flowers were from Jaylon? Maybe because he'd rarely visited my place.

"He's bad news. Don't like those reporters camped outside the building."

"Me neither."

She scowled. "Makes it hard to go out and let Charles tinkle. Damn reporters get in my way."

"At least they weren't here tonight," I offered. "Maybe they'll stop coming around when they realize what a boring life I lead."

"Or that you're never home," she added. Charles whined when she shoveled him off her lap and began to push herself up from the sofa. It took her a while to get to her feet, and I wondered if I should help. "I'm about to cook beef vegetable soup — Charles's favorite. Why don't you stay and have some?"

I reeled in surprise as she shuffled to the kitchen. She'd never invited me for dinner before…Then it hit me: she'd heard about my mother and was trying to be nice to me. She wasn't the first person to treat me differently since that news report. *Ugh.*

"Thanks so much, Mrs. Marshall, but I'll just grab something quick in my apartment. I have to study."

"On a Friday night?"

I shrugged. "It never ends."

She struggled to reach the upper shelf of her cabinet, and I came up behind her to take down the pot she wanted. I towered over her — she was barely five feet tall.

"Thanks, dear. What's your major?"

Now she wanted to chat? Mean Mrs. Marshall? "Um, biochemistry. I hope to go to med school, if I'm lucky."

"I was a receptionist at University Hospital."

I hadn't known that.

"Back then, all the doctors were men," she continued. She opened a carton of beef stock. Before she poured it in the pot, she fixed me with a feisty stare. "You better get studying to show those boys how it's done."

I laughed.

"But come over anytime for some home cooking, dear."

Two dears *within five minutes. Wha?* "Thank you, and thanks for holding the flowers for me. I'll get out of your hair now." I lifted the vase with both hands and headed for the door, serenaded by high-pitched barks.

"Cut it, Charles!" I heard from the hallway as her door closed. Once inside my apartment, I searched for a home for the overgrown bouquet. I nudged some papers aside so I could set it on the coffee table. Without the overpowering smell of menthol — or of kimchi, thank God — I could inhale the fresh fragrance. Alejandro did such sweet things for me.

The feel of waking up in his arms a couple mornings ago returned. I'd never spent the whole night with any man, and at first I'd felt panicked by his closeness.

"Hi," he'd whispered as he gazed down at me.

"Did you sleep?" I asked.

He nodded. "It's past seven—I woke up right before you."

"We slept *ten* hours?" I bolted upright. "Shit! I'm late for practice."

"Wednesday's your morning off, remember? Lucy came in earlier to tell me." He'd massaged his left arm as he spoke.

That had been the arm circled under me as we'd slept. "Does it hurt?"

"I lost feeling in it around midnight." He shrugged.

"Alex!" My jaw dropped. "Why didn't you let go of me?"

His mouth had spread into a sexy smile. "It was worth it."

The memory of that seductive smile and the scent of roses and violets warmed me inside. I whipped out my phone, shrugged off my coat, and wrote a text.

You do know Valentine's Day was three days ago.

Sometimes Alejandro got so wrapped up in studying or exercising that he didn't respond to my texts right away. I grabbed some Greek yogurt from the fridge and was about to eat my first bite when my phone dinged. I inhaled a happy breath. Was it normal to be this giddy over a stupid text? I didn't recall feeling this way when I'd started dating Jaylon.

Yeah, but I won't let Dane one-up me on the flowers.

I giggled. Lucia wasn't the only competitive Ramirez. I hopped into the other room and snapped a photo of the arrangement to add to my next text:

**They're beautiful. Thank you.
You shouldn't spend so much on me.**

I returned to the kitchen to eat my yogurt.

**It's my pleasure to buy you things.
But does it make you uncomfortable?**

The spoon hovered in my mouth. *Was* I uncomfortable receiving that expensive flower arrangement? I knew his family was rich…

**I'm eating the yogurt you bought after taking the test
you helped me study for. I do feel a bit uncomfortable
with everything you do for me.
I want to do something nice for you.**

You're ALREADY doing the sweetest thing for me, believe me.

What's that?

Dealing with the media. Brad said they've hounded your apartment. I'm sorry.

They weren't here tonight. They'll let it go.

I hope. Brad said Sec Serv is considering getting you a detail, or maybe local police protection.

No way. That's going overboard. Hey, how was your exam?

Just think about it. I know it's rough having protection, but it's a dangerous world. I want you to be safe.

Apparently he hadn't accepted my topic change. But then he texted again:

My exam went surprisingly well. How was yours?

Good, but they haven't posted grades yet. Why surprised you did well?

Been distracted when I study lately.

My mouth curled into a smile.

Yeah? What's distracting you?

YOU, of course.

I was hoping he'd say that.

So what's your next module?

Psychiatry. Watch out, Dane.

A knock on my door startled me. Alejandro hadn't sent more flowers, had he? Or had Jaylon decided to grace me with his presence?

Hold on. Someone at the door.

Be careful, Maddie.

My eyes widened when I peeked out the peephole. My brother hadn't visited since he'd helped me move in here last summer.

"C'mon, Maddie, open up. This is heavy," Braxton said.

I opened the door to find him holding two casserole dishes stacked on top of each other. "Food from Nana?" I asked with hope in my voice.

"Yep." He handed them to me and stomped inside. "Put the lasagna in the oven. I'm starved."

I scowled as he peeled off his winter hat and collapsed on the sofa. His short dreads looked new. "Make yourself right at home, Brax."

He ignored my sarcasm and glared at the flowers. "No space to prop up my feet with this monstrosity. They're from *him*, right?"

I decided I could ignore him, too. I set the heavy dishes on the kitchen counter and retrieved some plates. My phone buzzed again in my pocket, and I found several texts from Alejandro, all asking if I was okay.

My brother's here. I'll call later?

Braxton charged into the kitchen and turned on the oven. I shook my head as I turned it off. "It'll be faster to heat up individual portions in the microwave."

He looked at my phone. "You're texting Ramirez?"

"Okay, Brax." I sighed. "You obviously have something to get off your chest. Let's talk."

"Oh, we'll talk. But first I'm getting something to eat." He grabbed a spatula and slid a substantial block of Nana's lasagna onto his plate.

"You didn't have to drive all the way down here to tell me you don't like Alex. You could've texted."

He paused with the spatula midair. "I did text you. You didn't respond."

Whoops. He was right.

"You were probably too busy texting *him*."

Just then my phone buzzed.

OK

Alejandro's short, delayed response made it seem like he wanted to say more. He and I hadn't discussed my brother other than mentioning the police station protest, and I wondered what he thought about Braxton's visit. Another text arrived:

Ocupará mi mente toda la noche, Señorita Arroyos.

He'd started texting in Spanish from time to time, even though I didn't speak the language. Nothing Google Translate couldn't handle. I copied and pasted to read *You'll be in my mind all night long, Miss Brooks.*

"You're grinning like a damn fool."

I looked up to find Braxton scowling at me. My face felt hot. "Maybe I am a fool."

"There's no maybe about it."

"Stop acting so sanctimonious. You're not a PhD *yet.*"

"Not that you care," he mumbled.

"What?"

He covered the plate with a paper towel. After punching buttons on the microwave, he spun around and leaned back against the counter with his arms crossed. "You never asked me how my exams went."

Exams…what exams? I searched my memory. "Oh! Your…doctoral exams?" He gave a curt nod. "When were they again?"

"Wednesday."

"Sorry, Brax. I've not been thinking clearly lately." Maybe I needed some food to help my addled brain. I scooped lasagna onto my plate. "How'd they go?"

He whistled through his teeth. "Tough." He shook his head. "But I passed."

"Congrats!" I licked tomato sauce off my thumb. *Yum.* "So, uh, what does that mean exactly?"

"My coursework's done, and I can start my dissertation, hopefully graduate in a couple years."

I remembered more about his program as he spoke. "Right. And part of your exam was your dissertation proposal defense?"

He relaxed as he nodded. The microwave dinged, and I started heating my portion after he'd moved his plate to the little dining table behind my sofa.

"Did they like your proposal?" I asked.

"Mof coursch."

Thanks for waiting for me. "What's your dissertation about again?"

"White supremacy in the Republican party."

Oh, no. I zipped out of the kitchen. "You're kidding."

"No, I'm not." He gave me a hard stare for five seconds before he started laughing. "You're so gullible."

"And you're an asshole." I retrieved my warmed plate as he continued laughing behind me. He didn't stop chuckling until I joined him at the table.

"What's a guy gotta do to get a drink in this place?"

"He's gotta treat his sister with respect." I arched an eyebrow before I took a bite. *Gooey mozzarella heaven.*

When it was clear I wasn't going to fetch a beverage for him, he went to the kitchen. My anger dissipated when he returned with two glasses of milk. Nana had always served us milk with dinner, and he continued the habit at age twenty-six.

"Looks like you just went to the grocery store," he said.

I studied him as I took a swig of milk. "Alejandro stocked up my fridge."

His fork clanged on his plate. "So it's true? You're dating that right winger?"

"I already told Nana and Gramps I was."

"How can you be attracted to him, Maddie? Don't you know his dad just slashed food stamps? How can you like someone who absolutely hates the poor?"

I sighed. "I already told you I don't care about politics."

"That blows my mind, too! How can you stick your head in the sand like that?"

"I've been busy. You don't know what it's like to be a D-one student-athlete." Braxton had been a top high school basketball player, but he hadn't pursued a college scholarship. He'd claimed athletes in revenue sports brought in so much money that the universities should pay them salaries on top of tuition. Since that didn't happen, he refused to be a "slave" to the white man.

"So you don't follow politics," he said. "But you have to know his dad's a total poseur."

I shrugged. "I've never met President Ramirez. But I like Lucia." *And Alejandro. A lot.* "She's become a good friend. She's helped me."

"How?"

I looked down at my plate. "This semester has been difficult. I, um…" I glanced up at him. How would he take the news? Would he judge me? "I…have clinical depression."

His eyes darkened. "Says who?"

"Dr. Valentine, my sport psychologist. She's pretty cool."

"She's white, right?"

"Why does *that* matter?"

"How can she possibly understand what you're going through if she's white?"

Oh, Braxton. "Rez sees her for an eating disorder. Are you saying Dr. Valentine needs to have an eating disorder in order to help her?"

"That's different."

"How?" This eating disorder talk made me hungry. I wished Nana would send food down every week.

"Because she's part of the white hegemony that can't wait to slap a mental illness label on black people."

"But I'm not mentally ill. I'm depressed. Dr. Valentine said depression can run in families, so maybe you'll get it too."

He scowled. "It's not contagious like the common cold. And I'm not depressed."

"Well, you might be one day. Dad seems to get down sometimes—do you know if he's depressed? Is there a family history of depression?"

"Will you shut it with all the questions?" he roared.

Stunned, I leaned back in my chair. He shot up from the table and marched his half-eaten lasagna back into the kitchen.

I followed him and watched him stretch some plastic wrap over his plate before sticking it in the fridge. What was his deal? "You okay?"

"I was hoping to spend the night—I need to talk to a Highbanks professor about my research tomorrow—but that's obviously a bad idea."

"Why?"

"You don't want me here."

"What're you talking about?"

"I'll go back to Cleveland." He made a beeline for his coat hanging by the door.

"Wait! It's too cold. What if your car breaks down? Drive back tomorrow, when it's light."

He hesitated.

"C'mon, Brax. Stay. You can sleep on Shitty." He eyed the scratched, saggy cushions, then frowned when his gaze returned to the flower arrangement. How could I convince him? "What if I make you hot chocolate?"

He turned. "With marshmallows?"

"Yes."

"The itty bitty ones?"

"Of course." *I hope I have them.*

He stood still for a moment, then nodded. "Okay." He folded his six-foot-three body onto the sofa.

I exhaled. *Wait*—why had I convinced him to stay when I hadn't invited him in the first place? My brother was infuriating. By the time I carried two steaming mugs into the family room, I noticed my coffee table was bare.

"Where are my flowers?"

He pointed to my bedroom. "In there. Couldn't see the TV with that damn pink jungle in my face."

"But the TV's not on." I set down his mug and curled onto the sofa.

He shrugged. "Couldn't find the remote."

"Because I don't have one."

"What the fuck, Maddie? Who doesn't have a remote?"

"Who has time for TV?" I blew on my cocoa.

He shook his head as he picked up his mug. "No wonder you're so uninformed." He lapped up some mini marshmallows. "So you didn't see the picture of our house on the news? Hear them talking about our family?"

I winced. "I saw."

"You heard what they said about…" His cheek twitched as he looked down.

At that point I realized the actual reason for my brother's visit: he needed to talk to the only person who could understand. I also realized why he'd almost bailed before he had the chance. I felt the same ambivalence.

"About Mom," I said.

He froze as he stared at his cocoa. After a slow sip, he sighed. "My advisor took me into her office yesterday, said she heard about Mom leaving me at a young age." His upper lip squeezed toward his nose. "So embarrassing. I didn't want this to be a *thing* at grad school — for people to see me as the poor black boy from a broken home. I don't want their pity."

"I know." My heart felt heavy. "I'm sorry."

"My advisor said it made my academic achievements all the more impressive. Asked if there was anything she could do."

"What'd you tell her?"

"Nothing. Just wanted to get the hell out of there. She's never been so gooey and sweet before."

Today's practice came to my mind. Nina and I had practiced quick-sets against Lucia's block for countless repetitions. Nina's first few sets were on the money, and I'd slammed them through the block, but then her timing struggles had forced me to hit into the net.

"Sorry," she'd told me, and the look of sincerity in her eyes had floored me. "I'll get it right this time." That *had* to be related to that news piece about my mother.

A ghost from twenty years ago still haunted Braxton and me. "You were six when Mom left. What was she like?"

Braxton looked away, and I clenched my fists. He'd evaded my childhood questions about Mom so often I'd stopped asking, but tonight I didn't want to give up. "Please. I was only two, and I don't really remember her."

He finally said, "She was so tall."

I nodded. I'd seen a photo of my parents on their wedding day, and my mother had stood only an inch shorter than our six-foot-two father.

"And pretty."

I knew that too, from the photo. I took a sip of hot chocolate.

He looked at me. "You have her mouth."

I skimmed my finger across my lip.

"She could be a lot of fun." He gazed at the blank TV, like he was watching a grainy home movie. "She took us to Cedar Point sometimes."

"I didn't know that." I'd visited the amusement park with my physics class in high school — I thought for the first time.

"You were just a baby in a stroller." With sudden energy, he sat up. "One time she got us ice cream with, with those rainbow sprinkles. My favorite. She fed you some from her bowl, but I got my own cone—my big boy cone. When I tripped, my whole cone flew into your stroller. Ice cream got all *over* you." He smiled as I'd never seen him before. "Your hair, your dress…You were licking it off your fingers—you loved it, and I didn't even care I'd lost my ice cream because you were giggling like a little monkey…" His grin faded. "But when Mom tried to clean you up, she started crying." He set his mug down.

My throat tightened. "Did she cry a lot?"

"Some days." He looked at me again. "Do you remember that?"

"I don't know." I would've been too young to recall. But a gnawing sadness spread through me as I remembered the whimpering sound of her sobs, and the sheer size of a colossal bedroom door. I would peer through the crack at the bottom of the door into a dark room, the carpet a thick forest blocking my view. "Did she…did she lock herself in her room sometimes?"

"You can't remember that. You were too young."

"Maybe." *But I do remember.*

"Dad said not to disturb her." He stared at the TV again. "He said she was having a bad day. She had them often." He swallowed visibly. "When Dad was at class, you would cry, but Mom still wouldn't come out. I learned how to change your diaper."

A five- or six-year-old changing a baby's diaper? No wonder he seemed angry. "Thanks for doing that."

"Of course I did it. Who *else* would?" His eyes flared. "Dad didn't do anything about Mom. He just let her hole herself off from the world. He's so fucking impotent."

Whoa.

"I don't know what he saw in her," Braxton spat. "Should've married someone else."

The fury of his words had pressed me into the corner of the sofa, and I straightened as I took a deep breath. "How did Dad and Mom meet?"

"Nana's never told you?"

I shook my head.

Braxton twisted one of his dreads between his fingers. "When our grandma on Mom's side was dying of cancer, Mom stayed with her at The Cleveland Clinic. Nana was her nurse."

"What kind of cancer?"

He scowled at me. "What difference does that make?"

"We have our maternal grandmother's genes, dummy. We're more at risk for that cancer, and probably other cancers too."

"Not sure. You'll have to ask Nana."

Yeah, like I wanted to do that.

"Anyway," my brother continued, "Dad came to visit Nana at the hospital one day, and that's when he met Mom. Love at first sight and all that bullshit."

Braxton seemed so jaded. He'd had a girlfriend in high school, but he hadn't dated anyone since. Just like Dad had never remarried.

"They were so different," Braxton said. I couldn't believe he was still talking. "Dad was headed to grad school, and Mom didn't even finish high school. She had to drop out to take care of her mom when she got sick. And she was so poor. Her dad had taken off after she was born, and she basically grew up in the ghetto, surrounded by drugs and guns."

Oh, Mom. I'd heard hints about her coming from poverty, but hadn't known she'd lived in such squalor. What horrors had she witnessed? The heaviness in my chest made it hard to breathe.

"Jeez, Maddie." He got to his feet and pressed hands to his back as he stretched. "You *have* to get a better couch."

Just like that, I knew the conversation about Mom had ended. I struggled for a calming breath as I faked a smile. "With whose money?"

"How about that rich boyfriend of yours? His family's loaded."

Braxton recognizing Alejandro as my boyfriend seemed like progress. But Alejandro would *not* be buying me a new sofa. I didn't deserve all of his largesse.

"I'm gonna reheat the rest of my lasagna. Want me to heat up yours, too?"

I nodded.

"Maddie…" He looked down at me as he picked up our empty mugs. "I know I can't stop you from dating that tea party tool. But I don't trust him. Be careful, okay?" He frowned. "Don't make rash decisions just because you think you're depressed."

He took our mugs into the kitchen, leaving me reeling. *Don't you dare give me false hopes about my future, Alex.*

16
Alejandro

"Who's considering psychiatry for a career?"

Dr. Moore's question hung in the air as my classmates and I looked around at each other. *Heck no*, I thought. *No way I'll sit in an office talking to troubled patients all day.* I wanted blood. I wanted action. Apparently my classmates felt the same because no hands went up. I glanced at my buddy Dave, who tilted his neck and crossed his eyes like a crazy person. I shook my head, but couldn't hide my faint smile. Sometimes my med school classmates were more immature than undergrads.

"Aw, c'mon, pussies," Dr. Moore said as he paced the front of the classroom. A few chuckles rang out. "You scared?" His longish gray hair swept behind him in a chaotic swirl, and his sinewy body never stopped moving. "This is why we have a shortage of psychiatrists in America—you guys don't understand the beauty and power of easing emotional anguish. But I'll teach you, starting today. And by the end of this module, I guarantee at least one of you will choose psychiatry."

Brad shifted in the seat next to me. "Confident bastard, isn't he?" he muttered.

"More like certifiable," I said.

Dr. Moore flipped to the next slide on the projector, and I advanced to that slide on my laptop. It was a cartoon of Mickey Mouse on the therapy couch. "What lies at the root of your problems is that you inhabit a fantasy world," the doctor told him. More chuckles.

On the other side of me, Dave sighed. I followed his gaze to my classmate Josie, who tossed her hair over her shoulder as she laughed. Dave was infatuated with Josie but hadn't asked her out; Mickey wasn't the only one living in a fantasy world. I touched my phone in my pocket, longing to text Maddie.

"What happened in nineteen-eighty-seven that rocked the psychiatry world?"

Dr. Moore's question brought me back to the lecture. Josie raised her hand. "Prozac hit the market," she said.

Chingar. I knew that. *Focus.*

"Fluoxetine was indeed the first SSRI introduced to America that year." Dr. Moore's eyes glowed. "We lit up the five-HT receptors, and suddenly the severely depressed had hope, without all the nasty side effects of the old tricyclics."

Brad shifted and grumbled under his breath.

"Selective serotonin reuptake inhibitors," Dr. Moore continued. "No matter what your specialty, these babies will be powerful weapons in your prescriptive arsenal. Not only for depressed patients, but also for those with anxiety, addictions, chronic pain, PTSD..."

I wondered if Maddie was taking an SSRI for depression. Would she tell me if she was?

"We'll get into the newer meds soon, but fluoxetine is still around. In fact, it's *the* medication for adolescent patients. We need more research studying the effectiveness of SSRIs for teens; at this point, fluoxetine is the only FDA-approved medication for teenage depression."

"What about the black box warning?" I asked.

Dr. Moore's toothy grin looked maniacal. "You read my mind, Alejandro. Be scared. Be very scared." He flipped to his next slide, titled *Depression and Adolescents and Black Box Warnings, Oh My!* with an image of *The Scream* by Edvard Munch.

"Now," he said, "you may have heard the media freak out about antidepressants causing teenagers to commit suicide. Here are the facts. It's true there's a risk of increased suicidal urges for a small percentage of teens starting a trial of SSRIs. But since suicidal ideation is symptom of depression, and fluoxetine helps reduce depression, the benefits of the medication *far* outweigh its risks. Just make sure to tell parents to monitor their kids for suicidal urges when you prescribe antidepressants."

"Sounds dangerous," another female classmate said. She always seemed worried—maybe *she* needed an SSRI.

Dr. Moore nodded. "No doubt about it, these psychotropic meds *are* potentially dangerous. They can be lifesavers, but they all may have side effects. That's why we'll teach you some treatments in addition to medication. One is psychotherapy. Psychiatrists rarely do talk therapy these days, so you need to refer your patients to competent therapists. Also, there's a treatment for mental disorders that's as effective as medication, with longer-lasting recovery and no side effects. Anyone know what that is?"

I smiled as I pictured the speed bag I'd punched over and over this morning.

"Exercise," Josie said.

"Ding, ding!" Dr. Moore raised his arm and hit an imaginary bell. "We've already covered how exercise improves physical health, but it's great for mental health, too. Now, how do we get our screen-addicted patients to exercise? That's the tough one. The Exercise is Medicine website gives some good ideas…"

I couldn't imagine how people lived without exercise. It was *my* absolute go-to for stress. In fact, my workouts had taken on an even more intense vibe the past few days, probably due to missing Maddie. My body thrummed with nervous energy every time I thought about her. *Sublimation*, Dane had called it. Whatever it was, I had it bad.

On the car ride back to my condo, I glanced at my watch and realized Maddie would likely be between class and practice.

¿Cómo estás, Arroyos?

Having a GOOD day.

"You're talking to Maddie," Brad said from the seat next to me.

I looked up. "How'd you know?"

"You've got that happy, horny look about you."

Like you looked after meeting with your supervisor? I almost asked, but decided to drop it. Brad could do what he wanted. He could do *who* he wanted. All I wanted was Maddie.

> *Great to hear. Why so good?*

> **Got a 92 on my exam. Set the curve!**

> *Not a surprise. You're beautiful AND inteligente.*

It took her a few moments to respond. Had I embarrassed her?

> **Thanks to you, Hotajandro.**

Lord, I got hard every time she called me that. I swallowed.

> *Nah, that was all you.*

> *How was class?*

> **Psychiatry's not bad, actually. Did you know talk therapy changes brain chemistry just like medication?**

> *Awesome. I need some of that.*

When she didn't elaborate, I decided to change the topic.

> *Hey, how was your brother's visit?*

A whole minute ticked by. I texted:

> *Maybe you're busy?*

> **Got 5 min before I have to leave for practice. Just not sure how to answer.**

Hmm. I typed another message.

> *Give it to me straight. Braxton doesn't like me?*

> **Well, he did call you my boyfriend.**

I grinned.

> **But he thinks I'm making a mistake. He's mad your dad cut food stamps.**

My dad and Congress had decreased funding to quite a few programs—we had to address the debt somehow. I was about to type that when I remembered she couldn't care less about politics. I didn't want to bore her or sound defensive. But what if her brother wouldn't let her see me?

> *Did he order you not to date me?*

> **Ha ha HA! I'd like to see him try.**

Nobody would mistake her for a shrinking violet. Another text came in.

> **Don't tell me you forbade Lucia to date Dane.**

Uh oh. Minefield ahead. I would've done just that had I known Lucia was with Dane in the beginning. But I hadn't found out until my parents did, right before the debate. My father had done the forbidding for me. Not that it had worked. How to respond?

> **Our families are different.**

> **Stop evading the question.**
> **Did you tell Rez to stay away from Dane?**

> **No. But I wanted to.**

> **So Brax doesn't like his sister's boyfriend,**
> **just like you don't like Dane. Ironic, isn't it?**

I groaned. I could imagine Dane laughing. Why did Maddie have to have a big brother?

> **The irony isn't lost on me, sweetheart.**

> **SMH. You boys need to learn**
> **to give your sisters RESPECT.** ☺

At least she'd added the smiley face—hopefully she wasn't too mad. My phone dinged with her next text.

> **Time to head to practice.**
> **You home from class yet?**

> **No. Bad traffic as usual.**

I paused, unsure if I should type the words I wanted to say. But my fingers decided for me.

> **I miss you, Maddie.**

Another long wait for her reply made me think she'd had to leave. Then my phone buzzed.

> **Estoy loca por ti.**

Arousal zipped through me. How did she *do* that? She made me feel like I'd just cured cancer. *I'm crazy for you.*

Brad chuckled.

"*Cállate*," I said, hoping he'd learned enough Spanish to know I told him to shut up.

Brad sat taller as he reached into the pocket of his jacket for his phone. "Yes, sir," he said when he answered. After a beat, he handed his phone to me. "Hold for the president."

My eyes widened. "Hello?"

"Alejandro."

I clutched the armrest. "Hello, Dad. Everything okay?"

"Your mother told me you aced your last exam."

He was calling about my insignificant test? "It went well, yes. How do you have time to call me?"

"I'll always make time for *mi familia*. I wish I could see you more often."

"Me too. How's Mateo?"

"Better."

"Better?" My heart rate spiked.

"His sugar was over five-hundred a couple days ago—"

"*¡Por dios*, Dad!"

"—but Karen got his numbers down. He didn't even need to see the White House doc."

Karen was a Secret Service agent, and also a nurse practitioner, so my brother had medical care around the clock. Still, I didn't like hearing such high glucose numbers. "You're encouraging him to get the insulin pump, right?"

"Yes, though not as stridently as your mother."

"You have to know Mom's on the right side of this issue."

Dad sighed. "I hear you. I also hear your mother. I can't *help* but hear your mother."

I laughed.

"But it's been tough for Mateo. He's had so many losses from this disease. He's been forced to watch you and Lucy shine in sports—watch you follow your dreams—while he stays on the sidelines."

I knew that had to be excruciating. It had killed me to watch another TCU pitcher give up a homerun, knowing I could've struck out that batter. It would've been awful never to get to play at all.

Dad continued, "He has to be careful about every aspect of his heath. And now with Secret Service, he has someone watching him twenty-four-seven. It's got to be rough for a seventeen year old."

China growled at a driver who cut her off. *It's rough for a twenty-four year old, too.*

"I'm hoping he'll come around to this pump on his own. I want him to have some choice in the matter. And we're lucky we have the luxury of medical care readily available until he does."

Why did my dad have to sound so reasonable all the time? "But what if Matty never gets the pump?"

"Hmm. Then you'll have to develop a cure for diabetes, Dr. Ramirez."

I rolled my eyes.

"Listen — they're telling me we're about to start our descent, and there's something I want to discuss with you."

"You're on Air Force One?" The connection was crystal clear, without any engine noise.

"Yes, on our way to deal with the mudslides in Malibu. I hear you've discussed Madison Brooks with your mother, but you haven't talked about her with me."

The president wants to discuss my love life? I shook my head. He wasn't calling as the president—he was calling as my dad. "She's pretty great." My lips tingled as I remembered her soft kisses. "I want you to meet her."

"I'm not sure I should."

What?

He cleared his throat. "You should know what you're getting into, son. The FBI briefed me last week."

"The *FBI?*" I caught Brad's curious glance a moment before China's eyes flicked up to meet mine in the rearview mirror.

"They showed me photos of the Glenville police station, in Cleveland. A group of protestors gathered there, yelling and making threats." He paused. "The main instigator was Braxton Brooks, Madison's older brother."

I exhaled. "Dad, I already know that."

"You do?"

"Braxton was protesting the shooting of a black man by a white officer."

"A shooting with no evidence of racial bias. It wasn't a peaceful protest, Alejandro. Braxton was throwing things, inciting violence. He held a sign that said 'Black Lives Matter…White Cops Don't.' He came this close to being arrested."

My breath caught in my throat.

"You should see his editorials in the Cleveland State University newspaper. He thinks the Republican party is a vast conspiracy to keep black people down."

"But, Dad, we all know people say stupid things in college."

"Are you *defending* him?"

I inhaled. *Am I?*

"Abraham Lincoln was a Republican!" Dad added. "The Republicans are the ones trying to ensure equal opportunity for all people—all races. Latinos face racism too, but you don't see us holding up signs saying 'Latino Lives Matter.'"

"Okay, but we haven't had a history of slavery in America like black people have."

"You *are* defending him. What is up with you? Don't you believe in individual responsibility? Nothing is given to us—we have to make it happen. We have to earn our way."

I sighed. "I do believe that. When minorities work hard and get educated, we can have success like anyone else. We can't expect others to do it for us. But Dad, Maddie doesn't want handouts! She works really hard. She goes after what she wants, full throttle. Did you know she plans to go to med school, after she tries out for USA Volleyball?"

Dad was quiet for a moment. "I know Lucy thinks the world of her. But what I've learned about her brother is alarming."

"Maddie isn't her brother. She doesn't even care about politics."

"But does she share his views?"

"I don't know. Issues like this aren't even on her radar right now. She's struggling with a lot."

"Like growing up without a mother."

My throat felt tight, and I forced a swallow. The thought of Maddie's cheek on my chest swelled my heart with longing. I knew she was a good person. I'd have to convince Dad he had the wrong idea about her.

I respected my father. Such respect made it difficult to say the next words. "You're not supposed to know about her mother leaving.

Nobody's supposed to know that, and it's so unfair that you do. You realize why they violated her privacy, right? Because we're in the public eye. Because *you* ran for president. I feel awful about that."

"I feel awful, too." Dad's voice had lost its edge of anger. "I never meant to make your lives harder with all of this."

"I know. But really, how many fathers find out dirt about their in-laws through FBI briefings?"

Dad actually laughed. "Not many." Then he gasped. "Did you say in-laws? Is there something you need to tell me?"

"No, I haven't run off to marry Maddie." As I chuckled, I noticed Brad's eyebrows almost hit the roof of the car. The next thought that popped into my head shocked me. How would Dad react if I said it out loud? I bit my lip, then blurted, "But someday I want to."

Silence. "I had no idea it was that serious, Alejandro."

"It's kind of knocking me off my feet, too."

"Well, now I definitely have to meet her."

What? "I know you're busy…maybe it can wait…"

"In my short tenure in this job, I've learned one thing: communication is the way to resolve conflict. I want to talk to this young woman. If she's knocked you off your feet, she's someone I want to meet."

My mouth hung open.

"I'll have my people arrange it with Lucy's agents. Okay, I need to run. Keep up the good work in school."

"*Adiós*," I said, but the line had gone dead. I blinked a few times.

I looked out the window and noticed we were less than a mile from the condo. My agents were quiet, and it seemed rather awkward inside the vehicle. "I guess you hear all kinds of things when you're on duty, ¿*sí?*"

"We keep it private," Brad said. "Part of the job."

China piped up from the front seat. "Especially if we like the protectee." One eyebrow slanted up with the hint of a challenge.

Hmm. Did she like me? She sure didn't seem to approve of me most of the time. Did that mean she would keep my secrets?

"Don't worry—your father's treated us well for the most part," she said. "Better than some prior administrations have, from what I've heard."

Brad laughed. "Broomstick One?"

China joined his laugh—it was a rare smile from her.

"That's what they called Air Force One when a certain previous first lady was on board," Brad explained.

"Ah." I nodded.

"That's Shandy's car, isn't it?" China said as we pulled into the driveway.

"Yeah." Brad leaned back in his seat. "Probably just checking in."

I tensed. The last time their boss's boss visited, they'd huddled in my condo's office and hadn't let me listen in. After he'd left, both my agents seemed jumpy.

"Someone threatened my father?" I asked as the car came to a stop.

China stepped out and slammed the door.

Brad shrugged. "There're always threats to your family, Alex. That's why you've got us."

China opened my door, and I walked inside in an agent sandwich.

"Mr. Ramirez," Captain Shandy said as he shook my hand in the foyer of my condo. "How're things going for you?"

"Good." I set my laptop case on the table near the front door.

"I need to borrow officers Hallowell and Jansen for a few." He cocked his head toward the office, and my agents sped in that direction. He turned to follow them, then turned back. "Oh, and FLOTUS, er, the first lady sent some food up with me. It's in the fridge, sir."

Hot tamales! I was starved. Sometimes Secret Service wasn't all that bad. I flipped on Fox News, inhaled Mamá's cooking, then opened my laptop. Dr. Moore had given us a week to read the entire diagnostic manual for mental disorders, so I pulled up the ebook and got busy. Though the door to the office was closed, a few times I heard raised voices. The loudest voice was the captain's.

Bipolar Disorder has a higher prevalence rate in artists, I read. *Creativity, high energy, and confidence coincide with mania and hypomania.* That was interesting. Dane's father was a painter—did *he* have Bipolar Disorder? What about Dane? He sure seemed to have high energy. I grinned. Dr. Moore had warned us not to diagnose people upon learning the symptoms of mental disorders. Yet here I went with the med student syndrome.

The door to the office blasted open, and I heard my name called. I set my laptop aside and rounded the corner.

"Mr. Ramirez, I'd like a word," Shandy said. "Would that be all right?"

"Sure." I shrugged. I walked in the room to find China looking pale and possibly fighting off tears. I'd never seen her come close to crying. Sitting next to her, Brad stared at the floor.

"I want to talk to Mr. Ramirez alone. Both of you, dismissed."

Without meeting my eyes, my agents left, closing the door behind them.

"What's wrong?" I asked as we sat, him behind the desk and me in the lounge chair vacated by China.

"I'm not here about a particular security risk, if that's what you're asking. In fact, officers Jansen and Halloway did an excellent job defusing a recent terrorist threat before it had the chance to materialize into anything dangerous."

"They did?" I swallowed.

"Yes, sir. But I'm here to address the officers' personal behavior." He leaned forward, his hands folded on the desk. "Have you been dissatisfied by any behavior exhibited by the officers assigned to you?"

What's he looking for?

"Anything bother you? Anything inappropriate? It's okay; you can tell me."

"I'm not sure what you're talking about. Brad and China have been fine."

He frowned. His fingers tapped on a manila folder I just noticed on the desk. He opened the folder and scooted a blown-up photo in my direction. Though the image was dark, I could make out China and Allison kissing inside the greenhouse.

"Who took that photo?" I demanded. "Can they see inside the house? Is Lucy safe?" Had they caught me kissing Maddie on camera?

"We've tightened up security around the house already. That's not your problem. What I want to know is how Officer Halloway's unprofessional behavior affects you and your sister. You say the word and she's gone."

I sat back, stunned. "You'd fire her over this?"

"The director may do just that once we gather all the intel. And your input is first on the list. Has her illicit affair with a coworker hurt her job performance?"

"No." I shook my head. "She's been nothing but professional."

He stared at me for a long minute, then scooped up the photo and folder as he stood. "Thank you, sir. I won't take up more of your time." He strode to the door and opened it. "Officer Jansen!"

Brad appeared. "Walk me out," Shandy said.

China wasn't in the kitchen or family room. I headed to her bedroom to find her door closed. I slumped against the wall, wondering if I should knock.

Finally I tapped on her door. "You okay?"

After a beat, she said, "No."

"I can't believe they want to fire you."

She wrenched open the door, her eyes puffy. "*I* can. It's called homophobia." Her mouth trembled, and she laced her arms across her chest. "They suspended my pay for two weeks while they 'investigate.'"

"That's awful—I'm sorry. You think this is about you being gay?"

"Of course it is. They haven't shown the president the photo, but they're scared it'll leak out. The media will have a field day about a man who's denounced gay marriage having his two kids protected by lesbians."

I took that in. That *would* be quite a shiny nugget. "But the captain made the issue your relationship interfering with your duty. Which it hasn't." I thought for a moment. "Wait a minute. Captain Shandy doesn't know about Brad and his supervisor getting it on, does he?"

China's eyes flared. "*You* know about that?"

"It's kind of obvious."

"Right. Brad's not the king of subtlety. The thing is, I bet Shandy knows. A lot of people know. But because it's a heterosexual thing, nobody cares."

"Even if it's with a supervisor?"

Her mouth tightened as she nodded.

"That's not right," I said. "Something has to be done."

She unfolded her arms as she looked up at me. "That's not the reaction I expected from you, Alejandro."

It wasn't the reaction I'd expected either. But there was a clear injustice here.

I heard the front door open and the beeps of Brad setting the alarm. He came down the hall to find us standing outside China's room.

"Well, that was a fucking shitstorm," he said. "I think I talked him down, though." He looked at China. "You okay, baby girl?"

"I'll live, Brad. But you call me 'baby girl' again, I'll choke you with my dental dam."

He guffawed, and though I had only a vague notion of what she was talking about, I laughed too. *That* was the China I knew.

Maddie

So this is how the other half lives. The private jet's engines were so quiet I barely noticed we were in the air. I couldn't blame the tremor in my spine on engine rattle. Its source had to be my first trip to meet the president. Who happened to be my boyfriend's father. *Gah!*

Two weeks after Braxton had referred to Alejandro as my boyfriend, I now thought of him the same way. We'd been texting throughout the days and studying together at night over video calls. On study breaks, I'd gotten him to try my favorite TV show, *Parenthood*, and he'd made me watch *The Kelly File* on Fox News.

I heard Lucia giggle and looked behind me to see Dane with a long piece of red licorice draped over his lip like a Fu Manchu moustache. His cheeks scrunched up to clamp Oreo cookies over his eyes. "Wax on, wax off," he said with an attempted Japanese accent. His hands made circular motions.

Allison shook her head when I glanced at her across the aisle.

I turned back around with a pretend glower for Dane, not that he could see it through his cookie lenses. "Why'd you come on this trip again, man-child?"

"To take the heat off you," Rez answered, though I'd meant my question to be rhetorical. "Dad will be so busy worrying about me and Dane that he'll forget to worry about you and Alex."

"Yeah, the prez loves me." When Dane grinned, his licorice fell. He fumbled to catch it, and the cookies tumbled to the floor. "Dammit!"

Despite her initial objections to my relationship with Alejandro, Lucia had since become our biggest champion. She said Dr. Valentine had pointed out that me dating her brother meant she would get to see me more often, even after I graduated.

I'd seen Dr. Valentine three times now, and I was feeling better. My performance in class and the gym had improved, too. But on top of all my studying, she'd given me the most difficult homework assignment of my life: write a letter to my mother. I wouldn't be able to send it, since I had no address for Mom, but writing it was supposed to help "clarify" and "process" my feelings toward her. I had no idea how to begin.

Lucia tapped my shoulder. "Bet you miss Alex, huh?"

I patted her hand and nodded.

"But you'll see him soon."

I grinned. His incisive dark eyes floating down my body, his warm scent...Nothing could take my mind off my complicated feelings for my mother like being around Alejandro.

One hour and countless security checkpoints later, I was in his arms, his hard, muscular arms. The ornate décor of the White House residence seemed less intimidating once Rez's agents had shown us to the room where Alejandro waited. Rez had taken Dane's hand and disappeared into the hallway, chattering about showing him the bowling alley and leaving Alejandro and me alone in a room colored in shades of watermelon and strawberry.

His hand stroked through my curly hair as he held me, and I breathed in his solid strength.

"Lucy told me you've been killing it on the court." His deep voice reverberated in his chest.

I looked up at him. "She's not doing so bad, either."

"How're you feeling about selection camp?"

I held my breath. Now that it was March, there was only one month until I went to Colorado Springs to try out for Team USA. "Nervous."

"You'll block like a beast. Hit like a…" He twisted his mouth, searching for a word. "Hamster?"

I laughed.

"Humpback whale?"

My eyes narrowed. "Careful."

He grinned. "Want me to come with you?"

I stilled. He wanted to come to Colorado? I'd traveled there alone the past two summers. I'd never considered asking Jaylon to join me because of his training schedule.

"Don't mean to invite myself. If you'd rather go alone…" Alejandro stepped back.

"Oh. I…I don't want to put you out. Could you get away from school?"

"We have a break between modules. But don't worry if you're used to doing your own thing."

I pictured him pitched over the arena railing, hollering at Coach, and a warm sensation spread through my chest. Alejandro could bolster my confidence, support me when I needed it most. "I actually like the idea of you going."

"You do?" His mouth eased into a slow, sexy smile.

That ignited a furnace of heat in my belly, cementing the idea. "Yes."

"Here you guys are!" Mateo loped into the room, one side of his black hair slanted over his eye with a punk rock spike on the other side. "Johnny told me you were in the Vermeil Room, not the library." He gestured behind him to a blond agent who didn't look much older than Alejandro.

"Sorry, sir," Johnny replied, then joined Brad by the room's entrance.

"The what room?" Alejandro asked.

"The V-e-r-m-e-i-l Room," Mateo said. "Vermeil means gold-plated silver. Across the hall from the library."

Of course we were in the library. I just hadn't noticed the shelves full of books until now. I also gawked at the bouquet of roses on a round cherry-wood table. There must have been at least five dozen.

"Where's Lucy?" asked Mateo.

"She took Dane to see the bowling alley," Alejandro said.

"Sweet."

As Mateo spun around to leave, I noticed a black cat at his feet.

"Hey!" Alejandro called, and Mateo turned back to face us. "*Rudo.* Come meet my girlfriend, Maddie."

With a shy smile and a blush reminiscent of his sister, Mateo approached. "Sorry," he said. "I know Lucy's eager to see *Escuincle.*" He nodded at the cat and offered his hand.

"Matty, meet Maddie." He laughed, and Mateo and I cracked up, too.

"It's like I'm meeting myself," I said with a grin.

"Except you're taller." He studied me. "Your block was epic against Penn State."

Lucia's family had attended the final four of the NCAA tournament, but Secret Service had whisked them away before I'd had the chance to meet them. "Too bad we still lost," I said.

Mateo shrugged. "Penn State's setter was better."

"That's an astute observation, little brother." Alejandro glanced at me and smirked.

"Well, I've been dragged to countless volleyball games," Mateo grumbled.

"And baseball games." Alejandro's arm extended like he wanted to sling it across Mateo's back, but he stopped in midair when his brother seemed to stiffen. Alejandro tapped his fist on his shoulder instead. "Thanks for being there for us."

Mateo looked down, and awkward silence descended. I tried to think of something to say. "Your music's *increíble.*"

His eyes shifted up, and I noticed they were lighter than Alejandro's. "*¿Hablas español también?*"

I looked to Alejandro for help, and he shook his head. "Maddie doesn't speak Spanish. She doesn't care about politics, either."

"Then I like you already." Mateo gave me a conspiratorial smile. "But how do you put up with Alex's Republican rants? They go on and on, like, forever."

I met Alejandro's dark gaze. "He's a passionate guy. I like his passion." His eyes smoldered, and for a second I forgot I was standing in the White House. If Mateo weren't here, I'd show Alejandro some passion of my own. To tamp down the tingle in my spine, I focused on Mateo. "Your lyrics are really beautiful."

The blush returned. He was so damn cute!

"I think that's a great way to deal with your illness," I continued. "Funneling all your frustration and sadness into songs."

Alejandro inhaled, then nodded. "*That's* what you're writing about. Diabetes has stolen your life away."

"Some of my songs are about that, yeah." Mateo tucked his hands into the pockets of his frayed jeans.

Alejandro's eyes traveled down my body, then back up to linger on my face, which warmed under his appreciative gaze. "Quite insightful, Maddie."

"It's the Maddie-Matty connection." I tilted my head toward the teenager.

"Squinky!" Lucia shrieked.

She jogged into the room with Dane, Frank, and a man holding a camera trailing her. I followed Lucia's horrified gaze to the floor, and watched the black cat rise from his crouch after depositing two pellets of poop next to Alejandro's shoe.

Alejandro jumped away. "Disgusting!"

"Ba ha ha ha!" Mateo doubled over in laughter.

"Stop laughing, Matty." Lucia's voice shook with suppressed giggles. "We have to clean this up before Mom sees."

"Yes, we do," Alejandro growled. "I'm surprised he didn't poop *on* my shoe. That cat's such a brat." He looked at me. "That's what *Escuincle* means in Spanish. *Brat.*"

Lucia *tsked* and scooped up the cat, cradling him like an infant. "Don't listen to him. How's my little Squinky-Squinky?" she cooed. "Did you miss me, baby?" Dane leaned over to tickle the cat's belly.

Over the cat's motorboat purrs I heard the clicking of a camera. Was that the White House photographer?

Alejandro must have heard it too, because he hurled himself in front of his siblings, blocking the photographer's view. "You can't take pictures of this brat cat pooping in the library, destroying our country's relics!"

The rich oriental carpet probably cost more than an entire year of my father's salary.

Dane laughed. "Not the image you want for the first family, Alex?" He seemed to notice Mateo just then, extending his arm for a fist bump. "How's it going, my man?"

"Good."

"Hey, Matty!" Lucia stretched her free arm around his shoulder and tucked him in for a hug. "Thanks for looking after the Squinkster."

"He's a cool cat."

Alejandro glared at the feline. "He's the devil. Now, how will we clean this up without staining the rug?"

"Housekeeping's been notified, sir," Frank said from across the room.

Click, click, click went the camera.

Alejandro ran his hands through his hair, looking stressed. I crossed over to him and clasped his hand in mine. "It'll be okay," I said. "I think it's hilarious Squinky pooped on the White House carpet. The public will love it."

"Really?" His hand relaxed a bit.

"Mr. Ramirez?" The photographer called. "Will you move over by your siblings? I want to get some shots of you three."

He gave me a guilty glance, and I released his hand. "Go," I said. I backed up against a bookshelf and Dane came to stand next to me.

Alejandro stood the tallest, but it was his demeanor that made it clear he was the oldest. His posture was straight and serious, his dark gray suit professional. Lucia wore yoga pants and long-sleeved black shirt that had "Talk to the Hands" spelled out in rhinestones with an image of two palms splayed out over a volleyball net, ready for the block.

The siblings' thick, black hair shone in the overhead lights. When Alejandro reached to pet the cat, the resulting hiss got his brother and sister laughing again.

"Damn, that cat hates him," said Dane.

"Do you wish your family lived here instead?" I asked him.

He stroked his chin. "It'd be pretty sweet, I guess. But all the other stuff? The security detail, the media…" He pointed to the photographer. "Luz can't even hang with her bros without some douchebag recording it all for posterity. No, thanks."

A woman in a light-gray dress with a white apron entered the room and quietly cleaned the cat's mess.

"Wonder where we can drum up some food in this place," Dane said as he scanned the room. "I'm starving."

I was hungry, too.

"Maddie," Alejandro called. He smiled at me and gestured for the photographer. "Take some photos of us," he told him.

"You sure?" I asked.

"Why wouldn't I be?"

He folded me into his side, and we stood in front of rose-a-palooza for several shots. How would Braxton react to my wide smile?

"*Niños*, you're all here."

I turned to see Mrs. Ramirez enter the room.

"I'm so happy!" She cupped her face in her hands.

The photographer spun around to snap some photos of her, and she raised her hands in front of her face. "Ay! No photos. I look a mess."

A riot of jewel colors splashed across her vibrant print dress, and she'd clearly spent time on her coiffed hair and makeup. I glanced down. What would she think of my suede jacket over black jeans?

Alejandro clasped my hand. "You ready to meet Hurricane Sylvia?"

"Should I be scared?"

He chuckled. "Nah. She's loud and blustery, but she's okay."

Lucia and Dane reached her first. Lucia embraced her mother, and to my surprise, Mrs. Ramirez hugged Dane as well. As she let him go, she peered up at him. "You staying away from alcohol, young man?"

Dane grinned. "*Sí, Señora* Ramirez." He glanced at me and explained, "The first time I met Luz's mother didn't go so well."

"You were *drunk*," Mateo offered.

Dane rolled his eyes at Mateo. "Thanks for your help." He looked back at me. "Hopefully *Señora* likes you better than me."

"*Mamá*, this is Maddie Brooks," Alejandro said.

"*Qué hermosa*. Beautiful." She cradled my cheek in her hand, and her light floral perfume floated between us. "She could be a model, Alejandro."

"I know." He beamed at me, and my face flamed.

In an instant, I was in her arms. Mrs. Ramirez patted my back and murmured, "Lovely to meet you, my dear." Her ample bosom pressed into my abdomen; she was so soft and warm. Her comfort overwhelmed me, and I was shocked when tears blurred my eyes. I thought I was done with crying!

When Mrs. Ramirez released me, I blinked to clear my tears.

"Of course I like you," she said. "One look at Mr. Morose grinning like an idiot over there tells me everything I need to know about you."

"I do *not* look like an idiot," Alejandro huffed.

"Dude." Dane shook his head. "Your mom's enchanted by your girlfriend. Don't ruin it."

"Well said, Dane." Mrs. Ramirez clapped her hands. "But where are my manners? Come, all of you; you must be hungry. We have food set up in the Palm Room." She headed for the door, and Dane and Lucia followed her.

Alejandro had turned to watch his brother and a female agent. She wore the business-suit uniform of the other agents I'd met, topped with fiery red hair. Mateo rolled up one sleeve, and she pricked his exposed arm with a lancet, testing his blood in some sort of device.

Alejandro frowned. "Fingertip pricks are more accurate, but Matty says they interfere with playing the guitar."

"How many times a day does he have to get tested?"

"Not sure. A while back it was around five, but Mom said his numbers have been crazy recently—you know, with hormones and everything."

"Hormones affect insulin?"

"Especially human growth hormone."

The agent nodded at Mateo, who glared at us. "You done talking about me?"

Whoops. "Sorry," I said.

"How is it?" Alejandro asked.

"It's fine." Mateo marched out of the room, and Alejandro sped behind him. I jogged to catch up.

"What's the number, Matty?"

His brother ignored him.

"Tell me."

Mateo whirled, his eyes flaring. "It's one-ten, okay? I manage just fine without you."

"Okay." Alejandro held up his hands in a gesture of surrender.

I tried to think of something to distract them. "When will we meet your dad?"

But Alejandro seemed to tense up even more. "Maybe for lunch. I don't know."

Brad and the red-haired agent followed us. The first room we passed had white walls and recessed red shelves, flashing recognition in my mind. "Is that the China Room? I saw that in a movie once, I think."

"Yes. I'll make sure we get the tour later."

Across the hall from that room was an opaque door. "Secret Service," Alejandro told me. He glanced behind him at Brad. "China's in there?"

"Yep."

I hadn't seen her since we'd entered the White House. Alejandro seemed worried about her, but I had no idea why.

Once we arrived in the room with the buffet table, my eyes went wide. I'd never seen that much food.

Mrs. Ramirez stood by an informal dining table. "There's a family dining room upstairs, but we typically eat down here, with only three of us for meals." She gave her eldest a pointed look. A jab about him not visiting more? "I love all the light coming in."

Sunlight streamed through the glass door and windows at one end of the rectangular room, silhouetting the two marines posted on each side. I was grateful the spring weather was more temperate in DC than at Highbanks, where it had snowed a few days ago.

"Plus, it's near the kitchen," she continued, "and the West Wing, so Adolfo doesn't have far to come. Staff can grab something from the buffet, too. Please." She gestured to the plates at one end of the buffet table. "Dane, I see you drooling over the enchiladas. You go first, but save some for the rest of us, ¿sí?"

His eyes lit up, and he piled food on his plate.

Mrs. Ramirez exchanged a look with Mateo. He nodded, and she smiled. Was she also checking on his blood glucose?

We quieted as we ate. I kept staring at a painting of Lady Liberty ensconced in the American flag. It looked straight out of the eighteenth century. Alejandro noticed my fascination and smiled at me.

"¿Me puedo servir otro plato, Señora?" asked Dane.

"Por supuesto." Mrs. Ramirez nodded.

Alejandro leaned in to whisper, "Dane asked if he could have seconds, and Mom said of course."

Dane returned to his seat with an even larger plate of food.

"That's repulsive," Mateo said, eyeing the food mountain.

"C'mon, we had a killer practice this morning." Dane swigged some ice water. "Jessica says I eat more than swimmers do." He puffed out his chest like he was proud. "Though they're tapering now, so they're eating less."

Mateo perked up. "What's tapering?"

"It's when swimmers rest more—swim fewer laps—before their big meet at the end of the season. Jess bounces off the walls this time of year."

"What's her big meet?"

Dane finished chewing his bite. "US Nationals, in April."

"So, like, what events does she swim?"

That was Mateo's third question about Jessica. *Interesting.* I glanced at Lucia and noticed her smirk. I'd have to ask her if Mateo had the hots for Dane's sister.

"Breaststroke and IM," Dane said. "Individual medley is all four strokes. Jess is really versatile."

His pride was heartwarming. I wondered if Braxton ever spoke about me that way. Probably not. He'd told me several times I'd sold out by accepting an athletic scholarship.

Once we'd finished eating, Alejandro stood and reached for my empty plate. A man dressed in a black uniform rushed in and took it from him. "I've got it, sir."

"Oh." Alejandro stepped back and looked around, tugging at his jacket sleeve like he was nervous. It *was* strange to be treated like royalty. I hoped I wouldn't make a fool of myself during this visit. Alejandro started as he looked toward the West Wing. "Hey, Dad's here."

President Ramirez glided through the door held open by one of the marines, and it was obvious where Alejandro got his grace. The president towered over the two agents shadowing him, but when Dane stood, I could tell he was a couple inches taller than President Ramirez.

Alejandro took my hand and drew me to my feet.

"Sweetheart," Mrs. Ramirez said as she popped out of her chair.

Mr. Ramirez fanned his hands to the side and pressed down on air a few times. "Please, stay seated, everyone."

"That's okay; we're finished. Let's get—" The president cut off his wife by grabbing her for a kiss. They hugged for a long minute, whispering and smiling at each other. Alejandro rolled his eyes. But I smiled.

"What was I saying?" When her husband let her go, Mrs. Ramirez's hair was ruffled, and her eyes hazy. I knew what it was like to be undone by a Ramirez kiss. "Oh! Let's get you a plate, Adolfo."

"I ate earlier," President Ramirez said. His wife started to protest but he'd already moved to envelop Lucia in a hug. "*Mija*, so good to see you here."

"Cool crib, Dad."

He laughed, but his expression sobered as he turned to Dane. Offering his hand, he said, "Tough game against UC Irvine."

Dane's eyes widened in apparent surprise. "We'll get 'em next time."

"How are your parents doing?"

"They're..." Dane frowned. "Good."

"Send them my best."

He nodded.

President Ramirez patted Mateo's shoulder. He was still seated, his fingers flying over his phone keyboard. "A hug for your dad, Mateo?"

"Dad, I just saw you, like, five minutes ago."

The president shook his head at Mrs. Ramirez but let Mateo stay absorbed. As he approached us, my breath caught in my throat.

"Son." He and Alejandro thumped each other on the back as they hugged.

Alejandro seemed to brace himself as he looked at me, then back at his dad. "This is Maddie Brooks."

The president's sharp gaze met mine, sending my heart rate soaring. Then he broke out in a megawatt smile as he shook my hand. "So *this* is my daughter's idol."

"*Dad.*" Lucia sounded embarrassed.

Alejandro had the same deep, dark eyes, but lines around his father's creased when he smiled. "Thanks for taking care of Lucy."

"She's taken care of me, too." I shrugged. I smiled at Alejandro and almost added, *And so has Alex.*

"Alejandro tells me you're trying out for the national team?"

Warmth flooded my cheeks. What if I didn't make it? "Next month."

"Mr. President?" An older woman with blond hair had entered the room. I took in her flawless beige suit jacket and skirt. She looked familiar.

"What is it, PQ?"

My eyes widened as I realized she was the Secretary of State, Paula Quinlen.

"Bill's on the line, hoping to discuss the pipeline sabotage," she said.

"Good. We need to address that." Mr. Ramirez tugged the hem of his black jacket to straighten it. "Alejandro, walk with me."

Alejandro paused and turned toward me with a question on his face.

"Maddie too," the president said, already heading for the door. "I want to get to know her better."

Alejandro scooped up my hand, and we scurried behind his father's entourage. Brad fell into step behind us. We headed outside, over a brick pathway, with a cool breeze wafting through my hair.

I leaned in to whisper, "Bill is Bill Nichols? The vice president?"

Alejandro squeezed my hand and nodded like it was no big deal.

18
Alejandro

★ ★ ★

The only way to improve my first visit to the hallowed Oval Office was to view it through Maddie's perspective. Her lips parted in a wondrous smile as we passed the manicured lawn of the Rose Garden and entered my father's workspace. The pale yellow wallpaper was reflected in her glimmering eyes as they scanned the smooth, cornerless shape of the room.

"You two can sit over there," Dad said, pointing at a grouping of plush sofas and lounge chairs. Maddie grinned at me when I led her over the carpet's presidential seal to the yellow velvet sofa.

"What?" I asked as we sat.

"That seal is surreal," she whispered, tilting her head over her shoulder. Behind her was my father's desk, where he spoke into the speakerphone.

I nodded. The entire Oval Office was unreal.

She leaned in with a secretive grin. "Back at Highbanks, there's a seal like that with the university's crest. It's at the entrance to the oval."

"So you have an oval, too."

"More of a quad, really." She looked at her lap. "If couples kiss on the seal…" Her eyes floated up, and her tongue skated over her lip. "It means they'll get married."

Dios. Her words shot through me like a flaming arrow. The blush of soft pink on her cheeks, the spark of delight in her eyes, the glisten of her wet mouth...I looked to make sure Dad wasn't watching. He sat on the edge of the desk about ten feet away, his back to us as he continued listening to the vice president. Secretary of State Quinlen stood next to the desk with her arms folded across her chest.

I leaned closer and folded Maddie's slender hand between mine. Her palm rested on my upturned left hand, hot to the touch. She inhaled a staccato breath, matching my uneven gulps of air. The tip of her tongue flitted to the corner of her sweet mouth. I glanced at the seal, then into her shining eyes. "If I kiss you on the seal, I promise to marry you, ¿*sí?*"

She gasped, and I wondered if I'd come on too strong. But she curled her fingers around mine and brought our conjoined hands to her mouth. Her soft lips and warm breath feathered my skin. With a sultry look from under her eyelashes, she pressed a kiss to my knuckles. A rush of blood drained from my brain.

"Sealed with a kiss," she breathed.

I smoothed my hands up her jaw, plunging my fingers into her textured curls. When she closed her eyes and a sigh of pleasure left her lips, I pulled her into me. I had to have her. My mouth found hers in an urgent kiss—a kiss I'd craved since she'd arrived to the White House.

She was so soft, so warm. When her lips parted and her tongue brushed mine, I felt a charge up my spine. The kiss deepened as our tongues touched and played, ratcheting up the heat flooding my chest. I felt her fingers sneak over my waistband, and she tugged me closer, my thigh pressing into her long, gorgeous leg. Pressure built inside of me, and I couldn't get enough of her.

When I heard the clearing of a throat, my mouth froze on hers. Unsuctioning our lips, I tilted my head to the right, which put me in the direct line of my father's stare. *Mierda.* Ms. Quinlen's widened eyes confirmed they'd been observing us for some time.

"They're *watching* us?" Maddie squeaked. Her eyes were huge.

I unlatched my hands from her hair and brushed them down my suit jacket. "Sorry," I said quietly. "Got a little out of control there. You have that effect on me."

"Me too. But in the Oval Office? Holy mortification." Her gaze remained on her hands twisting in her lap.

"If there's nothing else, Mr. President, I'll head out." Ms. Quinlen said.

"Let me introduce you to my son before you go."

Please, no. Don't make me look her in the eye.

"Alejandro?"

Pony up, Ramirez. I stood and swallowed. "Pleasure to meet you, Secretary of State Quinlen." I approached the desk with my hand extended.

"You look so much like your father." She smiled as she shook my hand. "And this is your girlfriend?"

"Yes, ma'am." Before I could bring Maddie over, she'd popped off the sofa, and Ms. Quinlen walked over to shake her hand as well.

"My, you're tall." She looked up at my elegant girlfriend.

I circled the sofa to stand next to Maddie. "She plays volleyball with Lucia."

"Ah. That's how you two met." The woman's expression seemed to soften. "Lucia the matchmaker."

I stifled my snort.

"Maddie does more than *play* volleyball," Dad said on his way toward the sofa across from us. "She *dominates* the game."

I exhaled. Dad complimenting her was a good sign.

"She apparently dominates my son's thoughts as well," Dad added with a smirk.

I wanted to crawl under the sofa. How to veer this conversation back on track? "Maddie's trying out for the national team soon."

"Wonderful! Good luck." Ms. Quinlen nodded at my dad, then left.

Dad gestured to the sofas. "Let's have a seat and talk. Or would you like the room to yourselves?"

Maddie's giggle betrayed her nervousness. Once we sat across from Dad, he patted his thigh as he studied us, like he was assessing the strength of our bond. Silence stretched between us, and I fiddled with my watch.

"Everything okay with the pipeline construction?" I asked.

One eyebrow arched. Was he on to my attempt to redirect the conversation?

"A few Montana building sites have been vandalized. But we'll catch the perpetrators. We already have a few leads."

Maddie's back straightened. "The Keystone pipeline's being vandalized?" I was impressed she knew of the pipeline project.

"Yes." Dad nodded. "We think the vandals are environmental vigilantes; they're angry Congress approved the project."

She rubbed her index finger along her lip. "The pipeline's bad for the environment?"

My shoulders tensed as I watched the exchange.

"There are some downsides, yes. Environmentalists are concerned with increased tar sands emissions. But the pipeline's much more efficient than rail transportation of oil, which reduces pollution. And we're creating thousands of jobs."

"Shouldn't we focus on alternate energy sources?" asked Maddie.

Dad leaned forward, his elbows resting on his knees. Nothing excited him like oil. "We *are* exploring alternate energy. But our technology's not there yet. Take hybrid cars, for example. They're not cost-efficient, they require more energy to produce, and their battery disposal can be hazardous."

Dad kept talking, but I heard little of his speech. My attention zeroed in on the striking girl next to me. I loved her jaunty curls. The slope of her long neck. Her caramel skin. My lips tingled with the desire to kiss every inch of her.

My dad's chuckle interrupted my thoughts. I looked up to find him shaking his head. "What's funny?" I asked.

"I've never seen you like this."

"Like what?"

"Like..." His smile faded, and he leaned back. "Never mind."

"Is it bad, what you're seeing?" I felt my heart rate increase. *Am I disappointing him?*

"No, not at all," Dad said. "You're growing up. I just...I don't want you to go too fast. You two haven't had time to get to know each other all that well." He looked at Maddie. "What does your brother think of you and Alejandro?"

"My brother?" She shifted on the cushion as she snuck a glance at me. "Well, he's not a big fan."

"And why is that?"

Maddie took a deep breath. "He believes Republican policies hurt black people."

She was brave—I had to give her that.

"It's more like progressive policies hurt black people, but that's a discussion for another day." Dad leaned forward, and my heart galloped. "What I want to know is, do you agree with your brother?"

"You're interrogating her, Dad." I tried to give her a reassuring look. "You don't have to answer that."

"It's okay, Alex." She patted my hand. "He needs to know if he can trust me. My dad's the same way. He'll probably ask you even tougher questions when you meet him."

¡Hijole! I hadn't even thought of that.

"I love my brother," Maddie continued. "We don't always agree, though. Racism still exists, but I don't look at everything as black or white. I know some wonderful black people, like my grandparents, but there are black people who cheat, steal, even murder—and white people who do the same. There are good and bad people in every group. It's ridiculous to paint an entire race with a broad brush."

Her low, impassioned voice mesmerized me, and I couldn't take my eyes off her. Then she grinned. "Black, white, Latino, gay, straight—if any of them came across a bear in the woods, they'd all taste like chicken."

I laughed, and my dad's mouth twitched.

"I just try to get to know individuals, try to know their hearts," Maddie said. "Lucia, she has *such* a loving heart. I'm lucky she came to Highbanks."

The curve of Dad's mouth resembled a smile more and more. Maddie was smart to tap into his soft spot for Lucy.

"And you're right, I don't know Alejandro all that well, but what I've seen draws me to him." She peeked at me. "It scares me a little, how much I miss him when we're apart."

Hail Mary! She felt the same way? "Me, too," I admitted, and we beamed at each other. I didn't want to become dependent on her, but I hadn't figured out a way to keep her out of my mind, out of my heart.

"The way I see it, our cultural differences don't hurt us—they help us. They enrich us. For example, I want to learn Spanish. It's such a beautiful language." She turned to me. "And I want you to come to my church in Cleveland. It's where I grew up, and I want to share it with you."

I nodded.

"You see?" She looked at Dad. "Alejandro and I actually have a lot in common. Faith's important to us. He gets what it's like to major in pre-med and play a sport. I want to become a doctor, like him. I try not to focus on differences in our skin color, but pay attention to similarities in our character." Her eyes glowed with conviction. "It's not what divides us; it's what unites us."

Dad blinked as silence stretched between us. I'd never seen him speechless before. Maddie's hands fidgeted.

"I should create a cabinet position for you, Maddie," he finally said. "Ambassador of Racial Relations." He grinned. "What do you think, Alejandro?"

I stretched my arm across her shoulders and gave her a squeeze. "I think she's rather busy right now, Dad. She has a lot on her plate. And that was *before* she added learning Spanish to the mix."

Dad spoke to me in Spanish. "You're falling hard for her, and I can see why."

Relief flooded me. It was so important that he understood how special Maddie was.

"*Solo ve con cuidado,*" he added. *Be careful.* When he glanced at my arm across her shoulders, I removed it.

"Dad, could I talk to you about something?"

"You can always talk to me."

"I tried to call last week, but you were too busy."

Dad frowned. "That's not right. I'll get on—"

"It's okay. We're talking now." I paused to gather my thoughts. When I smiled at Maddie, she misunderstood my look as wanting her to leave.

She scooted forward on the sofa. "I'll go."

"No, please stay. You already know about the situation." I glanced at the agent standing by the door. "But could Secret Service leave?"

Concern crossed Dad's face. "Joe, give us a minute."

"I'll be right outside, sir."

The soft click of the door signaled it was time to make my case to my father. "I want to discuss China Halloway."

"The agent protecting you."

"*Sí.*" I took a deep breath. "I know this isn't my call, but I don't think she should be fired."

Dad cocked his head. "Why would she be fired?"

"Because of the affair. She hasn't let it interfere—"

"*What* affair?"

I flinched at his sharp tone, and Maddie seemed to tense as well. "The affair between China and Lucy's agent, Allison."

Dad's only response was a slight widening of the eyes.

"So you obviously don't know about this."

"No. Tell me everything." His arms folded across his chest.

"A Secret Service higher-up — Captain Shandy — came to Baltimore to chastise China for her involvement with Allison. He docked her pay while he investigated whether her behavior had been at all unprofessional. But I told him it wasn't."

Dad glared. "And this captain spoke to Lucia as well?"

"I suppose." I shrugged. "I haven't talked to her about it."

His fingers tapped his arm as he frowned. Then he bolted up and hit a button on the phone on his desk.

"*Afternoon, Mr. President,*" came through the speakerphone.

"Danny, I have a problem."

I whispered to Maddie, "Daniel Guthrie, Chief of Staff."

"My son tells me there's an investigation into the professionalism of China Halloway — an investigation I know nothing about. Surely that cannot be the case. Tell me he misunderstood something."

Mr. Guthrie paused. "*There is an investigation, sir. The director's reviewing the findings as we speak.*"

"How can this be?" Fire blazed in his voice, and I reached for Maddie's hand the way I used to reach for Lucia's when we were in trouble. "How have you not informed me about this matter involving my children?"

"*I'm sorry, sir. We didn't want to bother you with this.*"

"Make it known that anything involving my family is a top priority. I don't care how busy I am. But you know that already, Danny — how could you let me down like this?"

After a moment, Mr. Guthrie said, "*We thought the press would use this against you, since you've spoken out against gay marriage in the past.*"

Dad glowered at the phone, and his voice seemed to tremble with fury. "Do *not* handle me, Danny."

"*Yes, sir.*"

"I want you and the director in my office ASAP."

"*Yes, sir.*"

The call ended, and Dad breathed out through his nose. "*They're* the ones who should be fired."

"I don't want to cause any trouble," I said. "I just want to be fair to China."

"No, I'm glad you told me." He circled the desk, and his expression lightened. "This is simply about clarifying expectations. Reagan encountered it in his first days of office, too." He looked at me pointedly. "Are my expectations of you and your siblings clear?"

I felt frozen. I was accustomed to him as the leader of the Ramirez family, but leader of the United States was another level entirely. "Yes, sir."

A soft knock preceded the entry of Dad's right-hand man. I stood and guided Maddie to her feet. After a brief introduction to Mr. Guthrie and a brusque goodbye from Dad, we got out of there. Brad waited for us outside the Oval Office.

"Everything okay?" he asked.

I tried to get my bearings as I looked around me. "This entire building is just surreal."

"Totally surreal," Maddie agreed.

Brad laughed as his large hand cupped my shoulder. "You'll get used to it. Hey, let me give you the tour, freak you out some more."

"Can't wait!" Maddie curled her fingers around mine, and off we went down the hallway.

Almost an hour later, we still hadn't completed our tour. If I'd had a pedometer, it probably would've reached nearly eight thousand steps, even without picking up a game of basketball like I'd wanted to do when I saw the sweet court outside.

Brad gestured to a bedroom on the second floor. "The first lady said this is your room when you visit. The Lincoln Room."

"Oh, my God. The Lincoln Room?" Maddie zipped inside. "This is incredible!"

I smirked at Brad as I followed her in and closed the door behind me. Opulent golds and deep purples framed the windows and canopied bed. "No way I could sleep here." I scrunched my nose. "Too frou frou."

"*I'll* sleep here," she said, and just like that arousal spiked my blood. She lowered onto one of the gold loveseats and gazed up at the massive mirror over the fireplace. "Stunning."

"*You're* stunning." She blushed, and I joined her on the small sofa.

"What you said to my dad about going beneath skin color…" I tapped my thigh, trying to find the right words. "It means a lot to me. There was truth in your words. There was…healing. It seemed to come from a place deep inside of you."

Her brow furrowed. "I sure babbled in front of your dad."

"Not at all. You were quite eloquent."

"It's something I've been thinking a lot about, I guess. Dealing with racial differences—all kinds of differences." She frowned. "Disconnection. Shame. I've discussed it with Dr. Valentine. She had me watch this talk online about the power of vulnerability. We shy away from being real because we're ashamed. We don't feel good enough. It made me realize how bad I am at being vulnerable. I try to be perfect, but I keep failing."

Though she seemed perfect to me, I nodded.

"I've been ashamed of my imperfect family. I always knew I was different from all the girls at school—the ones who had mommies waiting for them at home—and that difference felt shameful. I felt defective. I kept my distance from people."

What a risk she had taken to let me into her heart, after all she'd been through. "But you haven't kept *me* at a distance."

Her face lit up. "I can't stay away from you, Hotajandro."

Warmth flowed through me, and I squeezed her hand. "Thank God. But why me?"

"I think I was tired of my life. The depression is a sign of that. And when people found out about my mom, they didn't judge me like I thought they would. *You* didn't judge me. You make me feel important, like somebody who matters." She shook her head. "All those years I feared others' scorn, simply for being different." She sighed. "It's sad we let our differences come between us. I don't want that to happen anymore."

"I agree." I rested my hand on her leg and drew small circles on the inside of her knee.

"I can tell you and Rez really love your dad. You admire him. But you know something?" She leaned in, her eyes fierce. "It's okay to be different from your dad. You can think differently than him. You can make different choices."

I shrugged. "I know that."

"Do you?" Her eyes searched mine.

I stilled. *Do I?*

Her hand skimmed my jaw, almost lifting me off my seat. We gazed at each other for minutes or hours—I couldn't tell for sure. She kept coming closer, and when her lips met mine, the buoyant sensation intensified. My eyes closed as I rode the waves of her sweet kisses. We swam in a sea of gold, with no anchors, no land in sight. I clutched her waist as I deepened her kiss. I wanted to float here forever.

My eyes flew open when she unbuckled my belt. Her bright eyes flashed as she unbuttoned and unzipped my pants, undoing me in the process. Was I ready for this? I sucked in a breath when her hot touch brushed over my boxer shorts, lighting me up inside. *Hell yes, I'm ready.* I stopped breathing when she reached in and drew my penis through the opening of my boxers. My hips bucked the second she touched me, her hand igniting an electric charge.

One of her hands pressed into my shoulder while the other rubbed and massaged my growing erection. We both watched my body respond to her silky, stimulating touch. I arched my back, almost writhing against the sofa, and ran my hand through her hair to anchor myself.

She offered me a sassy smirk. "Oral sex doesn't count as premarital sex, right?"

Lord, her beautiful mouth on me? "Not according to Bill Clinton." I felt lightheaded with anticipation. "I did not have sex with that woman," I assured her in my best Southern accent.

Her throaty laugh brought new heights to my arousal. "You think Bill and Monica did it in the Lincoln Room?" She grinned as she slithered down my body, landing softly on her knees. She looked up at me, her eyes darkening, then focused her gaze on my crotch. This was happening? I couldn't breathe. Brad was right outside. Her mouth rounded as she leaned forward, her lips glistening from our kisses.

My father's voice floated through my mind. *Have I made my expectations clear?* Was I ready for this?

"Stop."

Her head yanked back, her eyes confused.

"I'm sorry." *I'm a jerk.* "I'm screwing this up. I just can't..."

She sat back on her heels. I sighed with frustration.

After settling down, I zipped my pants, then clasped her arms. "You're gorgeous. I want you so badly."

She let me guide her to her feet, but when I tugged her toward my lap, she hesitated. After a moment, I exhaled when she folded into me.

"I'm so sorry—I didn't mean to hurt your feelings. I just..." I pressed a kiss into her collarbone. "We're in the White House of all places, and I'm just not ready, I guess."

It sounded like she stifled a groan. "So embarrassing, me throwing myself at you like that. Talk about vulnerability."

"Please don't be embarrassed. This is about my hang-ups, not at all about your desirability. God, I desire you. It's this damn Catholic guilt eating me up."

She avoided my eyes as she took that in. Then she looked up at me. "Good things come to those who wait?"

She was adorable. "I hope so." I'd waited for someone like her for twenty-four years. "You totally turn me on, and I don't know if I can hold off much longer."

As she kissed my forehead, my mind processed what had just happened. Why had I stopped her? I'd always thought sex before marriage was wrong, but now that I was an adult, I had to discern if that was what I really believed or if I was simply parroting my parents.

Maddie had let me in, but surely she'd eventually kick me out I refused to have sex. The thought of losing her crushed me.

19
Maddie

"Cou-cou-cou-cougars!"

The cheerleaders' chant echoed in my head, annoying me. Typically they didn't show up at men's volleyball games, but playing our rival Bridgetown in mid-March drew them to the arena like buzzing bees protecting their honeycomb. Bridgetown's one-game lead over Highbanks in the conference standings made tonight's match key to an NCAA tournament berth.

"We never had cheerleaders at baseball games," Alejandro said. Delight bubbled inside of me, just having him here. His impromptu weekend visit had come only two weeks after I'd last seen him at the White House.

From the other side of me, Lucia said, "That's 'cause baseball's boring as hell."

"You clearly don't understand the finer points of America's favorite pastime," Alejandro shot back.

Lucia pointed her nose in the air. "Clearly." Her tone was mocking.

To my surprise, Alejandro chuckled instead of escalating the argument. "Baseball *is* pretty boring to watch." He took my hand and rubbed it with his thumb, sending prickles of excitement up my spine.

The referee blew his whistle, and Dane shot away from the net, clutching the side of his head. I flinched. When he straightened, his hand fell away to reveal an angry dash of red above his eyebrow. Lucia gasped. The Bridgetown setter stood across from Dane with his hands perched on his hips. Had that asshole just hit Dane through the net?

The referee tapped the taut string on the top of the net and pointed his arm to the Cougars' side of the court, indicating side-out for a net violation. Hadn't he seen the blood on Dane's face?

Dane spun to face the Bridgetown player, and though his voice was too low for us to hear, his words brought the player back toward the net.

Our athletic trainer, Tina, approached the sideline, but it wasn't until Dane's coach, Phil, came onto the court that the referee realized a player had been injured. The ref whistled again, halting play.

"I wonder if that needs stitches," Alejandro said.

A trail of blood oozed down Dane's sweaty face, but his extended arm prevented Tina from examining the wound as he continued jawing with his rival. Their volume increased, and I thought I heard "fucking Neanderthal" come out of Dane's mouth. Phil tried to talk him down but Dane leaned forward and jabbed his finger through the net, spit flying from his mouth. Josh tugged on Dane's arm to no avail. The sideline ref scowled as he approached the players. *Uh-oh.* Would Dane get thrown out of the match?

"*¡Tranquilo*, Dane!" Lucia yelled. He looked up at us, but when the Bridgetown setter said something, he whipped back toward the net. The head referee blew his whistle again and climbed down from the stand where he'd been perched. This was bad. Just when the arena quieted in anticipation, Lucia hollered something in Spanish.

Dane's head turned toward us again. I was amazed when his glare morphed into a brilliant smile. He stepped back from the net and allowed Tina to guide him to a chair on the sidelines, where she and the team physician examined his cut.

"*Madre de dios.*" Alejandro cupped his hands over his mouth and looked behind him at his agents. He scanned the crowd as his shoulders shook with laughter. "Please tell me nobody else speaks Spanish here."

"What'd you say to him?" I asked Lucia.

She looked across me at her brother, and started giggling.

"*Dios*, Lucy." Alejandro shook his head, but couldn't stop smiling. He waited a beat. "She just told everyone the Bridgetown setter had a tiny penis. But Dane's hung like a horse."

My eyes widened. "Sweet, innocent Rez?" I noticed her characteristic blush finally making an appearance.

"Not so innocent anymore," Alejandro said. But then he laughed.

Once the team doc had applied a butterfly bandage to Dane's forehead, play resumed. Almost immediately Dane set a perfect ball, which Josh slammed for a kill. Dane mouthed *Fuck, yeah* as he chest-bumped Josh. Bridgetown's attempt to rile him had backfired, pleasing me to no end.

"I think I'll get a drink," I said. "Want anything?"

"I'll get it for you." Alejandro let go of my hand.

Behind us I heard his agents shift in their seats.

"It's okay, really." I laid my hand on his chest, feeling the muscles beneath his button-down shirt. When would I get to see them up close? It had been so embarrassing to have Alex refuse my advances in the Lincoln Room, but Dr. Valentine had helped me take it less personally. She said I'd done a masterful job being vulnerable, but I needed to give him some time. The anticipation was killing me.

"I don't want to make a big deal out of it—I just want a drink," I told him. "You stay and keep Rez in line."

I expected Lucia to protest, but she was too absorbed in the game to hear me.

His mouth tightened, but then he nodded and stood. "Probably a good idea. Who knows what she'll say next."

I laughed as I scooted around him to exit the row. Brad stood as well, looking like he wanted to follow me. But both men had to settle for watching me as I headed slowly to the concession stand, out of their sight. My butt muscles ached from Coach B's monster lunge workout this morning.

The greasy smell of pizza awakened my hunger, and I considered ordering some food, but Alejandro planned to take me out for an anniversary dinner after the match. I was in a celebratory mood and didn't want to order boring bottled water. I'd lasted over one month with Alex, and he hadn't bailed yet. If anything, we seemed to grow closer each week. So I asked for my favorite: root beer. When I punched a straw into the lid, I heard a familiar voice.

"Soda's bad for you, Mads."

I held my breath as I turned to find Jaylon right next to me. He had that hungry look in his eyes he always had around this time of year, and his V-shaped physique appeared even more built and defined than a month ago. Woe to his opponents in the upcoming NCAA tournament.

"I think you lost the privilege of training me." I moved a few steps away from the counter to a less-crowded spot in the hallway.

He scowled. I had him there. "But you gotta be smart. You got OTC camp in April."

I took a sip of sweet pop as I considered his words. That was thoughtful he'd remembered the timeline of my selection camp at the Olympic Training Center. He stared at my lips as I drank. Then his gaze trailed up, meeting mine. I knew that flash in his eyes: his turned-on look. What was his deal? I hadn't seen him since Alejandro and I had run into him outside my apartment, and I'd figured he'd finally accepted the end of our relationship. But now he licked his lips, looking at me like he wanted to kiss me.

"You said you'd take me out for my birthday, but you didn't."

He blanched. "Yeah. I…" He shrugged. "Been busy. You know wrestling sucks up all my time, 'specially this time of year."

Nothing took precedence over his sport, even me, and I'd accepted that when we'd been together. I'd believed I wasn't good enough to rank higher on his list of priorities. Thinking about it now, though, the comment rankled me. "So taking me out for my birthday was just a threat. You didn't follow through on your word."

"Ain't true. Was gonna take you out after the season."

"Why?" He said nothing, and I asked again, "Why take me out? It's over between us."

He looked down, then stuffed his hands into the pockets of his low-hanging jeans. "Think I made a mistake." His head stayed down, but his eyes rolled up to assess my reaction. "Think we should try this again."

When the urge to laugh pressed up my throat, I swallowed it down. It would be cruel to laugh in his face. But my callous reaction told me one thing: I was definitely over him. "What about Nina?"

"It ain't serious."

Did *Nina* know that? She'd given indications they were hot and heavy. Despite all of her issues, I felt sad for her. And glad I no longer had to deal with his crap.

"You know, Jay, I think you're smarter than me."

His eyes bugged.

"No, hear me out. You're smarter because you knew our relationship was over long before I did. And you were right. We're just not compatible."

"Yeah, we are. You and me...we good together. We're the best athletes at this school."

"You're an amazing athlete," I agreed. "I know you'll kill it at NCAAs. And I'm grateful you pushed me so hard in the weight room. I'll be thinking of you at camp—you're a big reason I got invited." I searched for the right words. "But we don't have much in common beyond that. One day I'll stop volleyball, and you'll stop wrestling, and then where'll we be?"

He frowned, but looked at the floor.

"You said I didn't love you." That still stung. "I *did* love you, but I didn't know how to show it. I'm sorry I hurt you. I'm sorry I didn't let you in. I've learned a lot about myself this year, and you were right. I wasn't letting you into my heart. I felt too damaged to show you the real me."

He let out a long sigh as his gaze swept over me. "Girl, you're a bomb-ass trap queen, dontchu know that?"

I grinned. I would miss his unique way with words. "Thanks." *I guess.* "You're bomb-ass, too. We're just not made to be together." My smile faded. "It's still hard for me to be vulnerable—to let others in—but I'm trying."

His eyes rolled. "With *him?*"

I paused, then nodded.

"You're always with him." He grunted. "Or some stupid TV show's on 'bout him being with you. Thought you and him was just *friends*."

"Alejandro and I are together now."

I sniffed spicy cologne a moment before Alejandro wrapped his arm around my waist. "We are," he said. It figured he'd come to check on me. I leaned into his solid body.

Jaylon eyeballed him, then China.

"You doing okay?" Alejandro asked me.

"Yes. Just saying goodbye to Jaylon."

His hand pressed into my hip, and he kissed the top of my head. "I'll stop interfering, then."

When he stepped away, his warmth went with him, and I wanted to be back by his side. He and China went and stood about twenty feet away.

I returned my focus to Jaylon. "I wish you the best. Good luck with everything."

"That's it?"

"That's all I got." I held my hands out to the side. "Do you want to wish me good luck, too?"

After a moment, he nodded.

"Maybe we'll both be in the Olympics one day."

His mouth curled into a smile. "Ain't no maybe about it."

"Just promise me one thing," I said.

His eyebrow arched in a question.

"Don't ever, ever, *ever* sing karaoke again."

He shook his head. "That fucker, Dane."

I smiled. "Goodbye, Jaylon."

He studied me for a long while, his eyes sad. "Can I hug you?"

I looked over my shoulder, then back at him. "Better not. Secret Service might take you down."

"I'd like to see them try." But he nodded. "Bye, Mads."

I watched him walk off, feeling a twinge of my own sadness mixed in with relief. Now I knew what closure felt like.

Alejandro examined me as I approached. "How are you?"

"Really great." And this time, I meant it.

"Good. I won't have to teach that wrestler a lesson." He flexed his fist, and recoiled when I laughed. "You don't think I could take him down?"

"I'll do it for you," China chimed in with a wicked smile.

I blinked up at Alejandro. "I think you can do anything you set your mind to. You're very determined."

My response seemed to placate him. "The match is almost over. Want to say goodbye to Lucy and head out?"

I nodded, feeling giddy.

He gestured to my paper cup as we returned to our seats. "I'm thirsty—can I have some?"

I gave it to him, and he stopped short after a sip. "Root beer?" With a moan, he closed his eyes. "My favorite."

"Mine too. But I've never seen you drink it."

"My family gave up soft drinks when Matty got diagnosed. I used to sneak a root beer now and then, though."

"You rebel." I nudged his shoulder.

Five minutes later we'd settled in the back seat of the SUV. It was a mild night, and High Street teemed with college students emerging from their winter hibernation. "Where're we going?" I asked.

"You'll find out soon enough." Passing street lights gleamed in his dark eyes.

I pouted until his hand sneaked behind my neck, stroked under my collar, and shot tingles down my back. I inhaled. "Can we celebrate our anniversary every month?"

His low laugh multiplied the tingles. "Whatever you like, *Arroyos*."

The Spanish word for Brooks sounded so sexy with the double r rolling off his lips.

I grabbed his suit jacket and tugged him into me. He responded with a warm kiss, molding his mouth to mine. I unbuttoned the top of his shirt and inched my hand inside. His mouth stilled for a second, then he deepened the kiss, which I took as permission to smooth my hand down the naked grooves of his chest. The faint beat of his heart revved up under my touch.

Emboldened by his physical response, I grabbed his hand and guided it to my chest. Would he go for it? I licked his lower lip, and his tongue swept out to tangle with mine. This time he didn't hesitate at all. His fingers swirled my breast and kneaded my nipple. The warmth pooling between my legs turned to full-on wetness, and I swallowed a moan.

"Hey, look, we're here, Officer Halloway," Brad shouted.

Alejandro and I froze. Just then I realized the car had stopped moving.

"Oh jeez," China said. "I guess it's time to stop what we're doing and head inside, then, Officer Jansen."

"That's a swell idea." Brad's loud voice dripped with melted cheese.

Alejandro rolled his eyes as he buttoned his shirt. "Thanks, guys. We get it."

When we exited the vehicle, I noticed the sign for an expensive steak restaurant near downtown.

A voice yelled, "Alejandro!"

"Shit," Brad said, and I looked up to see reporters running toward us.

"I thought you checked out the restaurant earlier, made sure there was nothing going on," said China.

"I did. Something must've just happened. C'mon." He marched us toward the restaurant, but the vultures swooped in to block our path. The lights mounted on the cameras blinded me.

"Alejandro! What do you think about Dariana Romero's death?"

His hand tensed in mine. There was a hitch in his step, then he kept moving.

"What're you guys doing out so late?" China asked.

One reporter pointed down the street. "We were covering a fire at the Greek Orthodox church."

"Is everyone safe?" Alejandro asked.

The reporter smiled. "I'll tell you if you give me a quote."

He shook his head in disgust as we slipped inside.

I cringed as we headed to a private dining room. "I feel like I need a shower."

"They sell their soul for a story on a daily basis." Alejandro sat next to me. "You sure you're up for dealing with those *cabrones?*"

I narrowed my eyes. "I already told you I'm not leaving."

His hand clasped mine atop the tablecloth. "I promise I won't leave you either, Maddie." The sincerity in his dark eyes relaxed me.

"Hey. What are *cabrones?*"

"The closest English word is…" He looked down at his menu. "Illegitimate children."

He wouldn't say the word *bastard* out loud? Now that I thought about it, I hadn't heard him use one swear word in English.

"Is wine okay with you?"

Ooh, he'd drink with me? Maybe I could get him to third base if wine loosened him up enough. I nodded.

"Red or white?"

I winced. "I know zip about wine."

"I don't know much, either." When the waiter arrived, he ordered a bottle of zinfandel.

"Why zinfandel?"

He shrugged. "It's my dad's favorite. And red wine is supposed to pair well with steak."

I fiddled with the napkin in my lap. "Who's Dariana Romero?"

"She was a seven-year-old Guatemalan." He looked down. "She died when she and her mother tried to cross the US-Mexico border. Her mother pointed a gun at Border Patrol, and they accidentally shot the girl instead."

"That's awful."

He nodded.

"It seemed like you wanted to answer their question about her." He nodded again. "What would you have said?"

"I'd say her death was a tragedy. I'd also say that pointing a gun at police never ends well. There are consequences for breaking the law."

"If you said that, they'd probably edit out the first bit."

He scoffed. "They do it to my dad all the time. Make him sound like a cold, uncaring jerk. Hence, my forced silence."

"Sorry, potato."

His scowl lightened.

After the waiter returned with a bottle of red, I felt so mature sipping wine in a fine restaurant. I ordered the filet mignon, and so did Alejandro.

"Baked potato on the side, sir?" the waiter asked.

His eyes danced as he looked at me. "Should I order a potato, Maddie?"

"Sounds kind of like cannibalism to me."

His easy laugh was wondrous to my ears. When the waiter left, we clinked wine glasses.

"To many more anniversaries," Alejandro said.

"Twelve a year." I grinned.

"I can picture us now, years down the road." His eyes took on a far-off glaze. "We'll come home from the hospital after a long day, unwind with a glass of wine in front of the crackling fireplace. Swap stories about saving lives. Admire your shiny Olympic gold medal. Pet the dogs."

A few months ago the hint of such commitment would've freaked me out. But it sounded like a lovely future, up to that last bit. "Dog*sss?*"

"Well, no way we're getting a cat."

"Then they'll be big dogs. Not yippy ones like Charles."

"Deal." He drank some wine. "I always wanted a dog when I grew up. But the life of a major league ballplayer doesn't lend itself to pet ownership. I guess that's one consolation of my injury."

"Oh!" I held up my finger. "I forgot—Dr. Valentine gave me something for you." I dug into my purse to extract a handout.

He read from the paper: "*Emotional issues from sport retirement.*" He quirked an eyebrow. "You think I have issues, Ms. Brooks?"

"Too many to count."

His smile faded as he continued reading. "*Chingar.* I've had every single one of these."

"Oh yeah?"

"Isolation, sadness, losing my identity…Oh, and anger at the circumstances ending my career, frustration over losing my special status. Then there's uncertainty about the future…It's like they did a case study on me."

"But the feelings have grown less intense over time, right?"

He considered my question. "Yes."

"That's what Dr. Valentine says. They're just feelings. They can't kill you. Ride them out, and they'll diminish over time."

His eyes pulsed into me. I hoped my feelings for him never diminished.

The waiter placed our plates in front of us, and my mouth watered. Alejandro set aside the paper. As I cut into my buttery steak, he took a bite of potato.

"How do you taste?" I asked.

His slow grin got my girly bits tingling. "*Delicioso.*"

By the time Alejandro signed the check, I was buzzing from the wine and burning from the smoldering look in his dark eyes. "Ready for home?" he asked.

I nodded. Would he come up to my apartment with me?

"Is Brad all set with the car?" he asked China, and she nodded.

Alejandro rounded the table to guide me out of my chair. His lips snuggled into my neck and kissed near my ear. "Did I tell you how beautiful you look tonight?" Lightheaded, I shivered at his deep, honey voice. "And you smell lovely." He took my hand.

I like this Drunkajandro.

We followed China through the restaurant, and I could see the SUV a short distance away through the glass door. Brad waited by the vehicle as he scanned the parking lot.

"Good thing we have designated drivers," Alejandro said.

We emerged from the restaurant. *Pop, pop.* His hand jerked in mine.

"Down!" China screamed as she lunged in front of us.

Pop, pop, pop. I gasped when Alejandro fell and dragged me to the ground. I hit my chest hard, knocking the wind out of me. After a moment I looked up to see Brad crouched behind the open driver's side door, firing his weapon into a distant line of trees.

He spoke into his wrist. "Shots fired. Hyde Park on High Street."

Shots fired? The rush in my ears made it difficult to grasp the situation. I strained for air as my heart thundered.

Brad discharged more shots, then glanced back at us and added, "Fernando down."

What just happened? Who was Fernando? I tried to push myself up, but Alejandro rolled over me, covering the left side of my body. His groan shredded my heart—in an instant I realized he'd been shot. I groped behind me to touch him.

"Stay down," he wheezed.

Pop, pop. Holy shit, was that a bullet whizzing by? Glass shattered behind me, answering my question.

"Son of a bitch." Brad crept into the driver's seat, staying low. The engine was still running, and somehow he put the car in drive and turned the wheel, placing the vehicle between the line of trees and our prone bodies. Good thing he stayed low because the front window exploded. Pieces of glass rained down on him as he slithered out of the car. "Gonna gut you, motherfucker!"

He looked back at me. "Help's on its way." Then he left the cover of the car and sprinted toward the trees. Why wasn't China helping?

I looked over and froze when I saw her splayed on the ground, blood spreading from under her chest.

"Alex," I cried. When I wiggled out from beneath him, his hiss of pain stopped my heart. I maneuvered myself to face him. "Are you hurt?" His lack of response scared the hell out of me. I ran my hand up his body, and when I reached his elbow, he moaned.

"Oh, my God!" I pulled the collar of his jacket down over his right shoulder, revealing a dark stain that spread with sickening speed as I watched. His eyes fluttered closed, and his head sagged.

I heard a gasp and looked up to see the restaurant's hostess gaping at us from inside the shot-out door. "Call nine-one-one!" I shouted, a second before I heard a siren in the distance.

"Alex." I began to sob. "Stay with me. You promised you wouldn't leave."

Quick footsteps approached. "Fucking son of a bitch," Brad huffed. He dropped to his knees behind Alejandro, and continued cursing as he examined his body and saw the blood. "Are you hit?"

It took a second for me to realize he was talking to me. "I, I don't think so."

He shrugged out of his suit jacket and wadded it into a ball that he handed to me. "Apply pressure to his shoulder. EMS is on their way."

I swallowed, scared to hurt him, and pressed the jacket to the joint. Tears coursed down my face, but Alejandro didn't make a noise. *Stay with me.*

"Oh, baby girl." Brad cradled China's head in his lap, his hands red with blood. "I neutralized the shooter. We're gonna be okay. Fight, baby girl. You got this."

As the siren's wail increased, I smoothed my hand down Alejandro's olive skin. "Don't leave me," I whispered. Tears blurred my eyes. *Don't you dare leave me.*

20
Alejandro

A balloon pops in the distance. *"Get down!"* China screams. *Pop, pop. I can't breathe. Then I'm falling, falling in slow motion. Right before I hit the cement, my body jolts.*

I tried to catch my breath. It was quiet around me, and I realized I was on my back, not my side. The surface beneath me felt softer than concrete.

"He's coming to," Lucia said.

"*Ay, Dios.*" That was my mother's voice.

I opened my eyes to find my entire family and Maddie hovering around me. It looked like I was in a hospital bed, and I noticed Brad, Frank, and one of Dad's agents standing by the wall. I blinked several times, trying to make sense of the scene. One thing was clear: I made it. *I'm alive.*

"Is everyone okay?" I croaked. Mom handed me a plastic bottle of water, and I took it with my left hand since my right arm was in a sling. A few sips soothed my dry throat — they must have intubated me.

Mom floated over me, the back of one hand pressed to my forehead, her other hand stroking my cheek. *"Mi precioso niño,"* she murmured. It was a little difficult to breathe, and I wished she'd give me some space.

"You got shot twice on your right side—your shoulder and elbow," Dad told me. *Dios.* I hadn't heard his voice shake like that since Mateo had collapsed as a five year old. "Sylvia, give him some room." When she stepped back, he added, "But your surgeon says you'll be okay. They removed a bullet from your shoulder, and cleaned up the entry and exit wounds near your elbow."

My gaze found Maddie. "Are you hurt?"

"I'm okay. I didn't get shot."

I exhaled, though the fear in her eyes made my relief short-lived.

"China's in a coma."

Chills went up my spine. That could've easily been Maddie or me, if not for China's heroism. "What's her prognosis?"

Maddie pressed her lips together. "She got shot three times—once in her head."

I gasped. About ninety percent of gunshot wounds to the head were fatal.

"GSW to the right frontal lobe, a penetrating wound," Brad added.

"Did they perform a craniotomy?" I asked.

"That's where they remove part of her skull?" he asked.

I nodded. "Yes, to ease intracranial pressure."

"Yeah. Allie told me they did that."

"That's good—she has a chance." *Please, God. Help China.* Brad slumped by the wall, looking distraught. "Hey, jarhead." He looked up. "Sounds like you actually picked up some medical knowledge attending my lectures."

He shook his head. "Gotta get something out of those boring-ass classes."

"We're all grateful to Brad," Dad said. "He got the shooter. He and China are a big reason you and Maddie are alive."

"Who *was* the shooter?" I asked.

"Mr. President?" Dad's chief of staff walked in and handed him an iPad. "We've made the changes you wanted to your speech."

While Dad read the screen, Mom spoke in uncharacteristically hushed tones to Brad. I noticed Lucia crying.

"Lucy." I held out my hand, and the motion jarred my shoulder—I wasn't going to do that again anytime soon. Her eyes got big when she saw me wince. "I'll be okay, *hermanita*." I curled my fingers, and she finally stepped closer to put her hand in mine. She sniffed as a fat tear rolled down her cheek. She looked like she needed a hug, but I couldn't provide that in my current state. "Is Dane here?"

"He was." She sniffed again. "He had to go to practice."

Mateo's hands were stuffed in his jean pockets, and he stared out the window of the hospital room at the gloomy drizzle.

"Matty."

He kept staring out the window.

"Mateo."

He looked at me with glassy, vacant eyes.

"Did you get any sleep last night?"

"I'm fine."

Now that the anesthesia was wearing off, I noticed how tired they all looked. "None of you slept, huh?"

Lucia shrugged.

"Matty, you need to get some sleep. There's a lounge chair over there." I tilted my head to the corner of the room.

"Karen just checked my numbers. I'm fine."

I sighed and nodded. We were all too fatigued to argue. But I also sensed my siblings were freaked out. "Matty, Lucy." I looked them both in the eye. "The agents did their job, and they'll keep protecting us. We're all safe. We're going to stay safe."

"How do you know that?" Lucia asked, chewing on her fingernail. She wore a volleyball T-shirt that said *KEEP CALM AND ACE IT*.

"I trust our agents, Luce. They're a pain to deal with, but they do a good job."

Mateo frowned, but his shoulders lowered an inch.

Lucia whispered in his ear, and he smiled as he extracted his phone from his pocket. They looked at something on his screen, and she gestured to the chaise lounge over by the wall. When Lucia sat, Mateo sat next to her. He pulled out earbuds, and they listened to something together before Lucia handed one earbud back to him. After a couple of minutes, I was amazed to see Mateo lean his head back and close his eyes. Lucia reached for his jean jacket and draped it over him like a blanket.

"She sure has a way with him," Maddie whispered.

I smiled. "You catch more flies with honey than with vinegar."

Dad glanced at me. "I'll be back after I address the media."

Once he and his entourage left, it was just Maddie by my bedside. "The reporters," I said.

"What about them?"

"They alerted the shooter of our location."

She nodded. "That's what they think. Brad's kicking himself that he didn't call off the dinner once the reporters came 'round."

"Yeah, but how could he have known? It's not like someone's been after me. Who was the shooter?"

"Are you sure you want to talk about this now?"

"Absolutely."

"His name was Alan Eastman; he lived near Highbanks."

"An *American?*" I'd figured it was a Middle Eastern terrorist. That was a threat I knew. To think one of my own countrymen had tried to kill me…I shuddered. "Why'd he do it?"

"We think it was a hate crime."

Brad stepped toward the bed. "Your dad's about to speak—he'll explain it." He reached for the remote and turned on the TV set hanging from the ceiling.

"Now awaiting remarks from the president," the reporter said, "following the horrific shooting last night. We're at University Hospital on the campus of Highbanks University." She nodded. "Here's the president."

Dad approached a podium in the hospital lobby. "I'm relieved to tell you my first-born son, Alejandro, is in stable condition. He's going to make it."

Applause sounded from those gathered. It felt bizarre to be spoken about on national TV. What would their reaction be if I'd died?

"I'm so grateful my son will live. He's studying to become a doctor, learning to heal others just like the tremendous physicians at University Hospital do every day. Their care has been top notch.

"We ask for your prayers for Secret Service Officer China Halloway. She's done an outstanding job protecting our family, but we need to protect her now. She's fighting for her life after taking three bullets. She's in critical condition."

The crowd gathered was silent, and a ghostly pallor hovered in my hospital room.

"Officer Halloway's partner tells me she's a fighter, but she needs your prayers to help that fight." He gripped the podium. "Though details are still emerging from the shooting, we want to share what we know at this point."

Dad was following through on his pledge to be a good communicator.

"Last night, after the attack, Secret Service had to kill the shooter, Alan Eastman. He was an American, a thirty-two-year-old landscaper, married with a young daughter. He had two children, but his seven-year-old son died about a year ago." Dad's mouth trembled, and he took a moment to collect himself. "It appears Mr. Eastman's grief relates to his heinous crime. His son, Joseph, sustained an injury from gardening shears and bled to death waiting for the ambulance to arrive. Mexican gang activity in the area reportedly prevented help from getting there in time."

Dad swallowed. "To our knowledge, his son's death incited a hate for Latinos that burned inside of Mr. Eastman. His wife has cooperated with investigators. She reported that her husband stopped taking his medication for depression last month. He went to a dark place and suffered from paranoia.

"Our country struggles with race relations, like every other country on this planet. We descend into hate of the different, the unknown. But the tragedies I've witnessed, including the recent threat to my son's life, have taught me one thing: we bleed the same." He paused. "Mr. Eastman's son. My son. The brave men and women fighting for our country. Black, white, Latino, Asian, Muslim—we all bleed the same. The color of our skin doesn't alter the color of our blood.

"Our nation has bled with hatred and violence too many times to count. The fear of differences will likely continue, but I pray the bleeding will stop. I do not believe God put us here to tear each other down. We are here to lift each other up. We are here to pursue happiness—pursue the American dream.

"I admit I was terrified when I heard my son had been shot. How dare they hurt my boy! I had revenge fantasies—I felt hate. But when fear and hate threaten to overtake us, we need to turn to love.

"I look to the African Methodist Episcopalian Church in Charleston, South Carolina, for spiritual guidance. A white man shot and killed nine black parishioners who had welcomed him to their Bible study. At a hearing two days later, family members of the deceased addressed the shooter. Their loved ones had died, victims of a vicious hate crime, but they had the audaciousness to *forgive* the killer. They stunned the world by praying for the killer's soul.

"Stirred by their love, I have a message for Mr. Eastman and his family. I want them to hear the message loud and clear. I forgive you."

I gaped at the TV.

"God forgive you. May God have mercy on your soul. We have no room for hate, therefore we will forgive. We are the country love has built, and we will not let hate tear us down. We will get to know our neighbors—who they are beneath the skin. Go deep so you can know their hearts. They bleed the same as you. We all bleed the same. Thank you."

I absorbed Dad's words. Maddie patted my shoulder, and I looked up to find her smiling at me. Mateo had slept through the speech, but Lucia and I shared a knowing look—a look of pride in our father. It wasn't long before agents ushered Dad back into the hospital room.

"Wow, Dad," Lucia said.

I nodded. "That speech was *increíble*."

"Thank you. Really, the credit should go to the Charleston church. Religion gets a bad rap sometimes—people claim it can be stifling and judgmental, and sometimes it is. But that church showed the best Christianity has to offer: a message of love." He glanced at Maddie. "And Maddie deserves some credit, too."

"I do?" Her eyes widened.

"I liked what you said about getting to know someone's heart. If China was out of the woods, I might have used your 'we all taste like chicken to the bear' joke. But I thought it wouldn't be appropriate at this juncture."

Lucia rolled her eyes. "Good call, Dad."

"Speaking of forgiveness, I'd like to speak to my son alone."

Maddie gave my hand a squeeze before she headed to the door.

Dad frowned at everyone else. "Could I have a minute?" When they all cleared out, except for my sleeping brother, I smirked. I hoped Dad's absolute power didn't go to his head.

He sat in the chair next to my pillow. He rested his hand on my knee and exhaled. "I was speaking the truth down there. I was terrified when I heard you were hurt."

"I'll be fine."

"First Lucy gets an eating disorder, then you get shot, all because I wanted to be president." He shook his head. "What horrible thing will befall Mateo?"

"Dad." I frowned at him. "Eating disorders have multiple causes. One cruel photo didn't create Lucy's problem. She had other risk factors."

"Like dating a Democrat, you mean?"

I snorted, then cringed at the pulse of pain up my arm. "Don't make me laugh."

His eyes creased with sadness. "Will you forgive me?"

"There's nothing to forgive." I pointed to my sling. "This will heal. America won't. Our country won't heal without your leadership. The economy's already improved. Jobs are up—full-time jobs. There's more opportunity for every American, just like you promised."

"It's not worth it if my children are in danger. And you're telling only one side of the story—I'm getting hammered in the polls."

"You're getting hammered in the *press*, and your poll numbers are in line with those of any president who tries to make substantive changes. This takes time. Don't let one crazy man deter you, Dad."

He sat back in his chair and sighed. His fingers tapped his thigh as he stared at my sling. "This could be worse, I guess. That's your throwing arm. The wounds would've ended your pitching career if you hadn't given it up already." He shook his head. "The surgeon could've been in here telling us you were done with your major league career, on top of everything else."

I looked down and rubbed my thumb over the sheet. "Sorry."

"Sorry?"

"Sorry I had to give up pitching. I know you wanted to see me go pro."

"*¿Estás loco?*" He leaned over the railing of my bed, fury flashing in his eyes.

I heard the beeps of my heart rate monitor pick up speed.

"Don't you know how proud you make me? You're studying to become a physician! That's every parent's dream." His eyes narrowed. "For as smart as you are, you can sure be dumb sometimes. You thought I wanted you to be on some pitcher's mound? Entertaining fans, instead of saving people's lives?"

"I…" I didn't know what to say.

"Your surgeon came in here while you were still out, you know. The guy's brilliant. Thank God he didn't choose a career in professional sports over saving your life."

"But I don't know if I want to become a surgeon."

Dad widened his eyes, gaping at me like I was a socialist. "Then don't. Become whatever you want. You know, Alejandro, it's flattering you look up to me. But I'm a flawed man. I make many mistakes. I sin, and I seek God's forgiveness. Then I do it again. It's time you stop looking to me, and start looking to yourself. You need to become your own man."

La ceguera. I blinked at him with wide eyes. He'd just ripped me a new one, but not to punish me…to free me. And he was right. I needed to let go of trying to please him all the time. I was too old for that. "You might disagree with my choices."

He appraised me for a moment. "Then I guess I'll have to deal with it."

Both of us turned when we heard a rustling outside my hospital room.

"Let me in, *El Niño!*"

I turned to Dad. "You had my best friend flown here?"

A sly smile was his only response.

"Come in, Jake!" I hollered.

He began talking as he entered the room. "Figures I don't get one scratch on me in Afghanistan, and *you're* the one who gets shot, fucker." He stopped short once he saw Dad. "Holy shit, *El Presidente.*" In a nanosecond, his spine snapped straight, and he saluted. His desert camouflage tunic pulled tight across his chest.

Dad rose from the chair and returned the salute. "Good to see you, Second Lieutenant."

"Thank you, sir." Jake remained at attention.

Dad winked at me. "Should I tell your friend to stand at ease?"

"Hmm. I rather enjoy him forced to be silent like that. Silence from him is so rare."

Dad laughed, then rounded the bed with his hand extended. "Glad you're safe, Jake."

Jake's blue eyes narrowed at me before he smiled at Dad. "Thanks for helping us fight out there, sir."

"The gratitude is all mine. Thank you for your service. I'll let you catch up with my son." Dad left, followed by a couple of agents, and Jake sauntered over to my bed.

"I just got to salute the commander in chief. The guys will be so jealous." He eyed me. "You in a lot of pain?"

"Not unless I move. They've given me some analgesic, but I can't read the IV bag." My eyes strained upward. "Can you turn it so I can see it?"

Hydromorphone, I read once he flipped the IV bag.

"That's some serious shit, bro." Jake shook his head.

"I know that, but how do *you* know?"

"They gave that to my buddy when his foot was blown off."

He spoke so casually, but nausea stirred in my belly. "How do you do it, Jake?"

"It's my job. It's not so bad. We're finally making progress. No more of this limited-engagement bullshit. I'm thinking of staying after my commitment's up."

"You sure?"

"Fuck, yeah. They say leaving your unit's the toughest thing."

I nodded, thinking about my retirement from baseball. "It was tough for me to leave my team, my unit." Then I thought about Maddie. "But you'll find a new unit. A new home."

He aimed his salacious grin at my crotch. "I met Maddie in the hallway. *Your* unit's sure found a new home."

"You're disgusting."

He thumped my shoulder, and I hissed in pain.

He jumped back. "Sorry, *niño!*"

"You better be." A thought entered my mind. "But you can make it up to me."

"Yeah?"

I beckoned him closer and whispered a question that made his eyes light up. After he answered, he lifted his big hand to thump my shoulder again, but stopped himself this time.

He pretended to wipe a tear from the corner of his eye. "So proud of you, *El Niño.*"

"You can leave now. But tell Maddie to come back in."

His waggled his eyebrows. "I sure will, buddy."

I shook my head.

She came in, holding her cell phone.

"Dr. Valentine just called to check up on us." Maddie inhaled a deep breath. "She said we might experience post-traumatic stress."

I nodded. "Flashbacks. Hypervigilance."

"So you've already covered that in psychiatry. I thought for once I knew something you didn't." Her pout made me reach for her—pain be damned—and draw her toward me for a kiss.

She pulled back before her lips touched mine. "I don't want to hurt you."

"Then kiss me."

She grinned. Her hand skimmed through my hair as she gently kissed my mouth. I lifted my head to deepen the kiss, and a shot of pain bolted through my right arm.

Apparently she heard my gasp because she let me go. As she blinked down at me, her eyes filled with tears. "I thought I lost you." Her voice trembled. "I thought you left me."

"I'm sorry I scared you like that."

"You were lying there, unconscious…" A tear slid down her cheek. "China wasn't moving, and I was all alone."

A popping noise exploded in my brain, and I felt my body jerk. The room darkened as my heart thundered.

Maddie grabbed my hand. "Hey."

I squinted up at her, confused. *Where are we?*

"Breathe," she commanded, and I realized how tight my chest felt. I exhaled, then forced in a gulp of air.

"It's March eighteenth, and we're in a hospital room." Her voice soothed me. "What do you hear right now?"

I stilled. "Your voice. My heart rate monitor." The beeps gradually slowed.

"What do you see?"

"Your beautiful brown eyes." She smiled. "Why are you asking me these questions?"

"Grounding—you know, to bring your mind to the present when it's flashing back to the past."

"Oh." I nodded. "We haven't gotten to interventions for PTSD yet."

Her grin widened. "So I *do* know something you don't."

When I smiled, I noticed how much calmer I'd become. I felt anchored in the present, focused on Maddie's shining eyes. Maybe there was something to this therapy thing. I brushed away her tears, and she tilted her cheek toward my palm. Her eyes fluttered shut.

"But I also know something you don't," I teased.

Her eyes opened. "What's that?"

"When I was lying there on the ground, feeling you beneath me…" I took a moment to make sure I was breathing. "I thought I was dying. I thought I'd never see you again."

I watched her chin quiver.

"And I had this huge feeling of regret." I looked at my lap, then back into her eyes. "What if I died without ever having sex?"

Her mouth dropped open, then split into a huge grin that mirrored my own. "That would be quite the tragedy."

"Agreed." I nodded. "We need to act right away to rectify that situation."

Her giggles filled me with warmth. I didn't even mind the zap of pain in my arm when I laughed, too.

Brad poked his head into the room. "Hey, uh, Maddie?"

She looked over her shoulder. "Yeah?"

"Someone's here to see you."

Maddie looked back at me. "My dad must've made good time from Cleveland." She leaned in for a soft kiss. "Be right back, Hotajandro. I'm going to hold you to your word."

We're gonna do it! I bounced out of Alejandro's room and into a hospital hallway filled with agents and police officers.

As I followed Brad, another thought slowed my step. *He has to almost die to want sex with me?*

I shook my head and quickened my pace. There was my old negative thinking rearing its ugly meanness again. *He's shown his love for you in so many ways,* Dr. Valentine had said. *Helping you study. Buying you dinner and flowers. Kissing you.* My heart skipped remembering his kisses, how his touch sparked ribbons of fire through my hair. When his arm healed, I needed more of those. *Don't doubt yourself. You are enough.*

Brad pointed to a hospital room, and I entered. *I am enough.* Mrs. Ramirez stood inside the door, next to the bathroom, her forehead creased with apparent worry. I stopped short. "You met my dad?"

She glanced into the room, and when I saw who waited for me, my breath caught. There, in the flesh, sat the source of my negative thinking.

"Your mother came to see you." Mrs. Ramirez patted my back, though I was barely aware of her touch. I couldn't look away from the woman who rose from the lounge chair with a regal air. She'd filled out a little from her wedding photo, but she was still long and slim. Her skin and eyes were slightly darker than mine, and Braxton was right—she did have the same mouth as me.

"Madison." Her low, resonant voice made my nose burn, a sign of imminent tears.

I looked behind me, seeking escape, but Brad had closed the door.

"It's okay, *niña*," Mrs. Ramirez said. As she clasped my elbow, I realized I was trembling. "Talk to her. Find out why she's here."

But I couldn't move. *Don't cry.* Why had my mother shown up after twenty years? How could she think she even had to right to speak to me?

"You can do it." Mrs. Ramirez pressed my elbow with a gentle nudge. "Your mother loves you."

I shrugged out of her hold and spun to glare at her. "She *loves* me? Is that what you call leaving your two year old? *Love?*" I swiped at my cheek. *Goddamn it.* I was crying again. I didn't want to cry in front of my mother. I didn't want to give her the satisfaction.

My tirade pushed Mrs. Ramirez back. "I'm sorry. You're right—I'm interfering." She reached into her massive handbag and handed me a packet of tissues. "You've been up all night. You must be exhausted."

The fight inside of me disappeared, and I nodded. I wished I could curl up somewhere with headphones and a blanket like Mateo—just block everything out. I pressed a tissue under my nose as I turned back to my mother. She watched us but didn't approach. *Good.* I couldn't handle her right now.

I felt Mrs. Ramirez's hand on my shoulder and lowered the tissue. "I've been talking to your mother," she said. She tilted her head toward the seating area in the room. "She was so scared to come here. She knew you'd be angry. She knew you'd likely reject her."

What about how she'd rejected *me?*

"But she had to see you. She heard about the shooting, and she rushed here to make sure you were okay." Mrs. Ramirez blinked. "As a mother, I know how she feels. I was an absolute wreck when we flew from DC. I had to see Alejandro, hold him, feel him in my arms. And thank *Dios* you weren't hurt." When she looked up to me and stroked my hair, tears streamed down my cheeks.

"I hope you'll listen to your mother. Give her a chance, Maddie." She smiled at me. "I'll leave you two now."

Don't leave! I wanted to shout. But she was out the door before I could speak. I turned back to face my mother and saw she was crying, too.

"I'm so sorry," she choked out before crumbling back into the chair. She sniffed. "I knew this would be hard…"

I looked at her for a moment, trying to really see her for the first time. An intricate turquoise and red beaded necklace rested on her collarbone, paired with a silky black shirt and a turquoise scarf hanging artfully off her shoulder. I had to admit I liked the ensemble.

"But I deluded myself as to just how hard it would be," she continued. "How awful it'd be to see the pain I've caused to the ones I love." Silent sobs racked her body.

I clutched the tissues, feeling cruel just standing here saying nothing. But what could I say? She'd brought this heartache on herself. After a beat, I inched closer. "Would you like a tissue?"

She looked up at me with watery eyes and the beginnings of a smile. "I see you have Thomas's kindness." She plucked a few from the package.

If Dad's so kind, why'd you leave him?

"Does Braxton have that kindness, too?" She mopped the corner of her eye.

I hesitated, unsure if I wanted to engage with her. "Not really."

A small laugh escaped, and she cupped her hand over her mouth to squelch it. Braxton would have been ticked off to hear her laugh at his expense. Picturing his offended scowl made me snicker. Giggles soon erupted from both of us. I slid into the chair catty-corner to hers and let my laughter rip from my gut, freeing and fun. I must have been slaphappy from lack of sleep and the insanity of my long-lost mother sitting across from me.

After a few moments, I let out a long sigh — the conclusion of a good laugh.

Her smile faded as she kept staring at me. Wonder seemed to fill her shining eyes. "God, you're beautiful."

I glanced down. If she thought I was beautiful, she had to know her own beauty as well. I looked just like her. Fatigue weighed down my eyelids, and my vision blurred. "It's been a long night. I think I'm delirious."

"Lord, I thought you'd been shot." My gaze lifted to see her hands twist in her lap. "I thought I'd lost my chance to see you, to talk to you…" She blew out a breath. "To explain why I left. To apologize. You deserve that."

I stiffened. I needed to know why she left. But an apology wouldn't make this right.

"I'm so sorry, Madison."

I jutted out my chin. "It's Maddie."

"You go by Maddie? That's pretty."

How ludicrous that my own mother didn't know my damn name.

"You're thinking my apology is meaningless after twenty years."

I stilled as I met her eyes, wondering how she'd read my mind. I nodded.

"That's how my therapist said you'd react."

Whoa. "You're in therapy?"

She nodded. "I've been in therapy for years. I have recurrent major depression. That's why I had to leave," she added, as her eyes welled up in tears. "The depression."

I laced my arms across my chest to brace myself. "Tell me."

She smoothed out a tissue on her lap. "My first bout with depression was when my mother died." She sniffed. "You didn't know your grandmother. But she was my soul. My heart." Her hand flitted to her chest. "She died from ovarian cancer."

I made a mental note to look up the genetic risk factors.

"Don't worry—I don't have the gene mutation, so odds are you don't either."

"How'd you know about gene mutations?" I asked.

"Oh." She blinked quickly. "You don't know, of course. I'm a nurse."

I took that in. My mother was a nurse, just like Nana had been.

"Why are you smiling?"

"I'm pre-med."

"Wow. That's really impressive, Maddie."

But it has nothing to do with you. Dad and my grandparents were the reasons Brax and I had gotten so far in school. "You were talking about your first episode of depression."

"Yes." She inhaled a long breath. "I met your father right before my mother died, and he tried to help me through my grief. But I was such a mess—I could barely get out of bed. I don't know what he saw in me."

Jeez, she had zero self-worth. Apparently low self-esteem ran in families too.

"He deserved better," she added.

Hot anger rushed through me. "Dad has always loved you, don't you know that?"

Her eyes grew big.

"He never remarried! He's never been with another woman. You *ruined* him."

Her hand covered her mouth, then skated down her neck. "I always hoped he'd find someone."

An unpleasant thought entered my mind. "Did *you?*"

She stared at me, not comprehending.

"Did you find someone?"

She licked her lips, then nodded. "Warren's been with me for about seven years."

A stab of pain pierced my heart. Dad would never get her back now.

"He's the reason I've been doing so well. Warren gave me the confidence to fight my depression, go to school, get a job."

She sounded rather dependent on him.

"How is your father doing, besides his, uh, love life?" she asked.

"Fine." *Not any thanks to you.*

She nodded. "He's teaching history?"

"Yes." It felt strangely disloyal to tell her Dad hadn't finished his doctorate.

"He has his own place?"

"He lives with Nana and Gramps, and Braxton."

"Oh," she said softly.

I frowned at her. Yeah, Dad lived with his parents. Did she think we'd all be just great when she abandoned us?

"How's your brother?"

"He's working on his PhD in poli sci." Her eyebrows lifted. I noticed she hadn't asked about my grandparents. "And not that you care, but Nana and Gramps are doing well."

Her head lowered. "They never approved of me."

That wasn't true, was it? "Well, they took good care of Brax and me."

"I'm so glad. And grateful." She swallowed. "I…*wasn't* taking good care of you. You needed more than I could give." At some point she'd stopped crying, but now the tears started again. "After Thomas married me, I was doing better. I got a job in childcare. But then Braxton came along, and the depression returned. Maybe it was post-partum depression; I don't know."

I could see her hands shaking as she folded a tissue on her lap. A tear splashed on her wrist. "After Braxton was born, I was in a fog. The miscarriages didn't help."

"The miscarriages?" Her use of the plural sickened me.

"We had two. Or three." She shook her head. "I can't remember."

She *had* been in a fog.

"When we made it to the second trimester with a healthy girl..." She lifted her eyes to meet mine. "I felt some hope. I was going to give my baby girl a better childhood than I'd ever dreamed of." She looked away with a soft smile. "Good schools, food in her belly, pretty dresses. Two parents." Her smile plummeted. "But when I brought you home, the depression returned, worse than before. It strangled me." Her palm pressed over her necklace, cradled around her neck like a noose. Her fingers stroked her skin as she continued. "All I wanted was to end the pain. I couldn't stop thinking about killing myself."

I realized my mouth hung open, and I closed it. "Didn't..." My voice was raspy, and I cleared my throat. "Didn't doctors help you?"

"They gave me medication, but it didn't help. It just made me sleepy. I barely left the bed as it was." She dropped her hands to her lap and twisted a tissue between them. "Thomas tried to drag me out of bed, get me to take care of you." When she sobbed, a lump lodged in my throat. "I tried. Please believe me, Madison. I tried." Her voice quivered. "But all I could think about was death. You and your brother were there, needing me, after me all the time...what if I tried to kill myself and inadvertently hurt you? What if you found my body? I had no control over myself. I was panicked about what might happen."

She shifted in the chair, and I considered asking her to stop telling her story. But she kept talking.

"I had to leave. I had to go somewhere, take my life without endangering yours. It was wrong, but I didn't know what else to do. I was desperate. I left right before Thomas got home from school one day, and took a train west. Chicago was where I'd do it. A big city where I was a nobody—where I wouldn't hurt nobody."

Nausea stirred in my gut. My mother had come so close to destroying herself.

She shook her head as tears spilled down her cheeks. "God didn't let me go, though. There was a nun on the train." She exhaled. "That nun kept badgering me with questions, and finally I answered one, just to shut her up. We talked that whole train ride. She took me to a shelter in Chicago." She sniffed. "But I couldn't afford living in the city, working in childcare, so I went up to Wisconsin. That's where I've lived, all these years."

I tried to imagine her life there, all alone. "Where in Wisconsin?"

She seemed to shrink as she peered up at me. "Madison."

I stared at her as my breath whooshed from my lungs.

"I felt closer to you there," she said.

Tears swam in my eyes, and I clung to the armrests. I couldn't breathe, and I knew I was about to vomit. Twenty years of loss pressed down on me, crushing me, making me gasp for air. I cried out. I couldn't take this. I would disintegrate beneath the weight of my pain.

"Oh, Maddie." My mother kneeled by my chair, and her arms slid around me, wrapping me in their surprisingly strong hold. I hadn't given her permission to hug me, but I melted into her all the same. "My sweet girl. I'm sorry. I'm so sorry." She rocked me over and over, and I closed my eyes. I felt the spasms in my chest slowly ease as I breathed in her soft perfume.

"I planned to come back. I did." She smoothed circles on my back. "But I couldn't get myself together. I'd try new meds, a new job, but I kept landing back in the state mental hospital. The last time I was there, I met Warren. He has severe anxiety, so he understands what it's like."

I pulled back. My mother had met her boyfriend at a psychiatric hospital? "Thanks, I'm good now," I said. Miraculously, neither of us was crying at the moment.

She nodded and returned to her chair. "Warren helped me find a job when we got out—an administrative assistant job at the university, with benefits. He had a wonderful outpatient therapist, and I started seeing her, too. We finally found an antidepressant that works for me. And Warren encouraged me to enroll in some college classes—tuition was free for university employees. It took six years, but I got my BSN. Then I got a good job."

Wow. Maybe meeting Warren in the psych hospital wasn't such a bad thing.

"You're about to graduate, too, right?" When I nodded, Mom smiled sadly. "I talked to my therapist about you and my family, about wanting to see you once I got my life together. She was pushing for it, but I was scared to cause you more pain. Then I saw you on TV, holding Alejandro's hand. My daughter, with the son of the president." Her hand covered her heart. "You're so tall. So stunning. So accomplished." She frowned. "And I was even more frightened to see you. You've done so well without me. I don't want to bring you down."

My chin dipped as I gazed at her. How could she ever think I was better off without her?

"When I saw the shooting on the news last night, I didn't think twice. I jumped in the car, drove all night to get here. They wouldn't let me in until one of the agents—Brad is his name? He knew I was your mother the second he saw me. And you're okay. Thank God you're all right. And Alejandro's in stable condition?"

"He was shot twice." My heartbeat spiked just saying the words. "He's going to be fine. But Brad's partner, China, she's touch and go."

"I'll pray for her, then." Mom studied me. "You know this China?"

"Yeah. Pretty well, actually. Secret Service is with Alex and Rez, I mean Lucia, round the clock." I shrugged. "Lucia's my teammate—she's how I met Alejandro. It's a strange world they live in."

"Seems like you're part of that world now, too." A smile lifted her mouth. "Do you love Alejandro?"

I leaned back in the chair. Was she allowed to ask me that question? I barely knew her. But seeing the tracks of tears on her smooth, dark skin—the evidence of her pain from leaving me—I decided to answer. I'd known the answer for some time. "Yes."

Her smile widened. "Then I'm happy for you. But I'm scared, too." Her smile faded. "Will you be safe? Will they try to shoot you again?"

"I don't think Brad will let that happen."

Brad's ears must have been burning because the door opened, and he stuck his head in the room. "Hey, Maddie?"

"How's China?" I asked.

He stepped inside as he blew out a breath. "She's out of the coma. They think she'll make it."

I closed my eyes with a prayer of thanks.

"And she's mad as a hornet," he added with a grin. "Hey, uh, the rest of your family's here. Want me to let them in?"

I looked at Mom. She straightened and wiped her palms up her cheeks, then nodded at me. She seemed petrified.

"Please do," I told Brad.

He returned a moment later and held the door open for my family. Nana scurried in first. "Maddie! Oh, darling." She wrapped me in a hug, and over her shoulder I saw Gramps, Dad, and Braxton file in.

"Well," Gramps said as he stared into the corner of the room.

Nana let me go and gasped.

Dad's jaw dropped, and he jumped back like he was spooked. Spooked by the ghost of his ex-wife. "Ayana," he finally said.

"Thomas." Mom stood tall, but her wobbly voice revealed her anxiety.

I zeroed in on Braxton, wondering how he'd react. Frozen just inside the door, his gaze bounced back and forth between Mom and me. His voice sounded small when he told our mother, "You came back."

Mom nodded.

He rushed toward her, and for a second I worried he'd hit her, but instead he grabbed her in a fierce hug. "Mom!" he cried.

"My boy." She cradled the back of his head and pressed his forehead to her shoulder. "I missed you so much." Tears coursed down her face, and I had to look away so I didn't resume crying myself.

I noticed Dad off to the side, his hands jammed into his pockets as he shuffled his feet. I found my way to his arms, and he clutched me tight.

"How're you holding up?" he whispered.

My throat felt tight. "Not well. Kind of in shock."

He pulled back and gave me a half-smile, though his eyes seemed troubled. "Me, too."

"Mom was severely depressed, Dad. She thought she was saving us by leaving. She thought she wasn't good enough for you."

He grimaced as he turned to look at Mom. She spoke to Braxton as Nana and Gramps watched from the other side of the room. Nana did not look happy.

"Dad." I squeezed his hand, and he looked back at me. "It wasn't your fault she left. Not mine or Braxton's either." His mouth trembled.

"Now that she's come back to us, you can let her go." I squeezed his hand again. "It's time to let her go."

He stared at me for quite a while. Then he exhaled a long sigh. "She really hurt us, Maddie. I don't care how depressed she was—you don't do that to your family. But I don't want to talk about her now. I want to talk about you." He tucked a strand of hair behind my ear. "I was so worried! I can't believe Secret Service made us wait so long to see you."

"Yeah, they kind of freak out when a protectee gets shot."

"I can imagine. But Alejandro will be okay?"

I nodded.

"I know I suggested you date someone new after Jaylon, but does he have to be so high profile? What if *you're* the one who gets shot next time?"

"I'm sorry you guys were so worried. But there are no guarantees in life, Dad. Love means risk. And I do love him."

He scowled at me. "Then it's about time you introduce me to that famous boyfriend of yours."

I smiled at him. "You got it."

As expected, when they met, Alejandro impressed the hell out of my father. Even with the danger his position added to my life, Dad couldn't help but love his polite, intelligent responses. And when Alejandro had chatted with Nana and Gramps about the changing landscape of healthcare in America—from both clinical and administrative perspectives—they'd fallen for him, too. Braxton hadn't been such an easy sell. But at least he hadn't been too rude, considering Alejandro was stuck in a hospital bed. Mom had stood quietly to the side, taking it all in.

She'd only stayed one night before she had to go back to Wisconsin for her next nursing shift. She and Dad had taken a moment for a private conversation before an awkward family lunch at a restaurant, during which Nana refused to speak to her. When it was time for my family to return to Cleveland, it had been clear Mom wasn't welcome in Nana's home. So I'd invited her to spend the night in my apartment. It had only taken her one night of sleeping on Shitty to promise to buy me a new sofa. *Score!* She'd also invited Braxton and me to Wisconsin. But neither of us wanted to rush a relationship with a woman we barely knew. I'd been too busy with school and volleyball then, anyway.

I'd exchanged a few emails with Mom as I prepared for the national selection camp. And though Brad and China hadn't allowed Alejandro to attend my college graduation — too risky, they'd said — Secret Service had permitted him to accompany me to the Olympic Training Center in Colorado Springs, where there was already good security in place. He'd really calmed my nerves at the selection camp.

There I'd encountered volleyball players from universities across the country, including women I'd met last year from Stanford, Washington, and Penn State. The setter from Penn State was much better than Nina, and my hitting elevated with her talents. We'd all been star-struck upon meeting the national team coach, Karch Kiraly, who had completely dominated when he'd played. He was the LeBron James of volleyball, we joked. Coach Kiraly tested us in every way possible — blocking, hitting, diving, setting, passing, jump serving, strength training, plyometrics, mental training, video analysis…I'd complained how sore I was every night in the condo Brad had secured for Alejandro and me.

Alejandro started physical therapy in the training room at the center, and he must have been sore too, but he never complained. He'd just told me how well I was doing, and massaged my legs with his good arm while he quizzed me on p-chem. I knew how tough it was to come back from injury, and I asked him how he kept such an upbeat attitude. He'd just said he was motivated to heal as quickly as possible. His response had puzzled me — what was the sense of urgency?

Now that it was May, I had come to visit Alejandro in DC before my next trip to Colorado for the second round of tryouts. I giggled as he pulled me into a third-floor bedroom and closed the door in Brad's face.

"Wow, this room's huge," I remarked.

"Bedroom three-oh-three, madam." He extended his right arm with a flourish and no hint of a wince. He'd gotten out of the sling a month ago, and I was pleased to see how swiftly he'd healed from surgery. "My home for the past two months."

"Nice." I noted the masculine décor. Late-spring sunlight filtered in through the two windows. "But not as impressive as the Lincoln Room."

"I told my mother if they were making me stay at the White House, I wouldn't live in the Lincoln Room, of all places. That's for dignitaries, people more important than me. Besides, here I'm next to the gym for my PT, and on a different floor from my parents and brother."

"You forgot the most important reason for staying clear of that room." He cocked his head at me. "Hmm?"

"When they shot Lincoln, they killed him." A flutter of fear kicked up my heartbeat, and I stepped forward to lace my fingers through his. "You lived, thank God. You don't belong there."

"I lived for a very important reason." He drew up our enjoined hands and pressed a warm kiss to my knuckles. "I plan to make good on my hospital bed promise."

My heart now full-on galloped as his dark eyes seared into me. "You sure you're ready?"

"Absolutely sure. I've been pushing hard in PT, waiting for this moment."

I smirked. So *that* was his motivation.

"And after today, we won't get to see each other much while you travel the world, Ms. USA Volleyball."

"I made the first cut, but I still have another selection camp to go before I make the traveling team."

"Please," he scoffed. "You're ten times better than those other middle blockers."

I grinned. His presence at the first camp had helped my confidence soar. And now I wanted to help with *his* confidence. I knew his performance our first time sleeping together would be important to him — he performed so damn well at everything else in his life. He'd also shown such eagerness during the stolen moments the past month when I'd shown him how to pleasure me. As I looked up at him, awash with anticipation, I nibbled my lower lip.

"You have the sexiest mouth, *Arroyos*." He nudged in to kiss me, spicy and sweet. I tasted cinnamon from the Mexican dessert we'd just shared in the Palm Room. He let go of my hands and clutched my head as he deepened the kiss. My fingers darted down his chest, unbuttoning his shirt.

When my fingertips made contact with the hard planes of his chest, he shivered. "Are my hands cold?" I asked.

His headshake was instant. "You're hot. So hot."

"Why thank you, Hotajandro," I giggled. I ripped his unbuttoned shirt off his shoulders and delighted in his lean, sculpted chest. My gaze glided over the puckered, round scar near his shoulder and up to his face. "You can undress me, too, you know."

He had my shirt up over my head before the words left my mouth. I stood before him in my bra, blue miniskirt, and flats. My hands perched on my hips, waiting for him to make his next move. He stared at me, reading the challenge in my eyes, before pitching forward to nuzzle kisses between my breasts. When he unhooked my bra while keeping his face buried in my cleavage, I inhaled a staccato breath. Wetness gathered between my thighs, zinging a line of pleasure straight to my brain. I stood on my tiptoes, bringing me closer to his touch.

I fumbled for his belt as his mouth kissed hotness down my belly. His clever fingers kept kneading my breasts. When he straightened to kiss my collarbone, I shucked down his pants in one swift move, leaving him in black briefs with his pants around his ankles. His mouth lifted from my skin, and his eyes, bright and deep, met mine.

He smirked as he stepped out of his pants and kicked them to the side. His briefs tented with his arousal. "Let's see what's under your skirt, shall we?"

I closed my eyes as he smoothed his hands down my ribcage. He tucked his thumbs into my waistband and pushed the skirt down my legs, my skin on fire from the trail of his touch. As I opened my eyes, he stepped back. His gaze roved from my feet, over my panties, up my naked chest, to my face. "*Hermosa*," he murmured. "So beautiful." His eyes burned.

And I couldn't get enough of his powerful, lean body. His skin was the perfect shade of brown, an olive tone that highlighted the cut of his muscles. I loved his dark features—the black of his hair, the faint shadow where he'd shaved, and the depth of his eyes. His intense, intelligent eyes.

His Adam's apple bobbed with what looked like a nervous swallow as we stared at each other. I needed him to relax. "You're quite the fine specimen, Alex. You put the *sexy* in the XY chromosome."

He tossed his head back as he laughed. "Sexy science humor?" His eyes danced. "You're such a nerd."

"C'mon, you love it."

"Yeah?" He stroked his chin. "Well, *you* put the XX in exxcstasy, woman."

With a grin, I shook my head. "That was so dumb."

"You started it!"

We laughed into each other's mouths as we resumed kissing. My hands were everywhere—the sharp curve of his shoulder blades, the raised line of scars on his elbow, the firm muscle of his butt. He sucked in a breath as I reached beneath the elastic of his briefs to cup his bottom.

I unlatched my lips from his and looked up at him. "Let me see you?"

He looked down at me with a half-lidded gaze, and nodded.

I peeled his briefs over his springy erection and stepped back to admire him.

How could he have kept himself under wraps for so long? It was a crime against women everywhere. As I gazed at him, he grew bigger. I tried to remember the words I'd rehearsed.

"Estás como un caballo," I said sweetly.

His mouth dropped open as his eyes blazed.

22
Alejandro
★ ★ ★

I wasn't sure which was the bigger turn-on: Maddie telling me I was hung like a horse, or her saying those words in Spanish. Before I met her, I'd believed in waiting until marriage for sex. Ironically, meeting the woman I wanted to marry had challenged that belief. And I knew I needed her. *Now.*

I scooped under her arms to lift her and carry her to bed.

"Your shoulder!" she cried.

But I didn't feel any pain. I was done with injuries stopping me from achieving my dreams. When she figured out I wasn't putting her down, she wrapped her legs around me, and the exquisite brush of her panties against my erection almost made me come right then. She smelled so good, so enticing.

I lowered her to the sheets like the precious jewel she was, her gorgeous legs lengthening to the foot of the bed. I'd never seen a woman with such taut abs, practically a six-pack. Her curls fanned out on the pillow as she stared up at me. Her chest rose and fell with each panted breath, and I realized my breath had quickened as well. I swung my leg over to straddle her, and she grinned as her eyes traveled down my torso. My penis twitched from the heat of her gaze.

When she reached for me, my body seized. She took me in her grasp and gently tugged the base of my shaft while stroking her fist up and down my length. Her touch on the underside of my shaft was particularly mind-blowing. "W-W-Won't last," I stuttered.

"That's quite okay," Her grin took on an evil glint. "We've got plenty of time for more."

Dios, the pressure rocketed through me. The fire kept building, and I couldn't quench it. Nor did I want to. Her strokes were molten bursts, stoking the fire higher, more pressure, higher even still...in a second I released all over her panties.

My eyes rolled back into their sockets. Maddie stimulating me like that was a thousand times better than doing it on my own.

"Bet you wish you hadn't waited so long."

Understatement of the year. I nodded feebly as I opened my eyes. "I made a mess."

"Not at all." She grinned and lifted her hips beneath me. "Help clean up by taking these off, though."

I slid off her panties and tossed them to the floor. When I looked down at her neat patch of hair, I inhaled. My eyes feasted on her perfection...grooves of soft brown skin tapering into exciting territory down below. This was happening.

"I loved watching you come," she said.

I grinned, and she gazed up at me, her brown eyes intense.

"I love *you*," she added.

¡Cielos! Heaven. Having made the decision to have sex, I only felt more ready after she said that. I knew my love for Maddie was good and strong. My feelings for her didn't diminish my faith—they deepened it. God had given her to me, and I wanted her to feel my love and gratitude. I zoomed down to kiss her. "I love you, Maddie." Our tongues touched and played. "And I'll enjoy watching you even more than you liked watching me."

When my mouth moved south to suckle her breast, her chest rose with a gasp of air. I teased her nipple with my tongue and skimmed my fingers down the firm ridges of her abdomen. Her muscles tensed when my fingers feathered lower and touched her wetness. Her small cry egged me on, and I slid one finger into her soft folds. I lifted my mouth from her breast to watch her writhe below me. She squeezed her legs together, then opened for me, and her head tilted back with a long moan as I continued stroking her, now with two fingers. "Yes," she murmured, her husky voice accelerating the surprising return of my hardness.

"Keep going," she demanded as her bottom grinded into the sheets. I knew the moment I'd found her sweet spot—she gasped and her back arched. I planned to love the hell out of that spot. My fingers swirled, causing her breaths to come even faster. Her palms pressed against the sheets, and I swept her right hand into my left to draw it to my mouth. I pushed wet kisses to the pads of her fingers as my fingers pulsed into her swelling wetness below. She locked her eyes onto mine as her chest rode up and down. "Oh," she cried. "*Alex.*"

Her eyes clamped shut, her mouth opened wide, and her hips bucked off the bed. Her pleasure tightened around me, flooding my fingers with heat. She shuddered with a breathy moan, and I grinned broadly as I watched her come. I did that. I made her feel that way. My pride was a mountain, higher than any stupid athletic or academic achievement. Jake had given me some good tips.

I lifted her arm over her head as I climbed back up her body to swallow her moans with my kisses. *Dios*, I loved her mouth. A musky scent now mingled with her usual calming aura. Her eyes opened, gazing up at me with what looked like reverence. I certainly revered her.

"Bet you wish I hadn't waited so long," I teased.

She giggled. "Jerk." Her eyes twinkled. "But we're not done yet."

Her words sparked more heat inside of me. "I was hoping you'd say that." I reached for the bedside table and extracted a condom from the drawer.

"Way to be prepared," she said as she sat up.

Brad had slipped me the condoms when I left the hospital. It wouldn't exactly look right if the press caught me buying them.

"Let's get this on you." She ripped the condom open, and I forced a long exhale as she rolled it on. *You have excellent self-control*, she'd told me once. That control was definitely getting tested today. Her touch was like striking a match against my trembling skin, lighting a fire within.

She stroked me as she kissed my chest. Her tongue darted out and licked my sternum. My hands wove through her curly hair, and I lowered us to the mattress, hovering above her. "Yes," she breathed. I felt the building force of my insane attraction to her. When she guided me inside,

I stopped breathing for a second. She surrounded me, compressed me, squeezed me, owned me. The fire blazed, and my body went completely stiff. I rode the high and rocked into her, matching her rapid breathing. Moments later, her body lifted, almost floated off the mattress. She clung to me, cried out, then sank back down with a long sigh.

I rolled to the side and pressed her to me, our skin slick with sweat. My eyes were closed, and I focused only on the feel of her in my arms. I was still buried inside her, and it wasn't a bad place to be. My pounding heartbeat made it feel like I'd just run a 5K.

"We have explosive chemistry, Dr. Ramirez," she said.

I opened my eyes to see her grinning at me. "*Another* science joke, *Arroyos?*" But I was feigning annoyance. I loved our chemistry — physical, emotional, and intellectual. I couldn't wait to conduct more bonding experiments with her.

Bounce, bounce, bounce. It felt amazing to have a basketball in my hand again, like the ball was an extension of my arm. And playing three-on-three on an outdoor court on the White House lawn? That was special, too. Maddie, Braxton, and I faced off against Lucia, Dad, and Dane, and I was excited to have a Maddie-caliber athlete on my side. As I'd predicted, she had qualified for the national travel team. We were celebrating with one last June weekend together before she traveled to tournaments in Europe, and I started med school rotations.

I watched Maddie dart around Lucia in an attempt to get open, but my sister moved in place to guard her. When Dane reached his long arm in to steal the ball from me, I evaded him easily. But it wasn't so easy to see around his gargantuan frame. After a couple of dribbles, I looked to Braxton, who broke away from Dad and hustled to the basket. I lobbed my pass above the rim, and he leaped to dunk it. The timing was perfect, and the ball slammed through the basket with a satisfying swoosh.

"Yes!" I pumped my fist. Sweat slid down my back in the June sunshine.

After high-fiving her brother, Maddie panted with her hands on her hips. "That was a thing of beauty."

Dad wheezed as he retrieved the ball, then glared at Maddie. "I thought you said your brother hadn't played in eight years."

"He hasn't!" Maddie's grin was cunning. "I just forgot to mention he turned down several basketball scholarships."

"You turned down money for college?" Dad turned to look at Braxton.

Braxton shrugged. He *did* look like a natural in low-hanging basketball shorts. "Schools make too much money off their athletes. They should pay them."

"Universities do pay their athletes, with a full scholarship," Dad replied.

I exchanged a nervous look with Maddie. We'd wondered about the wisdom of passing along Dad's White House invitation to her brother.

Braxton shook his head. "The NCAA makes millions off their slaves. A scholarship's a drop in the bucket."

"For places like Highbanks, maybe," Dad said. "But so many schools lose money off their revenue sports. How could they afford to pay their athletes?"

"Are we playing, or what?" Lucia asked. "'Cause Maddie's going down."

"You wish, freshman." Maddie's eyes blazed.

Lucia stuck up her nose. "I'm a sophomore now!" Her T-shirt featured a player jump serving, with the words *Kiss My Ace*.

"Just be careful, everyone," Mom piped in from the sideline. "Don't get injured. Especially you, Maddie—your national coach would kill us." She sat under an umbrella next to Mateo and China, with other Secret Service agents standing nearby. "You too, Adolfo. You're too old to play with these kids!"

Dad grunted.

Mateo strummed his guitar and sang, "He's over the hill, he drives a Seville…" He played a lively bridge, and Dane nodded his head to the beat.

"Sing it, brothah!" he hollered.

"But he's got a strong will, he won't stop until, his heart will stand still, they'll have to defill…" His fingers flew over the strings. "…ibrate."

Dad glowered. "I *bought* you that guitar, traitor!"

When Mom smacked Mateo, Lucia and I laughed. "Don't sing about your father having a heart attack!" she chided.

"It's defibrillate, Matty, not defillibrate," I said.

"But that doesn't rhyme."

China shook her head, and I looked across the court to see Allison and Frank smiling at her. Though she wasn't ready to return to duty, she'd made good progress recovering from her injuries.

"Enough of this." Dad took the ball and dribbled it down the court with the rest of us flying behind him, trying to catch up. Dane's loping stride reached the paint first, and he caught Dad's pass to make an easy lay-up. Dad fist-bumped Dane as I took the ball behind the baseline. I passed it to Braxton and jogged toward the opposite basket.

Braxton executed a spin move that left Dad in the dust, and he shoveled a clean pass to Maddie, who drove for the basket. Lucia was on her like beans on rice, but Maddie pivoted and made a jump shot that found the basket.

That's my girl. I winked at her.

Dane received Dad's inbound pass, and blew by me as I contemplated kissing Maddie. ¡*Chin!* I was supposed to guard Dane. I sprinted behind him and was able to reach around to wave an arm in his face as he shot a three. The ball bounced on the rim but careened to the side. "Damn!" Dane said.

Braxton nabbed the rebound, and I backpedaled toward the other basket. He sailed a pass to me over Dane's head, and I snagged the ball. Dane was on me right away, and I dribbled behind my back to avoid his big paw. Lucia stuck to Maddie too tightly for me to pass to her, and Braxton wasn't in position yet. However, I saw a sweet lane to the basket. When I drove in for the shot, Dane jumped with me and collided with my right elbow.

Needles of pain shot up my arm but I managed to follow through with the shot, and the ball found net. When I came down, my hand cradled my elbow.

"Alex!" Maddie shouted. She pushed Dane to the side and lifted my T-shirt sleeve to take a look at my scars.

"Shit, I'm sorry," Dane said, his hands splayed open. "Are you okay, man?"

China stood and took a few steps toward me, worry evident on her face. The shaved patch of hair above her forehead hadn't grown back in all the way yet, making her eyes look bigger.

But Maddie's warm touch on my sweaty skin had already made me feel better. "Dr. Brooks is on it, guys. Don't worry."

Maddie searched my face. "Are you really okay?"

"The surgeon told me the nerves will take some time to heal," I told her. "I'll be fine."

"Come get some lemonade, *niños*," Mom said. She smiled, but I could hear the tremor in her voice. She was still on edge after the shooting.

To appease her, I said, "Okay, let's give the other team a break. They're probably tired of losing."

"*You're* the losers," Lucia said.

Maddie grinned as I poured her a drink.

The fresh-squeezed lemonade went down easy on such a hot day. I had to admit I hadn't minded eating food prepared by the White House chef the past few months. But I was itching to return to my condo so I could study for boards in peace.

"Alejandro, Alejandro," sang Mateo, playing a salsa beat on his guitar. He continued, "Fernando..."

I stopped short and looked at China. "*That's* where you got my code name Fernando? The Lady Gaga song?"

She nodded. "You're quick, Fernando."

"And I'm Roberto," Mateo said, then sang, "Don't call my name..."

I rolled my eyes.

"What am I?" Lucia asked.

Dane grabbed her. "You're adorable." She giggled as he leaned in for a kiss. "And sweaty," he added.

"You sweat *way* more than I do." She pushed him toward one end of the court with a smirk.

Maddie and Braxton had drifted to the other end of the court. I had an idea what they were discussing: visiting their mother in Wisconsin. Maddie wanted to go before she left for Europe, but Braxton was still waffling. I noticed Mom sneaking glances their way as she pretended to listen to Mateo's song.

After meeting Maddie's mother and learning about Maddie's own struggle with depression, Mom had identified her platform as first lady: mental health. She'd already started planning an education program for the upcoming school year, in collaboration with the National Alliance for Mental Illness.

Mateo continued strumming the guitar as he shifted into another Lady Gaga song. I brought my glass of lemonade closer to Dad, and we watched him play for a few minutes.

"I can't believe my youngest is almost done with high school," Dad said. "Mateo sure grew up fast."

I nodded. "That *is* weird he'll be looking at colleges soon. But he's still a snarky teenager."

"He has his moments. He's a sensitive kid, more sensitive than most. Probably helps him as a musician."

Holy hell, did my younger brother just sing about riding a *disco stick?* I glanced at Dad but he hadn't seemed to catch the reference. "I hope he finds a girl to take care of his sensitive heart," I said.

"It's probably just a matter of time. If he's like his older siblings, that is."

We watched Lucia gaze up at Dane, her eyes lit up like firecrackers as she laughed at something he said.

Dad slumped. "My children are growing up—they don't need me anymore. I feel old."

"You're not old."

"You try playing against twenty year olds when you're almost fifty, and you'll see how it feels."

I chuckled.

He turned to me with a measured gaze. "What do you see for your future when you're my age?" His dark eyes bored into me. "What do you want, Alejandro?"

I swallowed. "I want to marry Maddie."

"I gathered that already."

I smiled. "And three kids would be nice." I stared at the soft curve of Maddie's hips.

Dad's eyebrow lifted. "This should be good—you with three screaming children. What goes around, comes around. And what about your career? Or do you plan to be a stay-at-home dad to all these children?"

I grinned. "Oh right, my career." My smile faded. "I think I want to be an orthopedic surgeon." I gauged his reaction. "I'll do a sports medicine fellowship after residency, so I can work with athletes. Help them through their injuries."

"That sounds perfect for you." Dad nodded. "So you'll be done with your training at age forty, then."

I laughed. "Just before that, I hope."

However long it took, I knew it would fly by with Maddie at my side. I turned to see her hand cover her mouth as Braxton spoke to her. She must have felt my stare because she turned and smiled. She said something to her brother, then headed toward me. I couldn't take my eyes off her.

"Looks like a bright future for you, son." Dad patted my shoulder.

I know. Her smile lit up my world.

"Mr. President?" Dad's chief of staff had materialized on the court, and Dad went to speak to him as Maddie reached my side.

"You look happy," I said.

She clasped my hand. "Brax just told me Dad might have a girlfriend."

"Really? He moves fast."

"Yeah, it only took him twenty years." She nudged her shoulder into mine, and I smiled.

"Twenty years is nothing." I leaned in and whispered, "I want to love you for a lifetime, *corazón.*"

Her eyes gleamed. When she kissed me, I felt her love flowing into me, filling my heart.

Excerpt from book three, *Spiked*,
coming late 2016

I. JESSICA

The stale odor of spilled beer and unwashed laundry assaulted me as I walked down the humid hallway, confused by the blown-up Disney images of Elsa, Anna, and Olaf lining the dorm walls. Was this a university or a preschool?

Next to me, Mom wrinkled her nose. "I wish Highbanks had placed you in one of their newer dorms."

"No, this is perfect," Dad said, behind me. We'd piled my stuff into a cart that he now pushed, and it was difficult to hear him over the squeaking wheels. "The quintessential college experience: fifties architecture, no air conditioning."

I pursed my lips. Why had I wanted my parents to stay together again? They disagreed on everything.

"Guys," I said, "we already went over this. Canfield Hall is where most of the freshman swimmers live, 'cause it's close to the pool." I rolled my wheeled suitcase to a stop in front of room 220.

From our online chats over the summer, I knew my roommate had planned to arrive on campus yesterday. She'd said she'd need time to adjust to a new time zone. Australia was a long ways away. I knocked on our door, but there was no answer. A thrill zinged up my spine when I extracted my key from my pocket. *My new home.* The key signified freedom and fun.

When the door opened, the contrast between the two halves of the room startled me. My side was ugly, sterile, plain. Mackenzie's exploded with color and energy. She'd lofted her bed frame to provide more space, and posters of shirtless men covered every centimeter of wall below and above the mattress. A fan on her desk rotated, pulsing the warm air.

"Well." Mom set down her handbag and approached a muscled sportsman with a critical eye. Despite the heat, she looked perfectly put together in a pale pink silk blouse, black pencil skirt, and beige pumps. "Alex Rance, Richmond Tigers," she read. "From the AFL. What's that?"

"Australian Football League." I heaved my suitcase onto the naked mattress. A bead of sweat slid down my spine. "Mackenzie's a huge sports fan. She wants to become Australia's equivalent of Erin Andrews."

"Who?" Dad asked.

"She's an ESPN reporter," Mom said, her eyes still on the poster. "I met her once at a fundraiser." As a US senator, Mom attended plenty of those. "We discussed the challenges of working as a woman in a man's world."

Dad and I shared a smirk. Mom was a staunch feminist.

He scanned the bare walls, hands on his hips. "You need to spice up this room. Want me to paint something for you?"

I straightened. He would do that for me? "Sure. I guess."

He fiddled with the collar of his light blue button-down shirt. "If you don't like it, you don't have to display it."

"I love all your paintings, Dad." He'd inspired me to major in art at Highbanks.

"That will get you going again, finally," Mom said to him. "You always love immersing yourself in a new piece of art."

Dad didn't reply, but from the tightness around his eyes, I knew what he was thinking: *Get off my back.* His last gallery show had been almost a year ago, and Mom had been on his case to start painting again. But his muse wouldn't be rushed, especially since the arguments between them had increased. Their spats poured ice water over his creative flame.

Mom fanned herself. "You sure we can't convince you to live with your brother, honey?"

Before I could reply, Dad said, "Jessie wants her own life, Lois. She doesn't want to live in Dane's shadow. Plus, she'll be closer the art building here."

"Don't lecture me like I don't know my own daughter." Mom folded her arms across her chest, and my stomach clenched. "I appreciate the value of struggle for building resilience." She waved her hand toward the chipped wood bedframe. "Like living with this cheap furniture. But, Patrick, she'll endure enough stress as a college student-athlete. Do you have any idea how packed her schedule will be?"

Dad scowled. "This is a dig about how I haven't been involved with Dane's volleyball career?"

I stifled a groan. Two years ago, right before my mother lost the presidential election to Adolfo Ramirez, we'd learned my dad had cheated on her. He'd been distant for some time, and after that revelation it all made sense. But he'd ended the affair, and my parents had committed to saving their marriage. They'd gone to couples counseling and for a while I'd been simultaneously embarrassed and relieved to see them kiss and hold hands. But after my dad's gallery show didn't do so well last September, he'd become grumpy. They'd started to bicker more. And I couldn't stand listening to their arguments.

Tuning them out, I texted my older brother. Maybe his flight from Colorado hadn't left yet.

Save me. They're fighting again.

Fuck. They suck.

I grinned, grateful Dane didn't act like the twenty-one-year-old college senior he was. He texted again:

Just boarded in CO Springs.
Layover in Denver then home at 5.
I'll rescue you.

This was the second Olympic developmental camp he'd attended, and he had a good shot of making the national volleyball team after he graduated from Highbanks next May. I would *kill* to be on the national swimming team. I had less than two years of college training before the Olympic trials—two years to prove I was the best breaststroker in America. Just thinking about it made me giddy.

I replied:

The rents will be long gone by then.
Mom has a thing at the Statehouse.

Not too late to change your mind and live with me.

I sighed as I looked at the scratched linoleum floor. Dane lived in a sweet two-bedroom condo off-campus with probably ten times the square footage of my dorm room. But living with him meant I wouldn't get to know my teammates or other students as well. I wouldn't live a normal college life. And after all the publicity of my mother running for president, I wanted normal. Besides, I didn't want to be a third wheel.

You and Lucia don't want me around.

Luz loves you, you know that.
We're psyched we both have our sibs here.

I gulped, picturing olive skin and dark, soulful eyes. Lucia's younger brother, Mateo, was new on campus this year, too.

My choice to attend Highbanks had been a no-brainer, given I'd grown up here in the Midwest and the school had a top-ten NCAA swim team. Mateo's decision had been more of a surprise. He reportedly liked the music school, but I bet it had come down to security. Secret Service already had Highbanks figured out. They planned to house him with Lucia in a safe off-campus house.

Did Mateo move in yet?

Not sure. Sec Serv won't tell Luz anything.
Boarding door just closed. Will call when land.
Tell Dad to stop being a dick.

It was more like Mom was being the dick, but I'd have to save that discussion for later.

I felt Dad's hand on my shoulder as I texted goodbye.

"Bested by the cell phone once again. We're clearly not needed here." He smiled.

Mom looked in the mirror and brushed her fingers through her hair. Hers was blond, short, straight, perfectly coiffed. Mine was blond, long, curly, imperfectly feral. "Sorry we got heated, honey." She patted her hair, then looked at me. "I know you don't like it when we argue."

Then why do you do it?

"You'll be okay, then, Jessie?" Dad's deep blue eyes assessed me.

"More than okay." I grinned. "I've been waiting for college for forever."

Mom approached me. "I remember feeling the same way, my first day at Yale. You too, Patrick?"

"Sure." Dad paused and shook his head. "Actually, I was scared shitless. The other art students seemed so sophisticated, and here I was, this poor kid from Ohio."

"Aw." Mom rubbed his shoulder. "I didn't know that. I wish I'd been there for you back then."

Dad nodded. "Me, too." He reached for her hand.

I exhaled.

"So your mother didn't take you to school?" Mom asked.

Dad shook his head. "She couldn't get off work. I had to make the trip to New York by myself."

As much as my parents annoyed me, I had to admit I was glad they'd helped me move in. But now it was time for them to leave. "Thanks for helping, Mom and Dad."

"That's code for *Get the hell out*." Mom laughed, then hugged me.

Dad squeezed me tight. "I'll miss you. We'll be at all your swim meets; we promise."

Butterflies fluttered in my stomach in anticipation of my first college swim meet.

Once my parents left, I finished unloading the cart and returned it to the dorm lobby. I was stuffing my last shirt into the overcrowded closet when the door swung open.

"Roomie!" Mackenzie squealed as she bopped in.

She was about five-five with a dark brown ponytail. What I would give for that straight, sleek hair…She wore a Highbanks Swimming T-shirt, and her gym shorts showcased tanned, muscular legs.

"Hey. I'm Jessica." I reached out my hand.

She frowned at my hand and scooped me into a hug. "Good onya, you're tall!" She looked up at me. "You're almost two meters, then?"

I chewed on my lip. "Um, I'm six feet."

"Ace." She scanned the room. "So, what do you think?"

"Too hot in here." I grimaced. My curls had seized up from the humidity, and I felt sweat at the nape of my neck. "Love your posters, though."

She brightened. "Right? He's my favorite." She ducked under her bed and patted the muscles of an intense-looking guy with a shaved head. "David Zaharakis, from Essendon footie." Her hand fluttered over her heart. "He's scored over a hundred goals."

"Awesome." I had no idea what she was talking about. Were goals like touchdowns?

She straightened. "Hope I meet a guy as cute as him here. You're coming to the swimmer party tonight, right?"

"I didn't know about a party."

"Now you do. It's at the swimmer house. We're going."

The giddy feeling returned. My first college party!

She held up her phone. "Elyse texted me about it. She wants your number, too. What is it?"

Elyse was a senior on the team who had followed me on Instagram. After I told Mackenzie my cell number, I asked, "What's the swimmer house?"

"A bunch of senior guy swimmers have a house on south campus." She stripped off her T-shirt and turned to her closet. Like most swimmers, she had no need for modesty. "Is your mum here?"

"She had to leave."

"Oh, poop. Dad wanted me to meet her." She tugged a camisole over her bra. "He says she's famous."

She didn't know my mother? "You know she ran for president, right?"

Mackenzie blinked at me. "President of the United *States?* Rack off!"

I laughed. How could she not know that? "She lost the election two years ago."

"Damn. That must've been heaps of bummer."

I shrugged. "It's not too bad. I wouldn't have been able to live in the dorm if I had Secret Service all the time, like Lucia."

"Lucia?"

"I told you about my brother, right? He's a senior on the volleyball team here. His girlfriend is President Ramirez's daughter."

"I'll be stuffed. Dad didn't tell me that." She tossed her backpack onto her desk chair and rummaged through it. "I wonder what it'd be like to date the president's kid."

I wonder, too. I'd met Mateo at the presidential debate two years ago, but hadn't seen him since. Back then, Secret Service agent Johnny Zucko had guarded me, and Dane told me Johnny was now on Mateo's detail. I hoped I got to see them both soon, as well as meet the hot men on the swim team. The sweetness of eye candy awaited me.

I studied my closet, wondering what to wear to the party. "Hey, what's up with *Frozen*-palooza in the hallway?"

Mackenzie laughed. "Zoe — she's the RA — she said our wing theme is *Frozen*."

"Whatever."

"Right?"

As I selected a turquoise sequined halter-top, I thought about Anna, the younger sister in the movie. First she fell for the handsome and confident Prince Hans, but then the unassuming Kristoff had wormed his way into her heart. One betrayed her, and the other earned her love.

"Love your shirt," Elyse told me. Thankfully she'd leaned in to shout in my ear so I could hear her over the pounding bass.

I was glad I'd stuck with sequins despite Dane's arched eyebrows when I'd met him for dinner. His only advice: "*Don't drink too much.*"

"Yours, too!" I yelled back.

Elyse's crimson cap-sleeve top complimented her long vampire-black hair and dark-framed glasses. We both wore jeans. Her high heels brought her almost to my height.

"Want a beer?" she asked.

I nodded. I despised the taste of beer, but tonight was a chance to whip my taste buds into shape. When she left, I felt self-conscious, standing by the wall alone. A cute blond guy had captured Mackenzie's attention, and I hadn't met anyone else yet. I tried to fade into the woodwork, which was hard to do as a six-footer.

"Hey, beautiful."

I turned toward the deep voice, and my breath caught in my throat. He towered over me, his gaze pinning me to the wall. He'd gelled his short brown hair into a peak over the middle of his forehead.

"Um, hi," I said.

His smile revealed perfect, white teeth. "About time you got here. The girls' team needs a fast breaststroker." His eyes flicked down to my chest.

My heart revved—he knew who I was. "You're a swimmer, too?"

"Of course. This is my house." He opened his arms, and I noticed a crack in the plaster behind the beat-up, striped sofa. "Instant swimmer, just add water."

I grinned. "What do you swim?"

"I'm a sprinter."

I should've figured that. Sprint freestylers tended to be tall. And cocky.

Elyse sidled up to me and thrust a can of beer into my grasp. "I see you've met Blake." Her voice dripped with disgust, but he didn't stop smiling.

"How was your summer, Lyse?"

"Fine." She gave him a tight smile.

I took a swig of beer and couldn't hide my shudder.

Blake's chuckle was low and deep, resonating in my toes. "Not a fan of the brewsky?"

"It's great," I lied.

Elyse latched onto my elbow. "I want you to meet Hailey."

Blake shook his head as he smirked. "Catch you later, Jess."

I allowed Elyse to lead me away, but I knew I wanted to talk to him again. My spine tingled, and when I looked back, his eyes still tracked me. Woo! Eye candy sugar rush.

"Elyse!" a girl shouted, then grabbed her for a hug.

A little while later I was chatting with a couple of juniors on my new team when a commotion at the front door drew my attention. A red-haired woman in a business suit entered, and the second I noticed her earpiece, I gasped. Why was Secret Service at a college party? Had someone threatened my family? When I saw a spike of black hair behind her, I had my answer. Mateo was here!

A blond agent swept into the room, and as he neared me, I tapped his shoulder. He whirled to face me. When I noticed the alarm in his eyes, I jumped back. "Johnny, it's me!"

His eyes flashed with recognition. "Ms. Monroe. You've, ah…" He looked me over. "Grown up."

"It's so good to see you!" I'd spent over three months with him before the election, and I bounded into his arms for a hug. I felt him stiffen before he chuckled and patted my back. He let me go and scanned the scene around me. Elyse and the two juniors gawked at us.

"How're you liking Highbanks, Ms. Monroe?"

I'd missed his warm, blue eyes. "It's awesome." From the corner of my eye, I caught movement. Mateo now stood nearby, with the redhead behind him. He frowned at Johnny and me.

I gulped. "Hey, Teo."

His frown morphed into a smile, and I noticed a dimple on his right cheek. "That's what Dane calls me."

"Is that okay? I mean, I wouldn't want to use a name you hate."

He nodded. He'd shot up in height since I'd seen him.

"Mr. Ramirez, please join Agent Kennedy so you're not out in the open." Johnny pointed to a corner where the redhead now stood after clearing the area of partygoers.

Mateo's dark eyes studied me. "Will you…come with me?"

"Sure." I followed them. As I passed by Elyse, I waved at Mackenzie next to her. They both looked impressed.

We stood near the wall with the agents a few feet away, barricading us from the prying eyes of the party. When a new song started, a girl screamed and started to dance. Just like that, we were no longer the center of attention, and I let out a breath.

I turned back to focus on Mateo. He had the beginnings of a goatee—and it suited him. "Why're you here?" I asked.

He blinked at me for a moment, and I felt the urge to brush away the black hair hanging over one of his dark eyes. Finally he shrugged. "Probably stupid to come, drag Secret Service here. I'm not an athlete or anything."

"Did you know I was here?"

He nodded. "Dane told Lucy, and Lucy told me. I just thought I'd say hi, but she didn't want me to come—said it was too dangerous." He shrugged again. "Obviously, I didn't listen."

Mateo glanced at the beer in my hand, my second of the night and just as nasty as the first.

"Oh, you want one?"

He shook his head. "Somebody will take a photo of me drinking and use it to embarrass my dad."

"That's awful." I couldn't imagine dealing with such scrutiny. And now that I thought about it, standing next to a Ramirez put me in the spotlight, too. I didn't want to get into trouble with my coach, so I set the can aside.

"Everyone here's a swimmer?" he asked.

"Most of them, I guess. I heard there were some rowers, but I haven't met any."

"When do you start practice?"

"Not sure. We have a team meeting and physicals tomorrow, but we'll be in the water for sure by the time school starts."

"Four days." He shook his head. "What are you majoring in?"

I smirked. "You sure ask a lot of questions."

His eyes widened. "*Lo siento.* Sorry, I, uh…"

"*No problema.*" He was so cute! "I'm majoring in art."

"Really?" His head cocked to one side like he was surprised. "What medium?"

"I'm not sure. They told me it'll be tough to swim and major in art, but I have to try. Maybe painting? Or three-D? What about you? What do you want to major in?"

"Music performance."

"Wow." He was artistic, too?

"Hey, Jess?"

I turned to see Blake peering around Johnny. "Wanna call the dogs off?" He tilted his head toward Johnny, who didn't look pleased. "I got you a real drink." He held aloft a glass of clear liquid on ice. "You want it?"

Smoking-hot boy was offering me a drink? Of course I didn't want to turn him down. "Sure." Johnny's mouth set into a firm line as he let Blake through.

I took a sip through the small straw and tasted sweetness and lime…and a lot of alcohol. "Vodka tonic's my favorite."

Blake's face lit up. "I like a girl who knows her booze." He knocked back a swig of his own drink.

I realized Mateo was frowning again. "Uh, Teo, this is…Blake, right?"

"Blake Morrell." He shook Mateo's hand. "The president's son at my house. Epic. Why are you slumming with us commoners?"

Mateo started to speak, but Blake interrupted him. "How rude of me. What can I get you to drink, man?"

"I'm good," Mateo said.

Blake squinted. "You don't drink?"

"I..." Mateo looked at me for help.

"He doesn't want to get caught drinking underage." I looked around as I lowered my vodka. I didn't want to get caught, either.

"How old are you?" Blake demanded.

Mateo raised his chin. "Eighteen."

That was my age too, and I smiled.

Blake laughed. "Really? You look fifteen." He shook his head, and Mateo's eyes narrowed. "But it's a stupid law. If you're eighteen, you're old enough to die fighting for your country. You should be able to drink."

I agreed.

Blake draped his arm across my shoulders, and I smelled his musky aftershave. "This one gets it." He gestured to me. "Swimmers are strong. They can handle anything. Right, Jess? Five four-hundred IMs, descend one to four, number five all-out. Piece of cake."

I watched Mateo inch back, uncertainty flitting across his face.

"Swimming isn't everything," I said feebly as I took another sip. Blake's body heat was getting to me, and I felt sweat beading at my temples.

"I better go," Mateo said.

Shit! I didn't want him to leave. I wiggled out of Blake's hold. "You don't have to."

"It's okay." He gave me a sad smile. "Lucy was right. I don't belong here. I'll see you around."

"Teo—"

But he'd already signaled his agents, who led him to the door.

"Glad the kid knows his limits." Blake took my hand. "C'mon. I want to show you something."

I felt dizzy—how much vodka was in my drink? I allowed myself to be tugged along up the stairs, careful to climb each one without falling. At the top Blake pulled me into a room and shut the door. *Ah.* A blessed decrease in music volume up here.

I swayed a bit as I took in the navy duvet on the bed—a neater space than I expected for a college boy. "Wow, I'm tired."

"Yeah, move-in day can take it out of you."

That must've been it.

"But now the real party starts." He grinned as he crossed over to his dresser. After closing the drawer, he held up a small cigarette. "Time to get high, baby."

Oh shit. That was a joint? I swallowed.

He sat on the bed and patted the spot next to him.

"What about drug tests? I don't want to get in trouble."

He shrugged. "They never test the freshman athletes. You'll be fine." When I remained perched by the door, his eyebrows drew together. "C'mon, Jess. I was eighth in the country in the fifty last year. You really think I would do something to jeopardize my career? Studies show weed helps your lung capacity. You'll see. It actually helps your swimming."

The bed *did* look inviting. I floated over to him and set my drink on the floor.

"I rolled this myself." He lit the joint and handed it to me. "This is your first time, right?"

I chewed on my lip and gave a small nod. He probably thought I was lame and naïve. I'd turned down weed in the past because I'd heard it would hurt my swimming, but now he was saying the opposite. "Smoking can't be good for you."

"Then why do they give it to cancer patients? This comes straight from the hemp plant, with lots of medicinal properties." He nudged my shoulder. "We're teammates now. I wouldn't do anything to slow you down. I just want you to feel how awesome this is; have a little fun."

The sweet, earthy scent invaded my nostrils. It was hard to think straight. *Should I?*

"Just relax. Getting high is so much better than getting drunk. No hangover, no calories. Breathe in and hold it."

I tried to hide the tremble in my hand as I inhaled the scalding smoke. Of course I started coughing, which made Blake laugh.

"You'll get used to it." He filched the joint from my fingers and took a hit.

We passed it back and forth several times—I lost count—and in a flash I found myself looking at the ceiling. When had I fallen back on the bed? The walls undulated around me as the air took on a hazy quality. Blake entered my line of vision, hovering over me.

"How're you feeling?" he asked.

I was too tired to speak. As my eyes closed, I thought I saw a smile spread over his face…

ACKNOWLEDGMENTS

Gratitude and blessings to:

Nicki Elson, critique partner. This series wouldn't be possible without you.

Jessica Royer Ocken, editor excelente. This is our seventh project together. Here's to many more. *clinks glasses*

Coreen Montagna, bomdiggity book designer.

Mitsy Princell, PA. Your enthusiasm is unparalleled. Thank you for all the encouragement!

Yelania Velasco and Nelly Guajardo, Spanish consultants. *Gracias* for your astute knowledge. (Any remaining errors are mine.) Special thanks to Nelly for her medical expertise as well.

My volleyball teammates at Kenyon College, particularly my bff: Gwynn Evans Harrison. Here's to Ahnold and the pursuit of pumpitude!

Supportive authors Darcia Helle, Lisette Brodey, Carol Oates, Debra Anastasia, Beck Anderson, Cherie Colyer, Joy Eileen, Alex Cavanaugh.

Encouraging readers Teresa, Jacki, Grace, Roche, Leisha, Kevin, Michael, Lorne, Janine, Cécile, Ina.

My friends and family.

ABOUT THE AUTHOR

Get psyched for romance with psychologist/author (psycho author) Jennifer Lane! By day she's a therapist, and by night she's a writer. She can't decide which is more fun.

Jen adores creating sporty heroines and hot heroes in her college sport romances. Volleyball wonder Lucia Ramirez found her love match in *Blocked* despite the glaring political spotlight aimed on her family. In *Aced*, the second book in the Blocked series, it's her brother Alejandro's turn to get lucky in love. *Aced* launches in December 2015.

A swimmer and volleyball player in college, Jen writes swimming-based romances as well: *Streamline*, a military mystery, and the free New Adult novella *Swim Recruit*.

Stories of redemption interest Jen the most, especially the healing power of love. She is also the author of The *Con*duct Series, a romantic-suspense trilogy that includes *With Good Behavior*, *Bad Behavior*, and *On Best Behavior*.

Ultimately, whether writing or reading, Jen loves stories that make her laugh and cry. In her spare time she enjoys exercising, attending book club, and visiting her sisters in Chicago and Hilton Head.

Visit Jen at:

JenniferLaneBooks.blogspot.com
Facebook.com/JenLaneBooks
Twitter.com/JenLaneBooks
Pinterest.com/JenLaneBooks
Instagram.com/JenLaneBooks

www.ingramcontent.com/pod-product-compliance
Lightning Source LLC
Chambersburg PA
CBHW061426040426
42450CB00007B/920